Dr. Khalsa's

NATURAL DOG

A Holistic Guide for Healthier Dogs

BY DEVA KHALSA, VMD

BOWTIE PRESS®

Irvine, California

Library of Congress Cataloging-in-Publication Data

Khalsa, Deva.
  Dr. Khalsa's natural dog : a holistic guide for healthier dogs / by Deva Khalsa.
     p. cm.
  Includes bibliographical references and index.
  ISBN 978-1-59378-647-2
  1. Dogs—Health. 2. Dogs—Diseases. 3. Holistic veterinary medicine. I. Title.
  SF991.K48 2009
  636.7'0893—dc22
                              2008051862

BowTie Press®
A Division of BowTie, Inc.
3 Burroughs
Irvine, California 92618

Printed and bound in Singapore
12 11 10 09   1 2 3 4 5 6 7 8 9 10

Dedication

For my mother and father,
and for Sam and Lucy,
who shared their love *and* chocolate with me

Contents

Foreword *by Dr. Marty Goldstein*..8
Preface..9

PART 1 EATING FOR LIFE...10
    Chapter 1 That Special Connection...13
    Chapter 2 A History of Dog Food..21
    Chapter 3 Nutrition for the Novice 35
    Chapter 4 Cooking Up Canine Health 47
    Chapter 5 Designing Diet..57
    Chapter 6 The Cure Is in the Cupboard...79
    Chapter 7 The Benefits of "Supplemental" Health Insurance 101

PART 2 THE NATURE OF HEALTH...110
    Chapter 8 Rediscovering the Natural Path..113
    Chapter 9 Eliminating Allergies...137
    Chapter 10 Cancer Prevention and Treatment..................................161
    Chapter 11 Dogs with Special Needs 183
    Chapter 12 When It Comes Time to Say Good-bye 211

PART 3 THE CANINE CAFÉ...220
    Toppers..222
    Meals in a Muffin 227
    Casseroles and Loaves 233
    Yummy Stews and Soups...238
    Toss and Serve...246
    Eggs and Omelets 250
    Raw Diets...252
    Industrious Stocks...256
    Fruits..258
    Snacks, Treats, and Biscuits 260
    Special Holidays and Birthdays...270
    Special Needs Dog Recipes..272

Acknowledgments 281
Resources 282
Index...296

Deva Khalsa and I were founding doctoral spirits as the movement of holistic veterinary medicine was being born in the United States back in the 1970s. We are now referred to as "The Elders"—a term of which I am still proud. To me, Deva was not just "one of us" but someone I respected, consulted with, learned from, and truly admired as she was one of the few, even back then, who "got it." There are two types of medical training: that in which medicine is learned and spit back in rote when treating a patient, or that in which medicine is learned, understood, incorporated within oneself, and ultimately applied within that same context for the betterment of the patient. Deva is an embodiment of the latter. She knows, feels, and practices healing, patient by patient. Importantly, she also has always been one of her own patients. You've heard it countless times: "practice what you preach" or "if you want to talk the talk, you better know how to walk the walk." Well, she damn well did, and she still does. In the decades I've known Deva, she has barely aged. She beams. That's called health. And, when you have it, you don't have to heal—but you sure can when needed for others.

This book that she has written is nothing more than a mirror of the incredible spiritual energy of a true healer. If you want to call it holistic, then use the term to its fullest capacity—not just the whole patient but the entire picture—mind, body, spirit, environment, human/animal bond, and most of all, good old common sense. Learn from this book not to simply practice its methods but to really understand its contents, make them your own, and apply them. It's not that much more complicated. It is pure and simple. Well done, Deva, and you'll always have my love and admiration.

— *Dr. Marty Goldstein,*
Author of The Nature of Animal Healing: The Definitive
Holistic Medicine Guide to Caring for Your Dog and Cat

The Scottie Who Watched TV

Once upon a time there was a Scottish Terrier who lived with a bunch of other Scotties. He didn't like his canine brothers and sisters very much, but he loved to watch television. His people had a super-big-screen TV that happened to have a very large and easy-to-use button for changing the channel.

His basic routine was to lie on the couch and watch television all day long. He liked only animal shows. When an animal show ended and something else came on, such as a game show, he would leave the sofa, go over to the television, and change the channel until he found another show with animals.

His people brought him to me so that I could give him acupuncture for his stiff joints. When they returned two weeks later, I asked, "How's he doing?" and they said, "Well, we can't really tell. All he does is lie around all day and watch television, and he still seems stiff when he stands up and stiff when he moves around."

I gave him a couple more acupuncture treatments, asking "How's he doing?" before each one. And we'd have the same conversation. On his fourth visit, his people said, "He doesn't seem to be getting any better at all." I thought some more and told his owners, "I think his problem is television. Pull the plug out for an hour or two each day (he knew how to turn it on), put a leash on him, and take him for a good brisk walk." I also changed his diet to 70 percent vegetables with only 30 percent of his regular healthful kibble.

A month later, his people reported that he was like a new dog, moving around just fine. He liked his new diet and looked forward to his walks, and he still had a lot of time for television.

This book presents the readers with a genuine path to better health for their dogs, which can be as simple as finding the right diet and getting them some exercise. Of course, designing the right diet takes some thought and a bit of familiarity with some real data about nutrition. But it will all add up to better health for your dogs and fewer reasons to run to the veterinarian. Not that I have anything against veterinarians—I happen to be one. But I became one to assist my patients to be healthier, and this book serves that purpose well.

Learning the truth about what really keeps your dog in good health will free you from any confusion and make it possible for you to have a healthier dog, one who will give you many extra years of companionship. Enjoy the journey!

Part 1

EATING FOR LIFE

L ooking out upon a majestic mountain or a tranquil lake, we see the splendor of nature. As we play with our dogs, we marvel at their joy in living. The beauty and complexity of life surrounds us. Every living thing on this earth has a system that sustains that life, a complex machine bustling with activity and full of energy. How well this machine is maintained will define how healthy your dog remains and how long his life will be.

There's no getting around the fact that the amount of attention you can lavish on your dog depends on how many other demands are being made on your time. But if you're fortunate enough to find time to devote to your canine companion, you may find that it enhances the quality of your life as well. And if you're among the growing number of people who have largely given up nutritionally deficient and additive-laden processed foods in favor of natural options, you're probably inclined to include your pets (who, after all, are members of your family) in this way of life.

Cooking is one of the ways that some people express their love for each other. While I find that our two-legged friends appreciate a great snack or meal, our four-legged friends are ecstatic over the same. Cooking for your dog, if that is what you want to do, can be an act of love, contributing in yet another way to your bond as a family.

Chapter 1

That Special Connection

For as long as I can remember, I have felt good and somehow safe in the presence of dogs. I've always intrinsically trusted them. Dogs have seemed so dependable, sincere, and genuine. They have all of the good qualities we hope to find in people and very few of the bad qualities that we sometimes do find in people.

I marveled, like many kids, at the frogs, butterflies, and squirrels that wandered through my little world. I tried to feed abandoned baby birds and I rescued "stray" cats, who just happened to belong to the neighbors; however, my attraction to animals went beyond a child's natural curiosity. Even before I could put thoughts into words, I somehow realized that, in my world, animals were special. I would sit and watch the cooperation among the ants in the colony in my backyard. On the morning of my second birthday, rather than dreaming of presents and cake, I was painstakingly loading ants onto a shoebox lid and moving them to a "safe" location so that my mother wouldn't kill them with boiling water before the party guests arrived.

Yet it was with dogs that I felt a special connection. When my parents took me out strolling in a carriage along the city sidewalks, I would call out a cheerful "Hello, how are you?" as strangers walked by with their dogs. Only the dogs understood that I was greeting them, not the people on the other end of the leashes. Actually, I was returning the dogs' greetings to me, which no one else seemed to hear.

I didn't know then that I was entering into the ancient bond between humans and dogs, one so solid and so old as to seem primordial. In their exploration of this special bond, scientists have speculated about the domestication of the wolflike ancestor of the modern dog. Although they disagree about how and when it came about, they agree that this special connection between humans and canines exists. I like the perspective told in the following Native American legend:

Once we communicated with all animals as our equals and we had great respect for all forms of life. But one day the Great Spirit opened a chasm between the human and the animals. This chasm was narrow at first. The dog looked at the human and he was uncertain whether to stay or go with the animals. So he jumped over to his animal friends. As the chasm widened he jumped back and forth, undecided, between the human and the animal worlds. Finally, at the last moment before the chasm was too wide, he took a great leap and forever joined with the humans. It remains this way to this day.

Evolving Together

The relationship with our "best friends" has continued to evolve in step with changing times and the changing needs for both species over the course of many millennia. Although humans no longer need dogs to ward off saber-toothed tigers, we have come to rely on their willingness to use their innate talents on our behalf in many other ways. Therapy and assistance dogs help people with various disabilities. Rescue dogs work alongside first defenders at earthquakes and floods. Police dogs sniff out explosives and track missing children. The burly Saint Bernard bounding through alpine snowdrifts and the diligent Border Collie rounding up a flock of sheep are quintessential images of the canine service and work ethic.

Dogs don't need special training or a purpose-bred body to fulfill a role among humans. The Westie who alerts the household that the mail has arrived, the Golden Retriever who waits with tail thumping for his young friend to come home from school, and the Beagle who curls up at bedside when Mom has the flu are all doing important jobs that improve the welfare of their chosen pack. "Work" of any type keeps dogs healthy and whole. It tones their bodies, engages their minds, and strengthens their relationship with the human species. How else can we explain why dogs risk, and sometimes lose, their lives helping humans if not for the bond with their extended families? We have the chance to experience the moment and to connect with our ancient past in a direct, elemental way when we make room in our hearts for a dog. Our brain fog clears, our senses are heightened, our emotions are accessible, and our spirits are elevated and refreshed as we relax with our four-legged friends. If you want to feel what I mean, it's as simple as taking a walk with your dog. Suddenly you will be able to smell the fresh air, see the beauty of your surroundings, and share the dog's thrill of adventure, even if you take the same route every day. You can let a wave of love wash over you that comes just from being with a trusted and trusting companion.

I feel sorry for someone who has never known the unconditional love of a canine companion. Too many people whom I meet are so busy going about their lives that they forget what living is all about. Our dogs provide an immediate and penetrating perspective into our real lives in a world where the value of joy of the spirit is too often forgotten.

The deep connection we have with our dogs is derived from a spiritual source. Dogs are a link to a spiritual—if you will, divine—dimension within all of us, a dimension in our lives from which we've become increasingly separated in our world of seemingly endless noise.

Both the story of the Garden of Eden and the aforementioned Native American legend remind us that we were once nurtured by the "family" of all living things, part of a harmonious whole. Today, our ears are filled with ringing phones instead of singing birds. We spend more time sitting in traffic than under the stars. No wonder we often feel empty and exhausted; we have lost touch with the pulse that beats through all life.

One way to become reconnected and recharged is through our relationship with dogs, reliable guides who can lead us along on a path toward oneness with ourselves, with others, with the world around us, and with whatever may lie beyond.

Best Friends

Our dog lends a sympathetic ear when we need someone to listen and a supportive shoulder when we need someone to lean on. If our emotional train is heading down a destructive track, our dog can throw a switch to divert it in a more positive direction. If we're happy, our dog knows it and celebrates with us. Always aware, even of minute shifts in the emotional breeze, dogs neither judge nor criticize or advise; they just love and listen unconditionally.

The root of the word *emotion* is *move*, and dogs can move emotional mountains. Big boys who don't cry shed tears at an old canine friend's passing, and Type A overachievers discover the joy of stopping to smell the roses (or the fire hydrant) by following a dog's lead. Over the years I've been heartened to see caregivers who are usually quiet or controlled break out of their shells to express uncensored feelings about their dogs. Those who are typically unaccustomed to going the extra mile will drive for hours to bring their sick pups for treatment.

Setting That Special Example

Dogs not only motivate feelings but also model them. Honest and not self-conscious, dogs wear their hearts on their furry sleeves. They display their emotions clearly, without calculation or hidden agendas, and respond spontaneously to the situation at hand. Dogs don't hold grudges. What would our lives be like if we could welcome home family members with genuine enthusiasm, no matter how hard a day it's been, instantly forgive a clumsy step on the toe, or feel vulnerable enough to seek comfort in a scary storm?

Dogs live closer to nature than humans do, without such layers of insulation as houses, cars, and clothes. Their paws are on the earth, their noses in the air, their eyes and ears alert to the faintest rustle in the leaves. As we go exploring at their pace, treading lightly as they do, we have the chance to get acquainted with the natural world, which evokes a sense of tranquility and wonder. While the "civilized" world makes constant demands on us, nature is constant only in sharing its abundant beauty, with no expectation of return, letting us know that we are all members of a peaceable kingdom. This is why witnessing a rainbow, watching a hummingbird hover, or wading in the ocean waves simply feels so good: the spirit is being showered with the gifts it needs to flourish.

Besides increasing our awareness of the world around us and our own selves, dogs help us tune in to others. Precisely because they are not human, dogs show us how to value diversity and cultivate tolerance of others, regardless how different they may be.

Spiritual Support

While humans often have trouble deciding who they are and tend to define themselves by their jobs and their possessions, dogs act from an unwavering spiritual core without being distracted by the irrelevant. Dogs see our essence, accepting and appreciating each of us for the unique beings we truly are. They make us feel loved, and we in turn become the loving beings reflected in our dogs' eyes. When we spend an extra five minutes playing ball with our dog even if we're exhausted, we are exercising our soul along with our body. And the stronger our spiritual muscles become, the easier it is to flex them in all of our relationships.

There is an old joke about the neurotic dyslexic agnostic insomniac who lies awake at night, worrying if there is a Dog. Of course, dogs are not the ultimate divinity (that would be cats—or so they think!). But dogs have a singular capacity to reawaken our slumbering spirits by reminding us that we two-leggeds, with our opposable thumbs and vastly inferior sense of smell, are also integral parts of the natural world.

Poetry of Canine Communication

Dogs expose us to new forms of communication, improving our ability to interpret subtle cues such as body language or facial expressions. This develops our empathy, which expands when we not only recognize another's needs but also put them ahead of our own—which, not coincidentally, is how dogs behave toward humans.

Several of my canine patients have learned to smile, and they also, of course, know within what social context to smile. They usually "grin" when they are saying hello or to show pleasure. Their owners often need to explain to the uninitiated that their dogs are not growling or snarling, just smiling.

T. S. Eliot once said, "Genuine poetry can communicate before it is understood." And so it is with dogs. You don't have to understand them in the same sense that you might understand the meaning of a spoken word to know their feelings, desires, or needs—and vice versa.

Clever Canines

We can forever put to rest the term "dumb animal." Although dogs, like humans, have different categories of intelligence that vary somewhat by breed and individual, dogs in general are quick studies in a range of complex cognitive functions such as processing new information, analyzing, drawing conclusions, and planning for the future (such as when a dog brings his owner the leash in anticipation of a walk)—all of which get a workout in the human-dog relationship. Dogs have even learned a "foreign" language. Some researchers believe that dogs can comprehend several hundred spoken words—not tones, but specific words—and even distinguish nuances in pronunciation.

Social Workers

Dogs come already equipped with a natural courtesy and deference to social order because of their evolutionary history. In their connection with humans, they have simply transferred their social graces to a different pack. Just as they detect friend or foe in the wild, dogs can evaluate, for example, which human is fun to be with or which one needs cheering up and whether it's appropriate to greet a stranger with a sloppy kiss, a polite wag of the tail, or bared teeth. This type of skill makes them effective "social workers."

They are also social icebreakers. Dogs relieve loneliness and lend a sense of belonging to those isolated from larger society, such as nursing-home patients, shut-ins, and prison inmates. When children play "tea party" with dogs as guests, they are rehearsing for social exchanges later in life. The self-esteem, discipline, and commitment they develop in caring for a dog are fundamental to a range of abilities necessary for becoming responsible members of a society.

Together Through Time

The dogs are at heel and matching us stride for stride as we progress on our journey through life. They thrive when they help us thrive; they experience the dignity and nobility of their spirits by giving us the oppor-tunity to experience ours. Most of all, in their connection with humans, they get to be their truest selves; they get to be dogs. In acting toward them out of love, we convey that we honor who they are, just as they are. When they fetch a stick, they get to indulge their senses with movement and togetherness. When they become eyes for the blind, they make contact with their reliability and selflessness. Snuggling with us on the sofa gives them a rush of devotion, barking at the delivery truck summons their sense of responsibility, and not stealing a juicy lamb chop off the table puts them in touch with their trustworthiness.

Whatever power you believe fuels the spiritual universe, dogs plug us right into it. They relay a divine spark of energy that transforms our burned-out spirits and propels our passage through life. Through our connection with dogs, we tap into a limitless source of meaning and purpose, a vital current of wisdom and values from which we draw such qualities as compassion, sacrifice, integrity, hope, and loyalty.

Dogs set an example in both the ways they lead their own lives and the opportunities they present to us in conducting ours. There are many accounts of dogs who endanger their own lives to save others and who in many other ways demonstrate character traits that we admire in humans. Dogs, more keenly than humans, understand the unity of all life and know that the good of the whole depends on the contribution of each part.

Admiration for a Forgotten World

We find ourselves noticing many of the sights and sounds of nature as we walk with our dogs. Unconsciously, we tune into a world we have largely forgotten, one meant to sustain and fulfill us with its life and beauty. This world is one discussed by contemporary author Thom Hartmann in his book *The Last Hours of Ancient Sunlight*:

> "Is there conscious life in you," I said softly, looking at the maple and spruce . . . I wondered if the entire forest might answer me with "We are alive," but instead I got a powerful sense of individual aliveness from each life-form I looked at. Each tree, the bird and the chipmunk, the soil under my feet teeming with microorganisms, each seemed to assert its own individual aliveness. Like the individual musicians in a symphony orchestra, they played together to create a beautiful sound. When you learn to communicate with other living things, you are, in fact, helping to rehabilitate a lost art of mankind—an intuitive skill known to more ancient cultures, but which the development of civilization, technology, and science have managed to obscure.
>
> I raised my hands, palms out, imagined my life comingling with that of the forest around me, and was filled with a thrill at touching the life of the earth. [Thom Hartmann, *The Last Hours of Ancient Sunlight: Waking Up to Personal and Global Transformation*, Mythical Books, 1998, p. 198.]

Dogs enable us to once again appreciate the aesthetics of this universe, loving and living fully within the moment. By extending ourselves to each other, we evolve toward wholeness, toward a more

Underestimating Dogs

A study published in May 2007 in the *Journal of Current Biology* proved to researchers that canines had surprising mental abilities. Dogs were able to do something that previously only humans were thought to be capable of: understand the concept within a situation and decide if and when to imitate that behavior.

Guinness, a female Border Collie, was trained to push a wooden rod with her paw to get a treat. Three groups of dogs were involved in this study. The control group had no contact with Guinness. When they were shown the device, they smelled the treat and used their mouths to push around the wooden rod to try to get the treat. A mouth is the handiest thing a dog has to get a job done, so it would naturally be what the dogs used.

Another group of dogs watched Guinness retrieve the treat with her paw, but she had a ball in her mouth every time she did it. When this group went to retrieve the treat, 80 percent of them used their mouths. The last group watched Guinness get the treat using her paw with her mouth free (no ball). A significant 83 percent used their paws to get the treat. The group that had watched Guinness get the treat while she had a ball in her mouth figured that the ball was preventing her from using her mouth, so that is why she had to use her paw. They did not have balls in their mouths, so they went for the far easier method—using their mouths!

The experiment stunned many researchers, for it showed that the dogs took in all of the nuances of Guinness retrieving her treats and decided accordingly what method would be best to use. In other words, the dogs assessed the situation. But as the researchers stand with dropped jaws, I am busy spelling out words like *walk* and *out* and adjusting my body language so my dogs cannot figure out some of the things I am up to.

complete version of ourselves, just as a tree grows fuller when it extends its branches to the light. Once you experience such a profound connection with your dog, the seed is nurtured by your relationship and blossoms into a love that forever changes the landscape of your lives. It has certainly changed, and immeasurably enriched, mine.

I no longer remember the presents I got for my second birthday; however, I carry the gift of the ants to this day. It is the foundation for the choices I've made in taking a different approach to healing, one that is shaped by reverence for life. That gift is the same one that is offered to each of us, each day, in our special bond with dogs—that when we open ourselves to another, we can reach beyond our limitations and touch the spirit that sustains, and connects, us all.

Chapter 2

A History of Dog Food

The very beginning of the human-canine relationship was probably a mutually beneficial hunting arrangement in which both parties shared the food. Fresh meat was necessary for the survival of a hunter society. As the ages progressed, the dog's role expanded. Dogs were used for a multitude of purposes, ranging from killing vermin and rodents to fighting in battle, wearing armor. Some dogs herded sheep while others fought bulls. The dogs who entertained the French and English nobility were the fellows with the cushy jobs.

As the roles of dogs changed as time passed, so did their diets. When we moved forward from raw meat to cooked and prepared meals, our canine friends marched on beside us. As written language was developed, the word *leftovers* must have had a special place in the doggy dictionary.

The Tables Turn

Up until the nineteenth century, our dogs ate what we ate. The more affluent the owner, the better the dog fared. The diet of a typical working-class dog living a couple of centuries ago may have consisted of bread, potatoes, and boiled cabbage, while the elite and privileged would lavish their dogs with roast duck and consommé. *Table scraps* had not yet become a bad word.

In the mid-1800s, an enterprising fellow named James Spratt noticed stray dogs eagerly consuming moldy biscuits (called hardtack) tossed onto the piers by sailors. That observation inspired Spratt to develop the first commercial dog biscuit, Spratt's Patent Meat Fibrine Dog Cakes, in 1860. Before long, similar products emerged. The sellers of dog biscuits claimed that they prevented all manner of canine ills, ranging from worms to distemper, and that everything necessary for a dog's health could be found in their products. Even the best "table scraps," warned Spratt, "will break down his digestive powers," making him "prematurely old and fat." "Fresh beef," Spratt claimed, could "overheat the dog's blood." Rival products, such as veterinarian A. C. Daniels's Medicated Dog Bread, were advertised as being free of the inferior ingredients contained in other biscuits that caused "constipation, indigestion, and skin ills." (See Mary Elizabeth Thurston's 1996 book *The Lost History of the Canine Race*.)

Enterprising individuals found that they could take table scraps to a new low, economizing by mixing moldy and rancid groceries into a dog chow. The real expenses were the processing, the bag itself, and the advertising. Food considered unfit for man was sold as the only healthy fare for a dog! Daniels had reason to advertise that his food did not cause skin ills and indigestion because his competitors' food did. Dogs were not nearly as healthy as they had been before this processed garbage was purchased and fed by misled owners.

Dog owners did not have much time to think about their dogs' diet, as the Industrial Revolution was in full swing. Historically, the Industrial Revolution transformed agricultural economies into industrial ones. Goods, including food for families and pets, which had been traditionally made at home, began to be manufactured in factories. Cities grew quickly as people moved from rural areas into urban communities in search of work. The time that was once allotted to household duties was now spent working for an hourly wage. The rural way of life, with mothers cooking for their families using products from their own farms, was quickly being replaced by a more frantically paced modern lifestyle.

Time for the Commercials

Cities now contained more concentrated populations, and the new working urban masses now needed to purchase their wares from stores. New businesses were formed, each competing with the other for sales.

Advertising first became a formal profession in the United States when Volney B. Palmer set up shop as an advertising agent in Philadelphia in 1841. Over the years, ads became more sophisticated and more cunning. Millions of dollars were spent on studies to discover what would encourage consumers to purchase a product. The phrase "truth in advertising" may make us think that what we see in an ad is indeed true, but truth, especially in presenting the results of research, can be ambiguous.

For example, I have always been amused by the Milk Bone advertisement claiming that these snacks help clean a dog's teeth. In fact, what the research showed was that dogs who ate only dry food had cleaner teeth than dogs who ate only canned food. While the previous sentence is true, it does not mean that dog biscuits work to actually clean teeth. People can become confused when they learn that their dog will need to have his teeth cleaned—he got his Milk Bone every day! When people express skepticism and disbelief after I tell them what I just explained to you, I suggest that they stop brushing their own teeth for two weeks and eat two Milk Bones a day instead. So far, no one has complied.

Today millions of dollars are spent every year to influence our choices and our thinking about dog food. Market researchers know when changes in public perception are starting to take place, and they are always scrambling to create the impression that they're helping lead the way. Often, after average dog owners become more aware of the unhealthy ingredients in many of the well-known brands of dog food, things suddenly become "new and improved."

Going, Going, Gone for Gullible

Supposedly healthier products begin to appear on the same shelves as the food that we were previously, and falsely, told had all the "balanced nutrition" your dog needed. Commercials tell you that now there is real chicken in the bag. As before, however, manufacturers do not tell you that chicken *by-products*, composed of feet, feathers, beaks, and eyeballs, make up the bulk of the "real chicken" in the bag. Pictures of vegetables now decorate dog-food packages, and some boast of added vitamins. Supermarket brands usually heat and compress these vitamins, so any remaining vitamin content is negligible.

Media Myths

To dispel the myths perpetrated by the big advertisers, we first have to realize the extent to which we've been misled. Most dog owners have come to accept what these mega-companies have perpetrated—that our dogs cannot eat the same foods that we eat (often disparagingly referred to as "table scraps"). Nothing could be further from the truth or better illustrate the manner in which advertising can corrupt our reasoning powers and plain common sense. A good starting point is to examine some widely held beliefs to see whether they make sense or, more than likely, are nonsense.

One such belief is that every single meal your dog eats must be nutritionally balanced. In nature, a wild dog achieves a balance over a period of time, rather than each time he eats. In any case, most prepared dog food is not balanced anyway, being abysmally lacking in some ingredients such as greens, which provide necessary enzymes and chlorophyll. Dogs may be trying to make up for this by eating grass.

Another nonsensical decree is that changing your dog's routine diet in any way will upset his digestive system. This media conditioning has gained a real foothold in the public mind, but it simply is not so. Feeding your dog different foods and offering a variety of wholesome, healthful ingredients is just about the healthiest way to feed your dog. It is true that dogs who eat the same poor-quality dog food for years and are then suddenly switched to another poor-quality dog food may get diarrhea. And there are dogs with unhealthy digestive systems who get diarrhea at the drop of a hat. Generally, however, a healthy dog's digestive system will adapt to new foods. In fact, many chronically ill dogs recover from their illnesses once they stop eating dog food and are fed a variety of home-cooked foods.

Yet another myth is that dogs are strictly carnivorous and that animal protein must be their chief or only source of nutrition. Like a person, a dog can be a vegetarian, subsisting on veggies, grains, legumes, oils, and spices, or, for that matter, a lacto-vegetarian, living on a diet of eggs and dairy along with greens and grains.

Dr. T. Colin Campbell wrote *The China Study*, a book recounting the most extensive study ever done on cancer. Dr. Colin participated in a groundbreaking study in which 2,400 Chinese counties were surveyed for death rates from cancer. Researchers then correlated cancer death rates with local dietary habits. Laboratory research confirmed the data amassed from the field. High animal-source protein levels in food predisposed people to cancer. Although the carcinogens in the environment do alter our cellular DNA and give cells the potential to change into cancer cells, it is a high level of animal protein in the diet that tips the balance and kicks off the actual transition into cancer cells.

As much of this research was done on a cellular level, the findings would also apply to dogs. In 2006 I watched a documentary in which the commentator stated that one in two dogs is now getting cancer. This statistic does not reflect dogs who die of unknown causes at home or dogs who die with undiagnosed problems. Changing to a lower-protein diet can reduce the incidence of cancer in our dogs.

No Dogs Named E.T. Here

The fact is that dogs are not alien creatures from a strange planet who can only eat "special food" from a bag or can. They need vegetables, whole grains, and high-quality proteins, just as you do. Good nutrition is vital to your dog's health, well-being, and longevity and could well make the difference in his ability to resist or get over disease.

Back in the pre-dog food days, the family dog would partake of the family's bounty, as mentioned before. If it worked for people and their dogs back then, there's no reason why it can't work for you now. That doesn't mean that a dog should be allowed to eat just anything that goes on the table; certain types of "people food," such as chocolate, grapes, raisins, and onions, should be avoided. In addition, a lot of the chemical-imbued processed products intended for human consumption are fit for neither man nor beast. Excluding these items, there's no reason why your dog can't enjoy the same wholesome and nutritious foods that you eat.

The Dog Food Recalls

In March 2007, a massive dog food recall of 60 million units of contaminated dog and cat food alarmed owners all over the United States. Dog food recalls are nothing new. Recalls had previously occurred in the years 1995, 1998, 2003, and 2005. The March 2007 recall was disconcertingly different, though, for many dogs that had partaken of the tainted food were rapidly dying.

Menu Foods of Canada is a very large corporation that produces pet foods for many major brand-name companies. They produce pet foods that I heartily do not recommend as well as those advertised and that have the deserved reputation as some of the top holistic brands. Menu Foods simply cooks up, bags, and labels the pet food for many companies. The March 2007 Menu Foods recall involved some 60 million units spanning more than 100 brands and labels that owners trusted.

The poisons found in the contaminated foods were thought to come from a single wheat shipment from China that had been delivered to Menu Foods in the United States. Thousands of concerned pet owners called their pet food companies only to find it an exercise in frustration. Many companies, to their credit, recalled foods that *may* have had contained wheat gluten from China even though no illnesses and deaths from their foods had been reported.

The Environmental Protection Agency had the job of figuring out what ingredient in the food was causing dogs to become ill. At first, a rat poison, aminopterin, was blamed. A few weeks later, the Environmental Protection Agency identified the contaminant melamine in wheat gluten purchased by Menu Foods from China. Melamine is a by-product of several pesticides, including cryomazine, a widely used insect growth regulator. Made from melamine, cryomazine breaks back down into melamine after an animal ingests it. Cryomazine is also absorbed by plants and converted into melamine. The level of melamine in the wheat gluten was very high, at an astounding 6.6 percent.

In April 2007, the *New York Times* reported that the Xuzhou Anying Biologic Technology Development Company, one of the companies that shipped the poisonous wheat gluten, had run an advertisement looking for sources of melamine. It seems that just a little bit of this stuff added to wheat gluten falsely increases the protein content on testing, thus increasing the value of the sale. If the wheat gluten is higher in protein, the bag of dog food can boast of more protein without the expense of adding animal protein.

More and more pet foods were being recalled—more canned pet food, dry pet food, treats, and biscuits—all found to contain the Chinese wheat gluten. Investigators tried to locate every place this ingredient wound up, and the recall expanded as more and more products made with the contaminated wheat gluten were found.

Some early articles stated that a large number of dogs and cats died from the tainted food and that many more had become critically ill, suffering irreparable kidney damage. Although many animals may not have died immediately, their lives may be significantly shortened and their kidneys will eventually cause their demise. In the July 23, 2007, issue of *USA Today*, FDA spokeswoman Julie Zawisza was quoted as follows: "The sad truth is that we will probably never know with any confidence the number of animals that fell victim." The FDA had received 18,000 calls by this time.

Melamine was not the only contaminated ingredient; cyanuric acid was also found. Both of these ingredients combine to form crystals in those who eat products that contain them. The crystals accumulate in the kidneys, causing kidney disease and, in a number of unfortunate cases, death from kidney failure. The life span of many animals whose kidneys were damaged will also be significantly shorter.

One month after the initial recall in March 2007, contaminated rice protein, in addition to wheat gluten, from China was also identified as being associated with kidney failure in pets in the United States. Rice protein is more expensive than wheat protein, and even some very well-regarded manufacturers of premium holistic pet food were shocked to find that they would need to recall their foods. At the same time, exported Chinese corn gluten was associated with kidney failure in South African pets.

A federal judge, U.S. District Judge Noel Hillman, approved a 24 million–dollar settlement hammered out a week before the *USA Today* article, aimed at compensating owners of thousands of pets that were sickened or killed by this recall. This settlement was not on the basis of emotional damage or pain and suffering, but was intended to reimburse pet owners for the expenses connected with the illnesses and deaths of their pets. The chief defendant in the suit, Menu Foods, Inc., and some other manufactures had already paid about 8 million dollars to settle claims filed earlier.

Shockingly, another scandal connected to contaminated milk powder arose in September of 2008. Thousands of Chinese infants became ill with kidney problems after drinking milk made from powder laced with melamine, the same poison found in the pet foods. Dairy farmers were suspected of lacing the milk used in Sanlu brand formula to, once again, boost its protein content. The Chinese health ministry knew the food to be contaminated but did not release the information until reports of sick babies began to emerge. More than 60,000 Chinese babies were sickened, more than 6,000 were hospitalized, and 4 died as a result of melamine in their baby formula.

Genetically Modified Foods

Renowned veterinarian and author Michael Fox states that many varieties of genetically modified (GM) rice have been planted in Asia and wonders whether other GM rice, corn, and wheat from China, as well as GM corn and soy from the United States, may be involved in the tragic poisoning. He feels that the fact that the pet foods were found to contain the rat poison aminopterin, also used as a genetic marker for genetically modified crops, notably wheat, was strong evidence that GM wheat, imported from China and not approved (yet) for human consumption, had been put into pet foods by American manufacturers. The manufacturers believed that what they had purchased was wheat gluten or rice protein, but it turned out to be wheat flour. This flour had been spiked by Chinese processors with melamine and cyanuric acid to make the flour test high in protein. When these two chemicals combined in dogs' and cats' kidneys, they formed crystals that resulted in kidney failure and death.

DNA provides the sheet music that instructs the body parts how to sing the song of life. Each cell plays the tune given to it with dedication. Each cell also plays the specific melody of the organ it composes. Cells and bodies are in harmony with the DNA encoded inside of them. This is also reflected on the planet, as all living things intermingle and coexist. Over millions of years, countless combinations have been played out, arriving at the ones that worked best.

Transnational life science corporations are in the process of disrupting the genetic music, or blueprints, of living organisms (plants, animals, and microorganisms) and patenting them for profit. An increasing number of scientists warn that the current gene-splicing technology is crude. In genetic manipulation, the genes of nonrelated species are randomly combined with each other. The results are not predictable and therefore are dangerous.

The biggest experiment in human history has begun, with planet Earth as the test site and us as the guinea pigs. The architects of life, in contemporary times, are a few gigantic international biotechnology conglomerates. The Native Americans made important decisions based on the effect they would have seven generations later. Corporations make decisions based on how they can profit now.

Hidden Changes

About 70 percent of all processed foods in the supermarket contain unlabeled GM foods. Many vegetables and fruits contain spliced genes to maintain freshness longer, to keep away insects, or to improve their color. GM soy formula for babies is commonplace. Genetically modified ingredients are also, of course, in your dog's prepared foods.

Genetically engineered soybeans, canola, corn, and potatoes are found in packaged foods on the shelves of our supermarkets. There is a hidden

Early Warning

menu, including GM squash, papaya, tomatoes, and dairy products, within the ingredient lists of prepared foods. Allergies skyrocketed after the stealthy introduction of GM foods to our food supplies.

It is more likely than not that soy is GM, as about 70 percent of the soy grown in this country is modified for herbicide resistance. There is little or no regulation and no labeling requirements, so the best you can do is look for is "non-GMO soy" or "organic" on product packaging to protect your health. In North America, all soy that is labeled as organic soy is guaranteed not to have been genetically manipulated or treated with herbicides.

A Chilling Bedtime Story

The horror stories involving GM foods are too numerous to mention, but the story of L-tryptophan, a supplement once taken by people for sleeplessness or anxiety, offers a double insight into the mechanics of corporate greed and the suppression of the truth about genetic manipulation.

L-tryptophan is an amino acid derived from foods high in protein, such as meat and dairy products. Turkey is particularly high in tryptophan, which is why so many folks get sleepy after holiday feasts. Tryptophan is transported to the brain, where it is broken down by enzymes and turned into serotonin. Serotonin is used in the process of neurotransmission.

It's important to note that the supplements that you and your dog take can come from natural sources or synthetic sources. Natural sources are better (see chapter 7). In 1989, thirty-seven Americans died after taking a particular brand of L-tryptophan supplement; five thousand people were permanently disabled. The culpable brand came from a company that used *genetically engineered* bacteria to generate the L-tryptophan.

When all of the lawsuits were tallied, the damages paid out to the victims came to more than two billion dollars. But the PR spin on this event never exposed the real reason that these innocent people's lives were destroyed. Instead, supplements were touted as dangerous and unreliable. The press never informed the public that the true cause was the use of genetically modified bacteria to produce this particular brand. So every single brand of L-tryptophan was removed from the shelves, and the supplement was no longer available to the people it had helped.

There are two powerful lessons to be learned from this event. First, take any news that would affect a prominent corporation's sales with a grain of salt and do more research to find the truth. Second, corporations without morals are creating "Frankenfoods" and taking no responsibility for the effect they have on the balance in nature. There appears to be little use of foresight regarding genetically modified foods although there are many analogous parallels about the dangers of introducing new species of animals and plants from one country to another.

What's Really in the Bag?

Back to pet foods. In the 2007 recall, one brand announced that it was recalling four foods containing rice protein concentrate that had been found to contain melamine, yet the package labels did not list rice. Dog food companies are legally required to represent on the labels what is in their foods. In addition, most pet food companies change the percentage of some ingredients from batch to batch. If they reformulate a food, they are required to note these changes on an updated label.

Several other companies were in the same fix. They recalled foods because of melamine-contaminated ingredients contained in their foods, but these ingredients *were never listed* on the labels. In short, it seems that the ingredients in dog foods have not been, and presently are not, represented accurately.

In an earlier pet food recall in 2004, dry food manufactured for Pedigree Pet Foods in Thailand resulted in reports of kidney failure in hundreds of puppies in Asian countries, but no toxic compound was actually found. A pet food recall in 2003 was caused by an unidentified toxin and also involved food from a contract manufacturer whose labels misrepresented the contents in the packages. In 1998, pets were sickened by food contaminated by an aflatoxin; aflatoxins are about the most potent carcinogens on the planet (see chapter 10).

Who's the Watchdog?

What's going on here? Isn't anyone overseeing the production of pet food? The Association of American Feed Control Officials, a nongovernmental advisory body with no legal clout, administers tests on dog food. To pass these tests, a dog food must keep a small population of test dogs alive and seemingly well for the specified trial period, which is twenty-six weeks for adult dogs and less than twelve weeks for puppies.

As previously noted, federal law requires that commercial dog food contain no harmful ingredients and be truthfully labeled. Although the Food and Drug Administration supposedly has responsibility for regulating pet food and food additives as well as drugs for animals, the actual job falls to the individual states; therefore, the food is subject to regulatory codes that vary by state. Typical regulations consist mainly of testing for minimum percentages of crude protein, fat, fiber, and moisture. That is all—simply minimum percentages. There are no state or federal controls on additives, toxins, carcinogens, and the like.

Measurements of minimum percentages are duly reflected on the labels—but let's face it, the protein content cited is a far cry from the quality, nutritional value, and usefulness to the body provided by, say, a steak, a chicken breast, or eggs. In addition, once such products are packaged for sale, there is no way to determine whether they actually contain the ingredients listed on the labels. You or I could cook up a great soup with vegetables and old leather shoes, then proudly announce the protein content to our guests. Like the protein in our soup, the protein in many dog foods is of negligible value, being of poor quality and almost impossible to digest or assimilate.

4-D Ingredients

The average bag of dog food is filled with a mélange of ingredients that would turn your stomach, and, more important, adversely affect your dog's health. The protein in such dog food typically comes from what are called 4-D animals, meaning dead, dying, diseased, or disabled. Many have received potent drugs, including euthanasia cocktails, which have been shown to survive the rendering process. In fact, at least half of the dry dog foods tested several years ago by the FDA's Center for Veterinary Medicine were found to contain residue of sodium pentobarbital, a drug used chiefly to euthanize dogs and cats, and occasionally horses and cattle, even though the Code of Federal Regulations forbids the use of such drugs in animals intended for food. (See FDA Center for Veterinary Medicine, *Survey #1, qualitative analyses for pentobarbital residue*, "Dry dog food samples purchased in Laurel, Maryland," March–June 1998.) Although the FDA concluded after an eight-week study that the levels detected were "highly unlikely" to have an adverse effect on dogs, the effects resulting from long-term dietary exposure aren't really known.

The names used to describe the beef and poultry by-products you find listed on the labels of nearly all commercial dog foods are euphemisms used to conceal the noxious ingredients they really contain. A better description of these by-products would be "slaughterhouse waste products." These normally include such items as chicken, eyeballs, feet, and beaks as well as cow hide and tendons that have been hydrolyzed into an unrecognizable mash. This recycled garbage can harm an older animal suffering from impaired kidney or liver function.

A practice similar to that of rendering horses, dogs, and cats from the pound and roadkill into a protein by-product brought about the scourge commonly known as "mad cow disease" in Britain and elsewhere. This brain-wasting condition, apparently caused by the replication of a misfolded protein known as a prion, is believed to have proliferated in the cattle population as the result of animal by-products' being used as animal feed. Basically, cows were fed the by-products of dead cows. The disease then crossed the species barrier, infecting humans unfortunate enough to have consumed beef from "mad cows."

The Consumer Makes a Difference

Consumer outrage and the work of courageous holistic veterinarians have brought about significant changes in the way dog foods are manufactured today. When consumers realized that a commonly used preservative, ethoxyquin, could promote cancer and contribute to reproductive problems, they wrote letters of complaint to dog food companies and government representatives. Consequently, most pet food manufacturers removed ethoxyquin from dog and cat foods in the early 1990s. One veterinary prescription food manufacturer added ethoxyquin back to its dry food formulas but announced in fall 2008 that it was to be removed again due to the requests from consumers and veterinarians.

Many new, healthier pet food companies were created in response to the consumer demand for healthy dog and cat food. In fact, the pet food industry began to self-regulate when companies began to check the ethoxyquin content of their competitors' pet foods while claiming their own foods were free of the preservative. In fact, this self-regulating procedure found several companies to be untruthful in their claims, and the rival companies used this in their advertising claims.

Although BHT and BHA are still used today as chemical preservatives in dog foods, most of the preservatives in today's pet food are chosen with a healthier philosophy. Vitamins C and E and rosemary are commonly used to preserve many brands of dog food.

Pet food companies are in the business of creating loyal and lasting customers. It's simply the way to do good business. The ethoxyquin story shows the strong influence that pet owners can have when they are informed and active in their responses to these companies.

Don't Be Misled

In summary, the labels on cans and bags of dog food do not provide a realistic indicator of what's actually inside. In both the wording and graphic presentation, labels are designed to remove all references to the true nature of the contents. Words such as *rendered*, which would truthfully define the ingredients, are replaced with appealing images and language that make the food seem healthful and appetizing. The appearances of the foods themselves are designed to be deceiving as well. Semi-dry dog foods, formulated to resemble real foods such as chunks of beef or cheese, are some of the worst offenders. These foods usually consist of poor-quality protein jazzed up with the likes of propylene glycol and corn syrup along with a number of harmful preservatives and dyes.

Misleading descriptions are employed by supermarket brands that have been making garbage for years. My favorite is "real meat," because pet food producers give themselves away with that one! Products may be labeled as "natural" or as containing supplements to benefit the older or arthritic dog. In actuality, the amounts of vitamins or joint supplements they feature are often so tiny that they are of no benefit whatsoever to the dog. Beware of major name brands that try to give the impression of being healthy or perhaps even holistic.

When a company spends millions to advertise a product, that cost goes into the retail price, at the expense of quality. You, in essence, are paying largely for the advertising used to entice you to buy the product, rather than for the actual ingredients. By contrast, one reason that smaller, holistic, and healthy brands (which we'll be talking about later) are likely to give you a lot more for your money is that they invest in quality ingredients rather than in costly advertising campaigns.

Separating the Good from the Bad

After reading this, you may want to learn how to prepare wholesome meals for your best friend. Yet you may still need to depend on store-bought dog food on occasion. The good news is that there are many pet food brands known for their wholesome methods of preparation and that take special care to exclude most of the noxious ingredients previously discussed. In fact, since the 2007 dog food recall, many such companies have gone to even greater lengths to make sure that they know where they get their products, what goes into their brands, and what the final product comprises. Dog-food producers know that their reputations and their future sales depend on their integrity.

With dog food, you get what you pay for. The smaller companies whose aim is to provide healthful prepared foods are typically advertised by word of mouth and are sold in smaller specialty pet stores. Their money goes into their foods rather than into advertising, but those foods are still significantly more expensive than the cheapest supermarket brand. Take my advice and look for these brands, for they are well worth the money. Better food means fewer health problems in the long run.

Look for words that indicate that whole foods are in the bag. The better food will have **chicken** listed rather than *chicken by-products* or *chicken meal* and **beef** rather than *beef by-products.* You also do not want *poultry by-products* or *poultry meal.* The same goes for *meat* and *meat by-products.* Meat is defined as "the flesh of an animal that is edible." If only the *meat* is listed, then what animal(s) are we speaking of? It is better to purchase a bag of dog food that listed **wheat** rather than *wheat bran,*

By~Products

By~products are defined by Webster's Dictionary as "derivative(s) made from other products." This includes such waste products as feet, beaks, tongues, eyeballs, connective tissues, peanut shells, and newspaper. For example, poultry by-products often consist of beaks and eyeballs, while typical beef by-products consist of hide and sinew.

wheat gluten, or *wheat mill run.* **Tomato pomace** and **beet pulp** are acceptable ingredients. *Peanut hulls* are a definite no-no, as you will learn in the cancer chapter. *Cereal fines* are also unacceptable, as is *corn gluten.* You want **rice** on label, but not *rice flour, rice bran,* or *brewers rice.*

Understand that the more generic and the more general the term, the more likely it is that the ingredient is undesirable. *Animal fat* is too general a term and can refer to restaurant grease. *Animal digest* is the enzymatic decomposition of animal tissue.

It is not in your dog's best interest to feed him foods containing artificial colors, artificial flavors, or toxic preservatives such as ethoxyquin, BHA, and BHT. Watch out for the imitation-meat moist dog food packs because they often contain propylene glycol to make them look moist and meaty along with sugars to make them tastier.

Don't let the pictures and advertising on the bag sway your selection. Beware of those vegetables dancing on the bags of super-market foods along with words like *natural.* As we've discussed, the healthy additives in such brands are most likely present in only tiny amounts, and the processing has destroyed just about any active ingredient in the food.

Purchase foods from companies that have open communication channels with pet owners, and don't hesitate to ask them your questions. You can shop at the superstores geared toward pets, such as PetSmart and Petco, but look for their superior natural and holistic products. You can also shop at boutique dog food stores that sell brands whose mission statement is to provide healthful foods for pets.

Compare the first five ingredients on the bag and look for whole foods to be listed, foods such as chicken, beef, salmon, venison, wheat, and rice. Look for products that use whole vegetables and grains. Organic ingredients are even more beneficial.

You should expect to have to look harder and to pay more for the better products. Once you have found foods that your dog does well on, it will be well worth it. Your dog is the ultimate indicator of what food is best for him.

Chapter 3

Nutrition for the Novice

Nature's wondrous and diverse rhythms weave through all living creatures. Each and every living thing on this earth has a system that sustains the life within it. Although each being is unique, dogs and humans alike have physical bodies that follow nature's designs. Lungs oxygenate our bodies as we breathe; our hearts pump blood through our vessels and into our organs. Our kidneys concentrate and excrete toxins, while our livers and digestive systems work to feed our bodies. To be better able to understand the intimate relationship between what your dog eats and his health, it helps to know more about how this machine—the body—works. The dog's body is a complex machine that is bustling with activity and full of energy. How well this machine is maintained will define your dog's health.

Food is the fuel that runs the machine; nutrition is the science that deals with foods and their effect on health. Let's look at what the words we hear so often actually mean. A synonym for *nutrition* is *sustenance*, meaning something that supports life. Good nutrition sustains life; a synonym for *sustain* is *prolong*.

Nourishing food sustains your dog, improves his health, and prolongs his life. Healthful food equals good fuel, and fewer toxins in the food mean less cleanup for the system. How well the body parts function will decide how long your dog lives and how disease-free his life will be. A healthy dog will fight off diseases, infections, and cancer more "doggedly" than a compromised dog will.

Your dog needs food for energy and raw materials to build and preserve his body. Before his cells can use the food, it has to be broken down into small enough molecules for the cells to accept. Food goes on quite a journey before the cells consider it acceptable.

Spot's Digestive Tract

The story starts in your dog's mouth. The journey begins when he chews his food with his teeth. The teeth grind up the food and mix it with the

> **WHAT ARE ENZYMES?** The word *enzyme* refers to a specialized category of organic substances that act as catalysts to regulate the speed of many chemical reactions.

dog's saliva. The saliva comes from the salivary glands. The saliva also contains an enzyme called lysozyme, which fights bacteria (from this comes the old adage that a dog's saliva helps fight bacteria). Most of the time dogs do not bother to chew their food long—but they seem to enjoy it a great deal.

From the mouth, the food slides down the esophagus into the stomach, which has many folds and ridges that help the stomach do its job. The digestive juices mix with the food, breaking it down further into smaller parcels. The stomach can absorb water but not food, so the food then travels on to the small intestine.

The Small Intestine: The Long and Winding Road

The small intestine works at absorbing the food. It has a great opportunity to do so, as it is about 20 feet long in a medium-size dog. This intestinal road is so long that its name changes along the way—first, the duodenum, then the jejunum, and finally the ileum. The small intestine ends at the large intestine, which becomes the colon.

The small intestine has friends—the liver and the pancreas—to help with its work. Located just outside of the small intestine, they help by releasing digestive juices that mix with the food. They give the small intestine these juices early on because just about all of the food is absorbed from the small intestine. The large intestine reabsorbs leftover water.

Friendly Bacteria: The Little Guys in the White Hats

The small intestine has other special helpers, called friendly bacteria, who reside within it and help it stay healthy. They fight the bad bacteria, keeping them at bay. Many of the good bacteria die in the process of helping the dog digest food and stay clean and healthy. The bulk of feces is composed of dead bacteria along with some undigested food residue.

Much of our experience with bacteria involves disease. Although some bacteria do cause disease, many kinds live on or in the body and *prevent* disease. Bacteria associated with your dog's body outnumber body cells ten to one. In your dog's intestine, a balanced community of bacteria is extremely important for health. In addition to protecting your dog from disease-causing bacteria, intestinal bacteria also provide your dog with needed nutrients, such as vitamin K, which the body cannot make itself, as well as B vitamins.

The communities of bacteria and other organisms that inhabit the intestine are sometimes called the normal microflora or microbiota. Friendly bacteria are often called intestinal flora, beneficial bacteria, and probiotics. Consider these bacteria as the "good guys in the white hats," for they are essential to good digestion. The B vitamins they manufacture help prevent digestive inflammation and upset. These bacteria also aid in the maintenance of a healthy pH in the body (more about pH later in the chapter) and fight off the dangerous pathogenic bacteria that wind up in the intestine. Additionally, they help break down the food the dog eats.

There are tens of millions of bacteria in your dog's intestine. Their Latin names, which you may see on bottles in the health food store, include *lactobacillus acidophilus, lactobacillus bulgaris, lactobacillus bifidus, streptococcus faecium, bifidobacterium bifidum, lactobacillus casei,* and *lactobacillus salivarius.* These bacteria can help with bad breath, gas, diarrhea, indigestion, colitis, and even constipation. Often, bad breath is due to poor digestion rather than rotten teeth, and these bacteria assist digestion in the gut. When beneficial bacteria supplements are given on a routine basis, they help maintain and protect your dog's health and build his immune system. It is very important to give your dog some beneficial bacteria when he is on antibiotics and after he finishes them. Antibiotics don't differentiate between the guys in the black hats and the guys in the white hats. Oral administration of supplements in the food will counter the adverse effects of the antibiotics on your dog's intestinal flora.

Available from health food stores, these supplements come in liquid, powder, and capsule forms. The same dose you take can be administered to your dog, whether a small dog or a large one. Plain yogurt made from a natural culture, usually found in health food stores as well, also contains these beneficial bacteria. Be aware that many of the yogurt brands available at the supermarket do not contain beneficial bacteria. In the supermarket, you can often find a product called kefir, which contains an adequate number of these good guys. You can give your dog a tablespoon or more by itself, or you can easily add some kefir to any meal. Any of these oral probiotic mixes will help reseed the intestine with friendly bacteria.

The Liver: The Big Guy on the Block

About forty years ago, *Reader's Digest* ran a series of articles titled "I Am Joe's (insert name of body part here)." The articles featured "talking" body parts who would discuss with the reader who they were and what they did. Prepare yourself for a similar introduction to your dog's liver.

I am Spot's liver; I'm the largest internal organ in his body. The kingdom I rule over is extensive because I perform more than 500 functions. I won't bore you by listing all of them, but I will tell you about my role in digestion.

I am the warden of digested food. After the food is broken down and absorbed in the intestine, it leaves the digestive tract and heads out to the blood to be carried to each organ to feed the cells—but not before seeing me. Everything has to go through me so that I can remove any poisons or wastes from the digested nutrients. This is essential. I have special cells that pick up and hold the toxic material so that it does not make Spot sick. The nutrients are carried at a superfast pace by the blood and blood cells to all of the other cells in the body once my job is done. Also, when Spot takes medications, I have to clean up most of them with my filtering system.

Within me, I have smaller ducts (called bile ducts) through which my bile flows into the gall bladder; together, these ducts resemble a branchlike plumbing system. The gall bladder uses that bile to help me digest and emulsify fats. Some mammals, such as horses, do not have a gall bladder, but Spot does.

I also function as a storage system for many proteins and chemicals in the body and amass reserves, such as fat-soluble vitamins (A, E, and D), keeping them until Spot needs them. I can make a variety of proteins using the foods that I store, including some that work in the immune system.

In today's toxic world, I can get extremely overloaded and tired. What helps me function better is good food and vitamins, especially the green foods that contain chlorophyll. With them, I can grow back cells that have been destroyed by short-term insult or injury. This makes me special because I can actually repair and regenerate myself.

I have several sections, called lobes. We all work together to share the load because nowadays we have a tough job. If I keep getting assaulted by toxins and man-made poisons, I can become very damaged. If I get fibrosis, then I cannot grow back. This is why healthy food and healthy living make my job a lot easier.

The Cells: Building Your Dream Home

Your dog's body comprises trillions of cells. These cells are organized into specialized tissues making up specific organs, such as the liver, kidneys, heart, muscles, nerves, and skin. Each cell is like a miniature city, bustling with traffic. The molecules in cell town are shuttled from place to place in a perpetual rush.

The mitochondria supply the power for the cell's machinery to work, converting sugar and other nutrients into something called ATP (adenosine triphosphate). ATP acts as an energy source for nearly every cellular process. In fact, the energy from sugars that are converted by the cell into ATP is used to move the proteins, fats, minerals, and vitamins.

To construct a house, you need more than just an energy source such as electricity. You also need materials such as nails, steel, wood, and cement and tools such as a hammer, a saw, a ladder, and a screwdriver. A cell can be compared to a microscopic house that is always under construction. The cell continuously re-creates itself, and when it can no longer do this, it fashions another cell and bestows on this new cell the same ability.

Sugars are used in the cell to make the energy source. Proteins provide the wood for construction. Vitamins and minerals are the nails, cement, and paint; the enzymes and catalysts are the hammer, saw, and screwdriver. Other nutrients, the antioxidants, act as the cleanup crew. They remove cellular rust, garbage, and toxins. (See more about antioxidants, vitamins, and minerals in chapter 7.)

The food your dog eats is not used only for energy. While sugars in the food are used for energy, almost everything else in nutritious food is used to facilitate enzymatic processes and build and maintain the body. The food your dog eats should be supplying all the nutrients he needs to meet the cells' needs. By now you know that most of the processed, packaged, big-corporation dog foods simply do not provide the essential nutrients for health.

Although each cell is a model of independence, it is also a member of the family of cells composing each organ. The organs interrelate like some superbly organized business, with everything running off nutrition. Every cell and every organ and every tissue is in the business of living, and they need all kinds of building blocks to stay alive. The more nourishing their environment is, the better they do. Your dog's cellular environment is largely created from what he eats. All the processes that cells complete—the errands they run, the items they deliver, the communication cycles they complete, the products they create, and even the cleanup after the party—could not be done without the help of nutrients.

Extracellular Fluid

Each cell is surrounded by a liquid bath called the extracellular fluid. It is from this fluid that the cell absorbs the nutrients needed for survival. Additionally, this fluid bath receives the wastes discarded by the cell. Cells have pumps to remove their waste products and send the rubbish into the extracellular fluid.

During the Middle Ages, human waste was commonly thrown out the windows. It eventually made its way into the rivers in the towns. When the first settlers from England came to America, they would not drink the water from the then pristine rivers and lakes because in England, disease and ill health came from drinking river water. Instead they brewed the water into a tea or fermented it into a beer.

Unfortunately, what the early settlers mistakenly assumed about American water is now true. Today we must carefully filter our water before we drink it.

A similar scenario exists within the cell's world. Pesticides, drugs, chemicals, toxins, and poisons all pollute the body, right down to the cells.

Each little cell dutifully marches on, working incessantly to clean up its own mini-environment. Plenty of antioxidants in the diet help a lot, as does keeping the cell's bath of intracellular fluid at the healthiest pH possible.

What the Heck Is pH?

The pH is one of the most important factors affecting health and organ function. The pH of the fluid around the cells in your dog's body will depend on the food he has eaten. The body functions best at a slightly alkaline pH.

The biological and chemical reactions in the body are controlled by enzymes, which function best at an optimal pH. Different systems within the body work and interact to keep the pH at the healthiest range for the body. The functions of the liver, pancreas, gallbladder, hormones, and other organs and systems depend on an alkaline situation. The more alkaline their environment, the better they perform.

Explaining pH

The letters *pH* stand for "parts of hydrogen." When you measure the pH, you find out if something is acidic or alkaline. In science class, you may have used litmus paper to measure the pH of a solution. Vinegar and lemon juice are acids, so they taste sour. Baking soda is alkaline and therefore tastes bitter.

Why Is the pH Important?

Predisposition to disease is directly related to the acid-alkaline imbalance around our industrious cells. Meats, poultry, and similar protein sources make the body more acidic. When meat digests, molecules of sulfur and phosphorus are formed, and the intestinal tract becomes acidic. Meat also contains nitrogen, which, when digested, transforms into ammonia. Ammonia is toxic to cells and so needs to be neutralized and excreted.

To manage these excess acids and toxins, the body stores away bicarbonate. These bicarbonate stores are pulled into the intestine to neutralize the acidic environment there. When these stores are released and lost into the bowels, the intracellular fluid then becomes acidic.

Three organs are responsible for eliminating the extra acids and toxic molecules that build up in the body: the kidneys, lungs, and liver. The liver is the most important of these three; it can process forty times more of these toxins than the kidneys can. Too much protein, particularly poor-quality protein, puts great stress on all of these organs.

Diet is one of the most important things that influence the body's pH. When the diet is too high in foods that acidify the body, the liver and kidneys cannot handle the load. The body becomes acidic and open to many diseases. Virtually all degenerative diseases, including arthritis, kidney problems, bladder stones, and heart disease, are associated with excess acidity. An acidic environment is also ripe for the establishment of cancer.

When cells are hampered by an acidic environment, they cannot perform their tasks of maintenance, cleaning, and generating cellular ATP. Their batteries run low, and toxins, including carcinogens, build up. DNA becomes altered, and cancer and other diseases set in.

All-Meat Diets

Although I do not disagree with using raw meat and poultry as *part* of a complete diet for dogs, I am heartily opposed to a diet composed predominantly of raw meat and bones. This type of diet is high in acid-forming foods and thus has the potential to predispose a dog to disease and stress on all of the organs. Of course, it has been established that most dogs do much better on any kind of homemade diet, as this replaces the poor-quality commercial-grade dog food. That's fairly easy to understand after reading the previous chapter. But a dog's diet must contain a *balance* of foods to promote health. This should include grains, greens, and other vegetables.

We know that the wild dog and his wolf cousins eat raw meat as a large part of their diet. However, this is only a part of their diet. The stomach and intestines of an herbivore, when eaten by a carnivore, provide a delightful array of greens and grains that are digested just right for the carnivore's assimilation. Your dog chews on grass because this is pretty much all that is available to him, while his wild cousins dine on a variety of greens and botanicals whenever they fancy a bit of chlorophyll.

We all know that our dogs' ancestors were wild dogs and wolves. Because of this, we assume that they evolved primarily as carnivores, living mainly on flesh from their prey. We forget that early man did the same thing when he was a hunter and gatherer. Long winters would provide only high-protein food from the hunt. Just as you are genetically far removed from, say, Neanderthal man, our dogs have far more genetic distance from their early ancestors, as their life spans are significantly shorter than ours. I not only enjoy vegetables and cooked grains but also need them to avoid many modern-day diseases. So does my dog.

pH CHANGES IN FOOD: The pH of the food that you and your dog eat changes after being ingested. For example, a lemon is acidic outside the body but will, when eaten and digested, make the body fluid more alkaline. Milk, an alkaline outside the body, will make the body itself more acidic.

What a Grazing Dog Tells You

To get a better idea of a dog's nutritional needs, take a look at how his first cousin, the coyote, eats. While some have said that meat is all that's necessary for a carnivore's diet, in the wild, the entire kill is consumed—this includes the prey's intestines and stomach, which are filled with predigested vegetables and grains. Consuming the liver, kidneys, and heart is important to the predator because these organs are filled with high-quality, easy-to-assimilate nutrients. Wild dogs and coyotes also chew on plant matter in the wild. They naturally know which plants are healthy and digestible. Although you will not see them grazing, they will occasionally munch on healthy greens, adding to the plant content they consume when they devour a herbivore. The wild wolf is really an omnivore, eating grains, vegetation, and protein.

Dogs need, even crave, chlorophyll, a potent detoxifier, purifier, and deodorizer. Your dog may try to fill that craving by eating grass, which, if it's sprayed with pesticides, is dangerous to consume. Dogs commonly throw up grass, which they cannot digest, in a yellowish fluid, or you might see it come out the other end looking much as it did when it went in. That's because the green grass on our lawns is decorative and was never designed to be eaten by a dog. Broccoli, sprouts, string beans, peas, kale, and other green vegetables, when lightly steamed or finely grated, are healthy and can be digested by your dog. See the section on vegetables in chapter 5 to learn how to prepare tantalizing veggies for your dog.

Protein—Once Thought the Perfect Food

The word *protein* is derived from the Greek word *proteios*, which means "primary." In its infancy, the science of nutrition equated protein with livestock products. This belief has been the status quo for more than a hundred years. The rich ate meat and the lower classes ate grains. More animal protein must therefore be good, right? The answer to this is *no*.

The fact is that too much protein has been proven to increase the incidence of diseases such as cancer, diabetes, high cholesterol, and high blood pressure, diseases linked to high animal protein intake. Be aware that protein does not only come from beef, chicken, fish, eggs, and dairy. The next time you are in the supermarket, pick up some food items that contain only vegetables or grains. Read the label and note the protein content listed. Grains, vegetables, nuts, and seeds all contain significant amounts of protein.

The animal-source protein content of your dog's food does not have to be as high as you have been conditioned to believe. I am not saying that

Dangers of High-Protein Diets

Large-breed puppy owners are warned to be careful of their pups' taking in too much protein. Owners mistakenly believe that this is because big puppies grow too fast on a high-protein dog food and, as a result of this speedy growth, tend to get bone disorders. In fact, the disorders are caused not only by accelerated growth but also by the acidic systems that result from too much meat protein. The acidity in the body fluids leaches the calcium out of the bones, weakening them.

You can help restore alkalinity to your dog's diet by feeding green and yellow vegetables. Well-cooked beans and dairy can be mixed in with grains and vegetables as a protein source to decrease the protein made available from meat and poultry. Cranberry powder also makes the *body* alkaline; cranberry makes the *urine* (which is excreted *from* the body) acidic. Adding probiotics to the food can also help maintain a more alkaline pH.

---

your dog must become a vegetarian, although I have found that dogs can do just fine as vegetarians. I'm simply saying that you have many choices, and most of us have been conditioned to lean toward too much animal protein in the diet.

Plant-based proteins supply all of the building blocks your dog needs to produce the required amino acids. Preparing meals for dogs from grains, vegetables, legumes, lentils, nuts, and fruit is relatively simple. Additionally, vegetarian dog kibble is readily available at many small boutique stores. You may be surprised to learn that 1 cup of cooked spinach contains about 5 grams of protein, while 1 cup of sunflower seeds contains about 32 grams of protein. A medium-size baked potato has roughly 5 grams of protein. One egg has 6 grams of protein, while 3 ounces of ground beef has 20 grams. Suffice it to say, there are many diverse protein food sources available

You should also be aware that the protein in many dog foods is from animal sources that are contaminated with hormones, drugs, and toxins.

For the past ten or more years, we have all been taught that if we eat a better diet we will improve our health, resist disease, and avoid cancer. Once again, while at the supermarket, take a look at the magazines that sit next to the checkout counters. There will be, every week, at least one magazine with an article that explains to the reader how consuming increased servings of vegetables, fruits, and grains is the key to people's enjoying better health. Headlines that advertise diets to help eliminate cancer will consistently talk about yellow, red, orange, and green vegetables and fruits.

Foods Promoting an Alkaline pH

Foods that your dog may enjoy that help promote an alkaline pH within his body can include:

✓ FRUITS: apples and bananas

✓ VEGETABLES: asparagus, carrots, celery, kelp, kudzu root, rutabaga, spinach, watercress, string beans, lima beans, peas, potatoes (if eaten with the peel), sprouted alfalfa seeds, and parsley

✓ GRAINS: millet and quinoa

✓ NUTS: almonds and coconuts

✓ MEATS: there are no alkaline-forming meats

✓ DAIRY: butter, cheese, yogurt, whey, and eggs, for the purpose of alkalizing, are much better than meats

✓ HERBS AND SPICES: cayenne pepper, garlic, rosemary, basil, marjoram, dill, sage, tarragon, thyme, cinnamon, cumin seeds, caraway seeds, coriander, fennel seed, and powdered ginger

Disease Starts and Ends with the Cell

It is important to recognize that the present-day dog does not live in the pristine environment that his ancestors and cousins did. Today, we are all constantly assaulted by toxins, in both our food and the environment, which daily threaten our health. One in two dogs gets cancer. Allergies are prevalent. Chronic diarrhea is a regular occurrence. Organs fail too early. The modern dog needs a correctly balanced diet and extra nutrients to promote the correct pH and to support his cells in their quest for health.

An essential fact about disease is that it did not happen in an instant. If a dog is diagnosed with cancer, for example, this condition did not develop in a day, a month, or even a year. It developed slowly, over a long period. Dogs (and people) can appear perfectly healthy for months or even years before a disease process reaches a critical condition. In many instances, by the time the disease is detected, the body is in serious crisis.

Why don't we detect disease earlier? It's because the disease begins on a cellular, microscopic level. With the advent of molecular and DNA studies, scientists are now absolutely certain that what happens on a cellular level is reflected, eventually, in the entire organism. One cell becomes diseased, and another takes over for it. This happens over and over again in healthy bodies. But when the insults to the cells begin to pile up and they do not have the necessary nutrients to repair themselves, they either die or change, no longer functioning as they once did.

Cells were designed in nature before lawn chemicals, toxic cleaning products, poisonous preservatives, and man-made carcinogens found their place on this planet. We now often purchase water in containers, but the plastic containers themselves leach their chemicals into the store-bought water. With each decade that passes, it requires more work to stay healthy. Fortunately, advances in vitamins and antioxidants are attempting to keep pace and balance the scales.

Our canine friends are fortunate that the cells in their bodies work tirelessly to survive. In payment for this work, they should have a high salary of pristine nutrients and a support staff of vitamins, minerals, and herbs. Instead, they get preservatives, highly processed foods, ineffectual vitamins that cannot be absorbed and utilized, and many toxins to excrete. A healthier diet will most certainly be of benefit.

Our relationship with our canine friends has grown and evolved over the centuries. They provide irreplaceable emotional support for us with their kindness and unconditional love. It's time to give a gift to our furry friends to thank them for their good deeds. We can show our love in a way that they will so easily understand—food. Provide simple, easy, nourishing diets that, I hope, will be fun for you to prepare. It's time for a change, and a good one at that!

Chapter 4

Cooking Up Canine Health

My grandmother loved to cook for her family. Of course, holidays served as the ultimate excuse. As a child, I used to pause next to the large stained-glass window in her foyer to experience the delicious aromas that wafted out from her kitchen. As my relatives poured into the house, I would stand quietly, my senses awash with the most delicious smells of freshly baked bread, pastries, homemade noodles, and cinnamon. My grandmother's kitchen was alive with love for her family, and I have always savored that memory.

We have instant meals, take-out food, and microwave ovens today. We also have grandmothers who are likely to be out working or volunteering. As Bob Dylan said, "The times, they are a-changin'." Nonetheless, the appreciation of home-cooked meals has not been lost.

When I did have the time to cook their favorite foods for my young twin sons, I thoroughly enjoyed watching their eyes light up with anticipation and gratitude. We moved into our new house when the children were young, and thoughtful neighbors arrived with a basket of fresh home-baked goods. This kind act transformed a stressful moving time into one in which we felt welcome and excited about our new life. My husband is still delighted when my sons get excited about the latest pie he baked for them.

Cooking is one of the ways that some people use to express their love for each other. While I find that our two-legged friends appreciate a great snack or meal, our four-legged friends are ecstatic over the same. Cooking for your dog, if that is what you want to do, can be an act of love and a special way of bonding. You all become, in yet another way, a family.

Love and Togetherness

Mealtime can be a celebration of family life as the table transforms into a place where the events of the day are shared. We relax and let the stresses slip away as we converse and banter. The aroma of the food and the sounds of our laughter open us up as we enjoy each other's company.

We can learn a great deal about our dog and about the relationship we have with him if we take note of our behavior when dining. Our dog will, just like us, be lured by the aromas of the food; he will also be drawn to the joy and fellowship of the group. Our dogs are quick to settle into the "pack," reacting to our laughter and reading our happy, relaxed body language.

Morse Code

We humans don't realize how many signals and messages we continually give to our dogs as we interact. Nor do we realize how astute dogs are at reading our nonverbal cues. When some of my canine patients arrive at my clinic for the first time, they are, understandably, nervous and worried. I yawn and then yawn some more. I explain to their owners that I am doing this because dogs yawn to calm themselves, and my yawning signals them to calm down. (If your dog is afraid of thunder and lightening, try yawning when the next storm hits and watch what happens!) Sometimes I forget to explain, and the poor clients think they are boring me to death. When I explain myself, we all laugh together and the dogs relax even more.

Dogs seem quite capable of laughing at themselves, like true wise men. Who can forget a dog who looks toward his tail quizzically, comically amazed after a loud flatulent sound erupts from his back end, and then wags his tail and happily looks up as his family breaks into peals of laughter? Rather than hide in embarrassment, he wags his tail even harder, delighted to be part of the fun and amusement. No wonder our relationship with our dog can relieve stress. Indeed, laughter is the best medicine!

Our dogs want to enjoy our company and be part of the moment because they see us as pack members. The cliché says that the way to a man's heart is through is stomach. In dog consciousness, that saying has been altered slightly and carved in stone, or, better yet, bone: the way to a dog's heart is surely through his stomach.

The Right Choice

If you decide to improve your dog's fare, this book will help you make the transition in a stress-free way. You may not have much free time. Maybe you don't even like cooking. Dry kibble, canned food, frozen meat meals (with or without grains and vegetables), quick-mix meals, and more are readily available from scores of companies that make good-quality products. Many of these are made with human-quality or organic ingredients.

Perhaps you have three young children, one small dog, and lots of leftovers. It's easy and takes just minutes to combine the leftovers into healthful meals for your dog.

You're going to decide which meal plan is best for you. Many of us are busy during the week but have some free time on weekends. Whatever your schedule, there is a path you can follow and many options to choose from; you will surely find something that suits both you and your dog just fine.

Whatever path you choose, the information I provide will support you in making a dietary transition for your dog and choosing the best way to do so. This does not have to be a gargantuan task. If you wish to prepare your dog's meals, I will make it easy for you with all kinds of recipes that are at your fingertips in The Canine Café section of this book.

When we make the decision to lead our canine companion down the path of natural foods, we add a pound more of love, a pinch more of sweetness, a cupful of fun, and a teaspoon of excitement to their lives and our own. When you reach your destination, your prize will be a happier and healthier dog.

While some of us might bemoan the loss of sweet desserts and French fries when we decide on more healthful fare for ourselves, our dog will delight in the delicious meals he is served. Some of the good food he has smelled for so long will finally be his. Mealtime for your dog will be an even more special event!

Dogs have had to eat whatever they have been doled out, and most of the time it wasn't nearly as scrumptious or diverse as the meals we ate. Consider also that dogs have over 500 times more sensory cells in their noses than humans do. Dogs can pick up a scent from a mile away. If those barbecued ribs smell good to you, imagine how they must smell to your dog!

The Wisdom to Know What You Can and Cannot Do

What does all this mean in practical terms? Do we have to do much advance planning or cook up specially prepared organic meats, grains, and veggies? Some dedicated dog owners are doing just that. However, many of us have lifestyles that leave little room to cater to our own dietary needs, let alone those of our dog. Before I moved to New Zealand, my busy schedule seldom allowed me any real time to cook for my dogs, as much as I love them. Now that I have more time, I thoroughly enjoy cooking for them, and so do they.

It's possible to rustle up good meals for your dog no matter how much or how little free time you have. First, you need to evaluate your own personal "hassle factor," the limits of your capability when it comes to canine cooking. If you don't consider this honestly, you risk turning what should be a loving effort into a major imposition on your time when you barely have enough to do everything else on your agenda. If you want to avoid feeling that those trips to the grocer or butcher on behalf of your canine companion are burdensome, you should use the following questionnaire as a guide in determining just how far you can comfortably go in changing your dog's diet.

A multitude of factors come into consideration when making the choice that fits your lifestyle best. These include time, your finances, your kitchen and refrigerator space, the number of dogs in the home, size(s) of the dog(s), whether you have children, the area you live in (city or country), the resources available in your area, and your interest in cooking, preparing, and storing meals.

Plan A

If most of your answers were in the A column, you'll want to follow Plan A. Essentially, this plan involves using a healthy kibble (preferably one of the brands you'll find listed in the resources section later in the book) as a base and augmenting it with a good vitamin-mineral supplement, nutritious leftovers, and perhaps some cooked fresh or frozen veggies (as mentioned as an "easy step up"). Healthy leftovers could consist of a variety of vegetables; potatoes; macaroni and cheese; spaghetti with plain or meat sauce; pieces of meat, fish, or poultry without the cooked bones; soup; or perhaps an unfinished slice of bread. They do *not* include leftover chicken and steak bones, sugary sweets, meat fat or gristle, bacon grease, spoiled foods, or moldy foods. Remember that the protein in good kibbled dog food is adequate, so toppers made of grains and vegetables would be more healthful for your dog than those made of meat.

Easy step up from Plan A: Add cooked frozen veggies. There are many different vegetable combinations that are precut and frozen in bags. For example, add a cauliflower, broccoli, and carrot mix to your dog's meal each day. Cook the whole bag (do not microwave!), perhaps toss in some olive oil, and dole out the following amounts each day: ? cup for a small dog, 1 cup for a medium dog, and 1 to 1½ cups for a large dog. Take another step and use fresh vegetables, frozen organic vegetables, or fresh organic vegetables. These can be lightly steamed or finely grated. No matter what type of veggies you use, avoid onions.

Plan B

If most of your answers were in the B column, Plan B is for you. Plan B centers more on home cooking for your dog, perhaps using some of the recipes we suggest later in the book, with the option of using a healthy kibble when that's more convenient. You can vary your approach by mixing a healthy kibble with veggies and leftovers on busy days, occasionally throw together a fun topper, and dedicate some spare time to prepare enough food to last a few days, such as a stew (portions of which can also be frozen). The Canine Café offers many options for easy, healthy, and often inexpensive stews and casseroles. The recipes for quick-fix meals are easy to make, requiring only some basic supplies.

Hassle Factor Questionnaire

QUESTION	COLUMN A	COLUMN B	COLUMN C	ANSWER (A, B, OR C)
1. How much spare time do you have?	None.	Limited amount.	Plenty!	
2. How much spare refrigerator space do you have?	None.	Limited amount.	Plenty!	
3. How much spare freezer space do you have?	None.	Limited amount.	Plenty!	
4. Do you like to cook?	No!	When I'm in the mood.	Bring on the pots and pans!	
5. How much can you afford to spend to feed your dog(s)?	As little as possible.	I'm on a bit of a budget.	Whatever it takes.	
6. How much do you usually have in the way of leftovers?	We're taught to clean our plates.	Enough for the next day.	Enough to feed a small army of unexpected guests.	
7. Do you eat a healthy, balanced diet yourself?	I some-times think about it.	I make an effort.	Religiously.	
8. How many dogs do you have?	More than three.	Two or three.	One.	
9. How large is/are your dog(s)?	50 pounds or more.	25 to 50 pounds.	Under 25 pounds.	

Plan C

If your answers were mostly in the C column, you will follow Plan C. Plan C means dedication to home cooking or raw-food diets. Your dog's diet can consist completely of food that you prepare for him, whether cooked or raw. The Canine Café will provide you with many delicious and nutritious recipes for meals to prepare on the stove or in the oven. There is also a section on raw food in which you'll find a guide to special food that you can order, either packed and ready for preparation or raw and ready to defrost. (Many raw-food regimens are somewhat stringent about what and when dogs should be fed.) Remember, if you're in the C category and routinely cook for your dog, it would be totally fine to feed him a healthy kibble in case of an emergency until you could get back to the cooked-food routine.

TOPPER IDEAS: Wondering what to do with that stale bread? In The Canine Café section, there are plenty of easy and healthy topper recipes that call for bread, and stale bread is just fine. The Canine Café also has recipes for muffins and loaves that can be crumbled onto kibble as healthy toppers. They can be frozen for weeks and defrosted when needed.

All Plans

All plans should be augmented with a vitamin supplement. The point to keep in mind is that allowing your dog to share your fare needn't involve an impossible commitment. A flexible "real-world" approach is always best, just as it's apt to be with your human family members. Ideally, you might prefer to prepare all of your family's meals yourself, utilizing only the purest and most healthful ingredients, but that doesn't necessarily mean you can always take the time and trouble to do so. There may be days when you simply grab some ready-made dinners out of the freezer or order a pizza.

The same goes for the way you feed your dog. It needn't be an "all-or-nothing" situation. One night you might simply fill his dish with one of the healthy brands of kibble, the next night you might allow him to share some of what you've prepared for the family, and the night after that you give him a combination of leftovers and dry food. A friend of mine had a dog who, whenever served something that the family was eating, no matter how much he liked it, never failed to cover the food with kibble from his dish before taking a bite. Perhaps he had been exposed to too much TV and was trying to cover up having strayed from what those dog-food commercials depicted.

You can put those dinner leftovers to good use without having to throw them away or store them in the fridge where, more likely than not, they'll get shoved in the back and have to be tossed three weeks later in petrified or putrefied condition. You'll find that your dog enjoys most of the same things you do—oatmeal and other cereals, yogurt, fruits, veggies, meat, poultry, and eggs—all of which can be either added to kibble or given to him in a separate dish.

Hassle Factor Scenarios

Donna has two Labrador Retrievers and three small children. She does not have a job, but she seems to always be on the run. After reading about the healthy kibbles that are recommended here, she decides to try one with her dogs. Her children typically don't finish things like vegetables, yams, potatoes, and pasta, along with other foods. Rather than throw away such leftovers, she saves them in plastic containers and gives each of her dogs a cup of cooked frozen mixed vegetables along with adding leftover macaroni and cheese and other table scraps to their food. She also gives them a good quality multivitamin and mineral supplement. She would be typical of someone in the Plan A column.

Vicky has three Pugs and a full-time job, but she still wants to cook for her dogs. She loves cooking, but does not have the time or money to justify the expense of the retail prepared healthful foods. Therefore, twice a week she cooks her dogs up a big batch of one of the dishes in The Canine Café recipe section. Many of the ingredients in her pantry, such as oatmeal and brown rice, are bought in bulk and store well. Her grocer saves her chicken necks and ground meat at a good price. Vicky can change the menu as she pleases weekly, watching the sales. Each batch lasts her about three days for all three of her Pugs. If she is in a pinch or if a meal runs short, she whips up one of the items in the quick-fix meal section. She also gives her dogs a good multivitamin-mineral supplement. She fits the Plan B profile.

Martha, whose kids have entered college and are out of the house, has three Golden Retrievers. A dedicated mom, she is used to making good meals for her family and wants to do likewise for her dogs. She favors a raw-food diet but doesn't want to shop constantly for the dog's food. She orders the raw food from one of the suppliers listed in the resources section of this book and feeds it to her dogs. She also prepares soaked or cooked grains and extra veggies to keep the protein percentage healthy. Martha purchases a special calcium supplement or makes one with egg shells (see page 251) to keep the minerals balanced, and she gives a good multivitamin-mineral supplement. Martha is more of a Plan C type.

Gillian is a wonderful cook and loves her time in the kitchen. She has plenty of freezer space and time to cook for her three Bulldogs. She has one teenage son. She chooses to follow the recipes in this book and cook for her dogs. Twice a week, she makes big batches, which she stores in freezer bags and defrosts as she needs to. She also remembers her dogs' daily vitamin-mineral supplement. She finds plan C easy to follow.

My husband, Monte, is a fabulous cook and loves being in the kitchen. He's also a busy guy. Before moving to New Zealand, we used good brands of kibble along with leftovers. Healthy dog kibble is extremely expensive in New Zealand, while healthy scraps of lamb and chicken, which are sold expressly for pets, are fresh and inexpensive. Monte found himself enjoying cooking up large pots of the "hearty dog" recipes while the dogs sat by the stove, wearing very happy expressions. We changed from Plan A to Plan C for financial reasons and found it to be rewarding and fun. When the protein content is adjusted to the ideal level and when oatmeal, rice, potatoes, and olive oil are purchased in bulk quantities, these healthy meals become very affordable. Add some plastic storage bags and a bit of freezer space, and you've got it made.

Every one of these scenarios results in actual health benefits for the dogs. Shining coats and eyes, reduced shedding, and boundless energy provide indisputable evidence of the advantages of a good diet.

BALANCING OUT: When you feed a wide variety of different foods to your dog, there is no need to make each meal complete and balanced. Over a two-week period, the variety will balance out.

When Buying Dog Foods

Because of all the dog food recalls, loving owners became distrustful and suspicious of many dog food brands. We all have doubts about the real ingredients in major commercial-brand dog foods, and there is good reason to expect more recalls in the future. Fortunately there are convenient new solutions to this doggy dietary dilemma.

There are now pet foods available that contain far more beneficial ingredients and are made from much higher quality food sources than the conventional brands. The brands of dog food I do recommend are those you'll find listed in the resources section. These are made by conscientious companies whose products are preserved with vitamins, offer various combinations of extra healthy ingredients, and contain neither toxic or carcinogenic additives or preservatives nor disgusting by-products.

Some companies market only dry products, while others supply both canned and dry varieties as well as biscuits and snacks. You'll even find companies that offer foods you can cook for your dog. Others will send you raw, organically raised meat or even full doggy dinners, either cooked or raw. There are also a number of brands of natural kibble, containing vegetables such as carrots, grains such as barley and oatmeal, fruits such as blueberries and apples, and vitamins. Several companies have actually made purely vegetarian kibbles available. All of these products offer a marked contrast to the noxious stew of chemicals and by-products from which standard preparations are made.

These foods are very palatable to dogs and more appealing to humans, too. For example, if you do opt for one of the healthy canned foods, you'll find them to be a pleasant change from the greasy and odoriferous products you buy in the supermarket. This makes it easier for the kids to feed the dog, since they won't be repulsed by the smell.

You won't typically find these healthful prepared dog foods on your next trip to the supermarket. You're most likely to find them at health food stores, holistic veterinarians' offices, or small boutique-type pet stores. The national pet-supply stores also may have a selection of them. Many of these foods are also available by mail or can be ordered online (see the resources section).

These progressive brands of dog food represent an ideal solution for those of you who, like I, have hectic and busy schedules, or for days when your own dinner might consist of nothing more than a take-home pizza.

Chapter 5

Designing Diet

Although it's true that what's good for you is, in most instances, likely to be good for your dog, there are also times when it's not particularly feasible to share your food. That's why you may want to make a little extra effort to prepare some cooked-to-order cuisine for your furry friend. If you do, I'd like to lend a helping paw by providing a few pointers.

You'll want to give your dog the benefit of a diet that contains as many nutrients and immune-boosting substances as possible, while reducing or eliminating his consumption of toxic or disease-promoting ingredients. Your dog's well-being depends on what you put in his dish. The time to keep illness at bay, after all, is before it's had a chance to develop. This is what a healthy diet can do!

Vegetables, fruits, grains, and herbs are sources of nutrients that your dog simply cannot get from eating a diet of commercial dog food. Keep in mind that vegetables and fruits are "live" foods filled with enzymes, vitamins, minerals, and other nutrients that disappear after heating and processing. Beyond their nutritional value, they possess the quality of freshness, the opposite of the "dead" products sold by the manufacturers of commercial dog food. Therefore, whenever you have the time to add, say, grated carrots to your dog's meal or give him a sliced broccoli stalk as a snack, do so. They will supply him with needed nutrients and help fill the void that a diet of processed or cooked food creates. The enzyme pathways of so many of a dog's organs need the vitamins and minerals only fresh foods can provide. That's why I strongly recommend that a "real food" diet include a variety of these commodities as well as a vitamin supplement.

It is also important to know what proportion of your dog's diet each category of "real food" should compose.

When you decide to create a meal from scratch, you'll need to know what your dog can eat and how to prepare it to make it appetizing. The following section will teach you how to make healthful food delectable and enticing to your dog. We all know the dog who loves his greasy, smelly can of dog food that is routinely mixed into his generic-brand kibble. Most of these fine fellows and gals will switch with absolute unequivocal joy to home cooking or just love the addition of nutritious toppers to a healthier kibble.

Believe me, if your dog seems to do fine on conventional dog food, you cannot and will not fail to make him healthier with some home cooking. And this is irrespective of whether or not you count calories or measure amounts precisely. You can't go wrong by taking this approach.

Portions and Proportions

The historical formula used to figure out proportions is the "one-third" rule, which means feeding your dog one third each of protein, vegetables, and grains on a daily basis. This formula has been around for a long time. More recent research has disposed me to recommend one-fifth protein, two-fifths vegetables, and three-fifths grains. The protein you will be feeding your dog will be a high-quality protein, and some will actually come from grains. Both the percentage and type of protein need to be considered in the quest for optimal health. For example, the recipe section has meal toppers that are purposely low in protein. When loving dog owners put more meat or poultry on top of a prepared commercial dog food, which has very adequate amounts of protein, they are doing a disservice to their pet's health.

Meals: How Big?

How big should a dog's meals be? You can refer to the following chart as a basic guideline for determining daily portions for your dog. If your dog is physically active, you can increase that amount. Just as with humans, each dog has his own metabolic rate. It's best to keep a watchful eye on your dog's weight and hunger level and alter the amounts if it's indicated by his condition.

Dogs are really a lot like we are in this respect. There are those who eat everything they want and maintain picture-perfect figures and those who stay heavy, despite eating well. Humans and dogs alike also tend to gain weight more easily as we age. Some people and dogs exercise routinely and some lie around all day. The combination of metabolism and lifestyle should strongly influence how much you feed your dog.

Weigh your dog first to get a reference point. If he is too heavy, he will lose some weight on this diet because of its roughage, fiber, and freshness. As his weight readjusts, you may find that you need to feed him less or more to maintain a desirable weight. The following chart will provide you with guidelines for where to start.

Weight and Portions

POUNDS	AMOUNT OF DRY FOOD A DAY (IF YOU FEED ONLY DRY FOOD)	AMOUNT OF COOKED FOOD A DAY (IF YOU FEED ONLY COOKED FOOD)
15	1 ½ cups	1 ½ to 2 cups
25	2 cups	1 ¾ to 2 ½ cups
40	3 cups	2 ½ to 3 ½ cups
60	4 cups	4 to 4 ½ cups
100	6 cups	5 to 7 cups

Portion Points to Remember

A dog's daily portion does not need to be eaten in one meal. Dogs are pack animals and they like to eat when their family does, which is usually in the morning and evening—breakfast and dinner. A 40-pound dog can have, for example, 1¼ cups of oatmeal and some yogurt or a "meal in a muffin" (see The Canine Café) in the morning. Then, later on in the day, he can have 2¼ cups of one of the stew recipes you'll find in The Canine Café section.

Most holistic healthy dog foods will have a chart on the bag with recommended feeding amounts. Each of these foods varies in the degree it is concentrated, how much fiber and roughage it contains, and the amount of oil and fat it contains, so suggested amounts can vary from brand to brand. However, this chart should help guide you as to the amount of dry food to feed your dog. *Use such product charts when they are available rather than the one given here, which cannot account for the variations in ingredients.*

When cooking for your dog, remember that ingredients such as oil add in calories, while vegetables serve as the "weight watchers." If your dog is eating loads of food and still seems to be thin, you may want to add more olive oil and other healthful high-calorie items in relation to the vegetables and fruits. For overweight dogs, the opposite is true. Use the portion chart as a guide as you keep tabs on your dog's weight, both with a scale and by watching his appearance. Ideas for specific menus for weight control can be found in the special needs section of The Canine Café.

Fresh Vegetables and Fruit

Vegetables

Vegetables can provide dogs with essential nutrients they aren't likely to get from other sources. The chlorophyll found in greens, for instance, serves to flush and clean the liver, an organ essential to your dog's good health that can also benefit from some of the other substances and enzymes contained in vegetables. Vegetables and greens can also help in maintaining a good pH balance, which is thrown off by an excess of protein. Then, too, water-soluble calcium that is present in leafy greens can be readily utilized by the body, in contrast to the calcium in dried bone or oyster shells, which is poorly assimilated. Cooking or finely grating vegetables makes them easier for dogs to digest.

My dogs love raw broccoli stems and carry them away to devour with great joy. I use mainly the tops, so we both win in the name of health. They will eat carrots only after they are cooked. In fact, raw carrots are hard for dogs to digest and come out pretty much the same way they went in, so I would rather cook the carrots anyway. Remember what your dog is used to eating. If you had eaten nothing but flavor-enhanced snacks like spicy corn chips every day of the year, steamed vegetables might seem bland and uninteresting. Come to think of it, plain steamed vegetables do seem uninteresting, no matter what you're used to. I like butter and salt on my vegetables, but dogs do not like salt, so please do not salt their food to suit your taste. Butter is another matter completely and is always welcome by the canine diner.

When you come right down to it, dogs can be a lot like little kids are with vegetables. And just like kids, some dogs need a little enticement to get out of the junk-food rut they're in. Many dogs truly enjoy certain vegetables, while others learn to enjoy them over time and need them doctored up a bit. Veggies that are lightly steamed until tender and tossed in butter or olive oil and then sprinkled generously with Parmesan cheese

Benefits of Garlic

Garlic in a dog's food will help prevent fleas. Dogs don't perspire as we do. When we eat a lot of garlic, it quickly comes out in our perspiration. In a dog, however, the garlic comes out over time in the oil of the coat. The essence of garlic will take some time to build up and have its flea-repelling effect. The trick is to wash your dog with nondetergent castile soap when you bathe him to prevent the coat oil from washing off.

Vegetable Dos and Don'ts

Below are recommendations for what to feed and what not to feed regarding vegetables.

✓ RECOMMENDED: Asparagus, brussels sprouts, beets (in small amounts), beans,* broccoli, carrots, cauliflower, celery, collards, cucumbers, kale, kelp, lentils,* garlic, green beans, parsnips, parsley, peas, potatoes, pumpkin, seaweed, sprouts, squash (all kinds), string beans, tomatoes, turnips, yams

✓ NOT RECOMMENDED: Onions in any significant quantity (although a little can be used for flavoring), onion soup

• Soak beans or lentils overnight, then pour off the water, rinse, and cook until nice and soft

are rarely refused. You can also cook vegetables in liquid flavored with beef or chicken by either putting a bone from the butcher (which is later removed) in the water or adding a beef or chicken bouillon cube to the pot. This will impart a meaty overtone to the vegetables. A meaty flavoring can also be accomplished by opening a jar of chicken or beef baby food, diluting it a bit with water, and stirring the watered-down baby food in with the steamed vegetables.

Sometimes grating or dicing the vegetables, lightly steaming them, and mixing them in with the kibble works well. I often mix vegetables with cooked grains and olive oil and place it on the kibble.

Root vegetables such as carrots and parsnips can be sliced into rounds, sprinkled with olive oil and garlic powder, and baked in an oven at 250 degrees Fahrenheit for about 45 minutes and then cooled. My dogs love these as snacks. Diced or grated raw veggies can be sautéed quickly in a bit of butter or olive oil. You can also sprinkle these lightly cooked veggies with some cheese. In general, though, vegetables work best when mixed in a prepared meal such as a casserole or stew.

Leftovers are an excellent way to add vegetables to your dog's meal. Dishes such as creamed spinach, baked yams or sweet potatoes, cooked squash with butter, and mixed vegetable casseroles that the family did not finish can be saved in plastic containers and dished out at your dog's mealtime. Most dogs love potatoes. Roasted potato wedges drizzled with olive oil and sprinkled with garlic are always welcome.

My dogs love Nori seaweed. These are flat sheets of seaweed that are used to roll sushi. Seaweed is an excellent source of kelp and minerals.

Fruit

The younger a dog is when you introduce him to fruit, the easier it is for him to love it. Apples are reliable favorites. Just slice up the fruit and offer some slices to your dog. If he seems uncertain, peel off the skin and try again. You can also dice up apples and put the pieces in a little chicken or beef broth to get your dog to try them. Bananas have always been a big hit. Mixing bananas and plain yogurt can make a yummy quick snack or a meal in itself.

Watermelon slices are often welcome on a hot summer day. Papayas are great for digestion, and fresh papayas or mangos can be added to cereal mixes. Many dogs also like a slice of avocado.

If your dog looks at you quizzically when you offer him fruit, don't give up. Offer the fruit a few times and, if needed, doctor it up to help him take the first step.

Organic Produce

Those toxic pesticides routinely sprayed on produce can be every bit as hazardous to canine health as they are to human health. That's why, whenever possible, you should make it a habit to buy organically grown

Fruit Dos and Don'ts

Below are recommendations for what to feed and what not to feed regarding fruit.

✓ RECOMMENDED: Apples, avocados, bananas, berries, figs, melons (including watermelon), oranges, peaches, pears. Pieces of fruit can be eaten raw, and a quarter of an apple or a piece of watermelon can help maintain electrolyte balance in hot weather.

✓ NOT RECOMMENDED: Grapes, raisins. (Recent studies have shown that eating grapes or grape skins can be toxic to dogs and can make them severely ill.)

products that are raised without poisonous chemicals. Otherwise, you should thoroughly wash and soak all fruit and vegetables. You can use products especially designed for cleaning fruit and veggies; these products are generally available in supermarkets and health food stores.

Organic crops are believed to contain far more vitamins and nutrients than produce grown with conventional farming methods. The farming methods employed by organic farmers work to rebuild the health of the soil and restore the nutrients lost by overuse of the land and heavy chemical fertilizers. By eliminating pesticides, organic agriculture does not contribute to the toxins in our water, soil, and air that threaten our health, our children's health, and our pets' health. The cultivation of genetically engineered crops, a source of great concern to environmentalists, is likewise banned in organic farming.

Grains

As discussed previously, a dog is not intended to be merely a carnivore; he also requires carbohydrates to remain in top physical shape. That's why grains in their various forms are such an important component of a well-rounded canine diet—as long as you don't try to feed them to your dog raw.

Healthy products made from prepared grains, such as whole-grain breads, cereals, and crackers, are fine for mixing with your dog's food just as they are. Thin slices or squares of whole wheat bread toasted in the

Offer your dog a more nutritious and tasty diet by including a variety of grains in his meals.

Recommended Cooking Time for Grains for Dogs

GRAIN (1 CUP)	WATER (CUPS)	COOKING TIME
Amaranth	3 ½	35 minutes
Barley	4	70 minutes
Basmati rice	2 ¼	20 minutes
Brown rice	3	75 minutes
Buckwheat	2 ½	30 minutes
Couscous	1 ½	7 minutes
Millet	3 ½	40 minutes
Oatmeal	2–3	15 minutes
Oats (steel cut)	3 ½	60 minutes
Quinoa*	3 ½	30 minutes
Wheat berries	4 ½	120 minutes
Wheat (cracked)	2 ½	30 minutes

Cooking tips: Sprinkle grains into boiling water slowly so that the water stays actively boiling. Stir only enough to moisten the grains. Reduce heat to a low boil in a covered pot, and don't overstir while cooking, to avoid mushy grains.

• Make sure that quinoa seeds are rinsed in cold water thoroughly before cooking to remove their naturally occurring bitter coating.

Wheat Bran

Wheat bran is a good home remedy for both constipation and diarrhea. Bran is not irritating to the bowels and is easy to add to food. Add a spoonful to one of the stew or casserole servings at mealtime. If used for constipation, you must make sure that your dog also drinks a lot of water.

• *Note: Constipation is not very common in dogs. If your dog is chronically constipated, please take him to the veterinarian for a thorough examination.*

oven at 200 degrees Fahrenheit for 30 minutes also make excellent treats that your dog will love to chew on. Leftover pasta, such as spaghetti and macaroni, will surely set tails a-waggin'.

Unprocessed grains are whole grains that have not been preprepared. Instant oatmeal is not an unprocessed grain, but steel-cut oats are. Whole grains are full of nutrition and are essentially intact. While unprocessed organic grains, such as oats, barley, brown rice, millet, amaranth, and quinoa, certainly contain important nutrients, a dog cannot easily digest such grains in raw form because carnivores have shorter digestive tracts than herbivores do.

Grains, when fed to a dog, should typically be cooked even longer than they are for human consumption and with more water. Brown rice, for instance, would ordinarily be cooked for 45 minutes on the stove, using 2 cups of water to 1 cup of rice. However, when preparing brown rice for a dog, you should cook it for one hour and fifteen minutes, using more water. Soaking grains overnight is a way to cut down on cooking time the next day. Oatmeal soaked for about twelve hours may require no cooking whatsoever, or you may choose to cook them. Generally speaking, oatmeal is easier than brown rice for dogs to digest. Oatmeal is the one grain that can just be soaked overnight, although I believe cooking makes it more digestible.

Grains intended for your dog can, if you wish, be cooked with a meat, chicken, or fish stock to add flavor. Grains and vegetables can be cooked together and added to a quality commercial kibble. The commercial dog food already has adequate protein, so there's no need to add more animal protein. Better yet, a stew containing grains, vegetables, and meat or poultry can be portioned out on a daily basis. If that's your preference, it's best to cook the grains first and then stir in lightly steamed or grated vegetables. Some examples can be found in The Canine Café recipes.

You also have the option to use prepared grain mixes, which are now being offered by a number of companies and can be purchased at a specialty pet store or ordered (see the resources section). While each has its own unique ingredients, the mixes typically consist of a combination of some of the following: oat flakes, rye flakes, wheat germ, bulgur, sesame seeds, kamut flakes, spelt flakes, and oat straw. They also normally include veggies such as potatoes, alfalfa, parsley, peas, carrots, beets, squash, and broccoli and herbs that include garlic, dandelion root, ginger, rosemary, and peppermint. All you need to do is add water and perhaps some protein to the mix.

Eggs and Milk Products

If your dog is the sort that rolls over to show appreciation for a favorite treat, he'll do flip-flops over eggs and cheese. Canines can receive many nutritional benefits from having these products, along with other dairy products, included in their diet.

Egg yolks, for instance, contain health-promoting fatty acids such as omega-3, a nutrient that is important for protecting the heart and is also good for the coat and skin. In addition, eggs contain high-quality protein that is also highly digestible.

Eggs can be fed to your dog cooked or raw. Unlike people, dogs are relatively impervious to the salmonella that raw eggs might contain. I would advise, though, if you feed your dog three or more eggs a day, that you cook at least some of them because raw egg whites can impede absorption of biotin, an important vitamin.

Dogs enjoy eating eggs, including crunchy omelets made with the calcium-rich shell.

> **DOGGY BREATH:** It's not just bad teeth that can cause doggy breath. A little bit of yogurt each day can help improve bad breath due to poor digestion. Your dog's teeth and mouth should be checked if the problem persists.

Since a taste for eggshells is something that also tends to set dogs apart from humans, here's another suggestion. Boil the egg in its shell for two to three minutes, then mash up the entire egg, including the shell, and feed it to your dog. I like to eat egg-white omelets for breakfast, and I find myself with a lot of leftover egg yolks and shells. A bit of butter goes into the pan, and I add all of the shells after I lightly crush them. After quickly beating the yolks, I pour them on top of the shells and flip when the first side is done. After the concoction cools, I break it apart and my dogs have their morning crunchy egg-yolk snacks.

An omelet filled with some chopped parsley and veggies and topped with cheese can be an ideal dish for your dog, particularly as a way of sneaking vegetables into his diet. Dogs like eggs done any style, whether scrambled, poached, hard-boiled, or as omelets.

Because dogs do not suffer from thickening and hardening of the arteries (arteriosclerosis), as some people do, and are not subject to high cholesterol, there's no need to worry about these problems resulting from their consumption of eggs and dairy products. So you can relax and let your dog indulge in some of the foods that offer him benefit and enjoyment.

Various types of cheeses will set your dog's tail a-thumpin'. Favorites include Swiss cheese, cottage cheese, farmer's cheese, and ricotta cheese. None of these relatively bland cheeses should cause any sort of digestive disturbance. Unlike meat, containing nitrogenous waste, which is hard on the kidneys, dairy products such as cottage cheese are excellent sources of protein and calcium. I also strongly recommend yogurt and kefir. Sold near the yogurt at supermarkets, kefir is a more liquid form of yogurt and is very tasty. Both are easy to digest and can help prevent diarrhea. The beneficial organisms used to produce these cultured milk products are very healthy for the digestive tract. Make sure you buy yogurt that has these beneficial bacteria, as the yogurts made from mixed cultures often do not have enough of them.

Milk powder is a concentrated source of protein, calcium, riboflavin, and other nutrients. When mixed with a cereal-based meal, milk powder can give your dog an inexpensive boost of protein.

Dairy products can be excellent sources of protein and calcium. The protein in dairy is kinder to the kidneys than is meat protein, which, again, contains nitrogenous waste that is hard on the kidneys. Many commercial foods designed for dogs with kidney problems have dairy as their main source of protein.

Meat

Now that we've reviewed the variety of canine-friendly foods that you might never have considered feeding your dog, it's time to discuss what many people still consider the main course: meat.

To Cook or Not to Cook

One source of controversy when it comes to meat is the question of whether the so-called raw diet is actually better for your dog than the cooked kind favored by humans. As in most debates, there are arguments for and against raw diets, but it boils down to what type of diet is best for your dog's particular situation. Most of the opinions I've heard have been subjective—that is, based on each dog owner's experience.

Many owners report that their dogs are thriving on raw diets. There are a variety of raw-food diet plans to guide dog owners, as well as data based on solid research and analysis of the most popular raw diets. One study, for instance, shows the calcium/phosphorus ratio and zinc content of raw-food diets to be inadequate. This is why supplementation is absolutely necessary. (See "Evaluation of Raw Food Diets for Dogs," by Lisa M. Freeman, DVM, PhD, DACVN, and Kathryn E. Michel, DVM, MS, DACVN. *Journal of American Veterinary Medical Association*, vol. 218, no. 5, March 1, 2001.)

Some dogs do well with raw meat, others do not; consult with your vet about serving it.

Tips and Yips

Preparing your dog's food in a microwave is not something I would recommend because microwave cooking destroys many important nutrients. Just two seconds of microwaving, for instance, can destroy all of the enzymes in grains and vegetables. Using plastic dishes in a microwave can also cause plastic molecules to end up in food.

First of all, it should be emphasized that dogs are generally better equipped to handle raw meat than people are. That is, their digestive tracts have better defenses against bacteria and parasites, such as *E. coli* and *Salmonella*, that would make us sick.

However, that's not necessarily the case with all dogs, particularly older ones whose digestive systems have likely slowed down and secrete fewer juices. That's why I would not recommend placing a senior dog who is used to cooked and processed food on a raw diet. The same goes for a dog with a weakened immune system. If you're not sure about your dog's ability to resist such microorganisms, there are compromise measures you can take, such as lightly steaming the meat or soaking it in grapefruit seed extract, which may help deter pathogens. I would also be careful about feeding raw meat or poultry to any dog prone to digestive problems.

That being said, a dog can benefit from eating meat in its uncooked state. Raw meat provides nutrients, such as essential fatty acids, that cooking destroys. There are stories of dogs making miraculous recoveries from serious health problems once raw meat was introduced into their diet. By contrast, I have heard of many dogs who have done very poorly on raw-food diets. Some of these dogs become painfully thin with no muscle mass and poor-quality coats. These particular dogs look and feel much better when fed a cooked diet with grains or even a healthy kibble. Each individual dog has its own metabolism.

Years of study have brought me to conclude that a diet consisting solely of raw meat is far from ideal. *The China Study*, as mentioned in chapter 2, provided evidence that a high dietary percentage of animal and dairy protein points toward increased cancer incidence. It is well documented that an acidic cellular environment (of which one of the causes is high levels of animal protein) is more prone to disease and cancer than is an alkaline one. Carbohydrates are needed for the brain, thyroid, and liver to function optimally. Vegetables are a live food source, providing enzymes and phytonutrients that prevent cancer and other diseases.

If raw meat is your preference, you can leave the fat on any uncooked meat you feed to your dog (a fat content of 20 to 30 percent is fine). Dogs do not suffer from such human problems as clogged arteries, high blood pressure, and high cholesterol and can actually benefit from saturated fat. Since fat turns into unhealthy grease when heated, however, it should be trimmed from meat before you cook it.

It's a good idea to freeze raw meat for fourteen days before you feed it to your dog. This amount of time in the freezer should kill any parasites encysted in the muscles and organs. Should you opt for cooking, you can do so by baking, boiling, or broiling after trimming the fat and perhaps adding organic olive oil as a fat source, as well as grains, vegetables, and herbs.

Meats such as beef and lamb are good sources of protein, vitamins, and minerals, whether cooked or raw. Pork and rabbit meat, however, should always be cooked because of the danger of diseases such as trichinosis (caused by the parasite *Trichinella spiralis*) that can infect your dog. In addition, pork should be fed to dogs only in small amounts and should not be used as a dietary staple.

It may also be best to avoid venison in those areas such as the Rocky Mountains and upper Midwest, where deer have been known to suffer from a condition similar to mad cow disease. No amount cooking or freezing will handle the prion "proteins" that cause this disease. The dictionary defines a prion as an infectious particle of protein that, unlike a virus, contains no nucleic acid and is not destroyed by extreme heat or cold.

Poultry

Fowl fills protein requirements quite nicely, although chicken is the preferred variety with dogs. It's second only to eggs, in fact, in its ability to be easily assimilated. *Be careful not to feed your dog cooked chicken bones, however, since these can splinter and perforate the intestine.* Exceptions to this rule are the back and neck bones, which consist of cartilage and are thus safe for your dog to chew and swallow. The subject of bones will be discussed in greater detail later in this chapter.

Beware of Hazardous Wastes

Since studies have shown that *E. coli* and *Salmonella* can pass through your dog's digestive tract and wind up in the end product, you should be especially careful about disposing of waste from a dog that is being fed raw meat. You should also be aware of the risk of exposure to children who might be playing in your yard, and be sure to scoop the poop as soon as possible.

Turkey is very high in an amino acid called L-tryptophan, a natural tranquilizer that has a calming and sedating effect. This is the reason why we tend to feel so sluggish and sleepy after a big holiday feast. During the holidays, I do see my share of dogs that have been "turkeyed out." Turkey can be added to stews or other items, including kibble. If available, game birds such as pheasant, duck, and quail can also be fed to dogs.

Organ Meats

Whatever you do, don't confuse *organ meats* with *organic meats*. By organic meats, we mean the kind that come from animals whose feed and environment were free of pesticides, hormones, antibiotics, steroids, and other toxic substances, residues of which are usually present in conventionally raised meat. I highly recommend organic meat and poultry, both for dogs and their meat-eating masters.

Organ meats, however, are those made from animal organs, such as the liver, kidneys, heart, and gizzard. These are often readily available from the grocer at a very reasonable cost. As a rule, however, organ meat should not be fed to your dog more than once or twice a week, and it should not make up the bulk of your pet's diet.

The source of the liver you choose to feed your dog is important, as the liver contains more toxic hormones and drugs than any other organ meat. Remember, the liver is the organ that pulls toxins out of the body. Commercial chickens, for instance, are fed hormones and antibiotics and live in quarters sprayed with pesticides. All of these compounds are cleaned by and are harbored in their livers. When your dog eats chicken livers, he is also eating the hormones, antibiotics, and pesticides that the chickens were exposed to.

I'd recommend organic chicken livers or liver from calves rather than cows. Full-grown cows, simply because they lived longer, had more exposure to poisons. Organ meat from sheep might also be preferable since sheep tend to have less exposure to toxic substances than do other commercial livestock. The only real reason I can think of for feeding a dog liver every day is if he's anemic, in which case I'd again recommend organic liver.

Fish

As a protein source for your dog, you can't do much better than fish—especially white fish, such as flounder and tilapia, and cold water fish, such as salmon, mackerel, and trout. The latter are also rich in omega-3 fatty acids.

But there are a number of caveats you've got to keep in mind, the first being that *fish should never be fed to your dog raw*. Your dog could fall prey to the parasites that raw flesh sometimes harbors. Second, make sure that all bones are removed, as they can cause damage to and even puncture

Any fish your dog eats should be well cooked and carefully deboned.

the intestinal wall. Third, while canned salmon and mackerel are fine for dogs, canned tuna is not, as it can decrease your dog's ability to utilize some fat-soluble vitamins. Remember, too, that tuna and swordfish are both very high in mercury. For that reason, the United States government recommends that tuna and swordfish not be eaten by pregnant women or eaten more than once a week by children.

Although there are no such advisories in regard to dogs, they can also do without the effects of mercury. I often opt for fresh farm-raised tilapia, which is relatively inexpensive, and canned salmon, which stores well and is handy in a pinch to make up a quick meal.

Nutritional Yeast

Nutritional yeast, also known as brewer's yeast, provides an excellent source of protein, B vitamins, and iron. On an ounce-for-ounce basis, brewer's yeast contains almost three times the protein of beef, although we do not consume brewer's yeast in such large quantities. For the most part, dogs love the taste of nutritional yeast, which has a meaty flavor and odor. It is available flaked or finely ground and can be added to just about any meal your dog eats. However, if your dog has either skin or digestive allergies, be careful about adding nutritional yeast to the food, as it is highly allergenic.

Keeping Your Dog Well Oiled

There are many kinds of oil you can use in feeding your dog. The supermarket shelves are filled with many different types of oil. Some are better for certain purposes than others, and some are healthier than others, the latter being olive, walnut, hazelnut, flax, and coconut oil. Healthy oils provide monounsaturated fat and other healing fats. As olive oil is readily available and is the least expensive of these, I highly recommend it for general use.

Olive Oil

For cooking for your dogs, I particularly recommend olive oil—more specifically, cold-pressed virgin olive oil. Olive oil has a high content of fatty acids and oxidative substances. It is very well tolerated by the stomach and helps maintain a good level of vitamin E.

Oils should be refrigerated after opening to keep them fresh and to prevent them from being degraded by heat or light. You can now buy olive oil in a cardboard box; a plastic bag of oil is inside, attached to a tap. As the oil is used, the bag collapses, keeping air away from the oil. Boxes of olive oil will stay fresher for longer outside of the refrigerator. This works well because olive oil firms up when left in the refrigerator, although it will liquefy when exposed to room temperature.

Depending on his size and his coat condition, a dog can be given anywhere from a teaspoon to a tablespoon of olive oil each day on top of his food. It is wonderful for the coat. You can also cook his food with it. Ordinarily the breakdown of other common oils during cooking creates ingredients that are not well digested. Because this isn't true of olive oil, it is the only oil you should use when cooking for your dog. I use loads of olive oil and rosemary in my dog's meals, and their coats shine. Dogs love olive oil in their food.

Flax Seeds and Their Oil

Flaxseed oil is another oil that is excellent for a improving the quality of a dog's coat, and I especially recommend it for dogs with dry skin. Do not cook with this oil; simply place some on your dog's food. The amount given may range from one teaspoon to two tablespoons, depending on your dog's size. A large-breed dog would benefit from up to two tablespoons of flaxseed oil, especially if his coat or skin is dry. I like to give my dog both olive oil and flaxseed oil, as they work together well.

Once opened, the oil should be refrigerated, as should most other oils, since they tend to go rancid when left out. Organic cold-pressed flaxseed oil is a most nutritious and well-balanced oil, containing both omega-3 and omega-6 fatty acids. It is used routinely to help relieve allergic skin disease in dogs. This type of oil can usually be found in any health food store, where it is much less expensive than when found in veterinary products.

As a less expensive alternative to flaxseed oil, ground flax seeds themselves can be sprinkled on your dog's food. They must be ground up first to release the oils and nutrients. Fresh ground flax seeds have the best nutritional value of the flax and are the most economical way to get a very fresh and potent product. Dogs do not seem to mind the taste of ground flax seeds, but I have encountered many a dog who did not like flaxseed oil.

Flax seeds are so tiny that the average blender will not chop them. You will need to purchase a coffee grinder and grind up the flax seeds this way. After you grind the seeds, you must store them in the refrigerator. Store no more than a ½ cup of flax seeds at a time. Give a medium-size dog about a tablespoon each day in his food.

Coconut Oil

At one time, coconut oil was a significant part of the American diet. The food industry considered coconut oil to be the superior dietary oil for use in baking and food preparations. However, during World War II, when the Japanese occupied most of the South Pacific and the Philippines, supplies of coconut oil were cut off. Americans had to turn to alternative sources for cooking oils, and this is when many of the polyunsaturated oils entered the market.

Coconuts and their oil are classified as "functional foods" because they provide many health benefits beyond their excellent nutritional content. Coconut oil possesses healing properties far beyond that of any other dietary oil and is extensively used in traditional medicine among Asian and Pacific populations. It is used around the world to treat a wide variety of health problems, including abscesses, asthma, baldness, bronchitis, bruises, burns, colds, constipation, cough, dysentery, earache, fever, flu, gingivitis, gonorrhea, jaundice, kidney stones, skin infections, toothaches, tuberculosis, tumors, and more. Coconut palm is so highly valued by Pacific Islanders as a source of both food and medicine that they call it "the Tree of Life."

Modern science is confirming that coconut oil, in one form or another, can be used to kill viruses, bacteria, and yeast; protect against osteoporosis; relieve the symptoms of Crohn's disease and stomach ulcers; prevent tooth decay; support thyroid function; dissolve kidney stones; and prevent obesity.

Only recently has modern medical science unlocked the secrets to the coconut's amazing healing powers. Researchers have known for quite some time that the secret to health and weight loss associated with coconut oil is related to the length of the fatty acid chains contained in coconut oil. Coconut oil contains what are called medium-chain fatty acids. These medium-chain fatty acids are different from the common longer-chain fatty acids found in other plant-based vegetable oils.

Vegetable oils are typically stored in the body as fat, while coconut oil is quickly burned in the body for energy. This is akin to adding kindling, rather than a big damp log, to a fireplace.

Coconut oil is nature's richest source of medium-chain fatty acids. They not only raise the body's metabolism, which leads to weight loss, but they also have special health-giving properties. The most predominant fatty acid chain found in coconut oil, for example, is lauric acid. Recent research has discovered the value of these lauric oils. Outside of a human mother's breast milk, coconut oil is nature's most abundant source of lauric acid and medium-chain fatty acids. The medium-chain fats in coconut oil are similar to fats in mother's milk, and both have been shown to have miraculous healing power. When lauric acid is consumed in the diet, either in human breast milk or in coconut oil, it forms a monoglyceride called monolaurin, which has been shown to destroy several types of bacteria and viruses as well as protozoa such as *Giardia*. Monolaurin is sold in tablet form in the United States, and I commonly use it to prevent or nip in the bud any flu or cold. Once word got out about how effective it was, I could not keep it on the shelf in my practice. Dogs love coconut oil on their food as a condiment. Its daily use results in a glowing coat with less dandruff and odor. It also supports your dog's thyroid function and hones his metabolism. Easily found in health-food stores, coconut oil should be kept in the refrigerator. Half a teaspoon a day for a medium-size dog is the average portion. A jar of coconut oil will last a long time.

Bones: The Bonus with a Caveat

Yes, it's OK for your dog to enjoy a bone or two. In fact, it's even desirable, just as long as it's the right kind of bone. The kinds of bones I'm talking about are marrow bones such as the large femur or leg bones and knuckle bones from a cow, which are practically impossible to swallow or chip. Even so, you should make sure such a bone is big enough for your breed of dog. A bone may be served raw, parboiled, or cooked (meaning baked, boiled, or broiled). It should always follow a meal, since it is too rich to be given to your dog on an empty stomach. The marrow may be a bit rich for some dogs, so you can remove at least some, if not all, of it at first—then, as your dog gets more accustomed to it, you can leave more in.

Boiling is the best way to prepare marrow bones. Keep them in boiling water for eight to ten minutes; then scoop out the marrow. To bake knuckle bones, put them in the oven on a baking tray at 300 degrees Fahrenheit for 30 minutes or so.

Chicken necks, because they are made from cartilage and will not splinter, can also be used as treats for medium-size dogs or as chews for a small dog. Chicken necks are easy to locate at butcher shops or in the meat and fowl section of most supermarkets. You can either feed them raw or prepare them by broiling or baking in a preheated oven at 350 degrees Fahrenheit for 15 to 20 minutes. After they cool, cut them into 1-inch pieces for small dogs or let your medium-size dog chew on the whole neck. Cook up several at a time and freeze the extra ones for a later date.

Because a whole chicken neck is small for larger breeds, watch that a large dog does not swallow it whole. Like chicken necks, chicken backbones are made of cartilage rather than bone, are easy to digest, and will not splinter. Although chicken necks and backbones are usually OK when raw, they should not be given to a dog who has no experience with bones, as he could conceivably swallow a chunk too big to exit the stomach.

The good news is that gnawing on a bone helps stimulate the gums and remove tartar from the teeth, a substitute toothbrush of sorts. It's certainly preferable to dental surgery for your dog. In addition, it can enable a dog to exercise his jaw muscles.

However, the wrong kind of bone can result in a variety of problems, some merely inconvenient, such as getting pieces stuck between the teeth, and others more serious, such as pieces' lodging in the stomach or piercing the intestinal wall. The most dangerous bones are those that can splinter or be swallowed, such as cooked chicken and turkey bones and bones from steaks, cuts of lamb, veal, beef, and pork.

You have to watch that a bone doesn't get too small; if it does, exchange it for a new one. In addition, a dog who gets overly enthusiastic about a bone can sometimes chip a tooth, which is why a dog who's savoring his very first bone bears supervision. When your dog is chewing on his bones safely, relax and enjoy the fact that his teeth and gums will be healthier for it.

Chapter 6

The Cure Is in the Cupboard

Exotic is the word I think of in relation to the history of herbs and other spices: perilous ocean voyages, colorful cultures, secret maps delineating spice routes, danger, and excitement. Commerce in spices began more than 3,000 years ago. Prior to this, the ancient Egyptians recorded and cataloged their knowledge of herbs, and a Chinese emperor published a book, *The Great Native Herbal*. Many plants mentioned in there are still used today in Chinese herbal preparations.

At first, Arab merchants controlled the trade routes to India in the Middle East and therefore the spice trade. Once sea routes were discovered, Egypt became a major commercial center for trading spices. Later, Venice monopolized the spice trade between the Middle East and Europe. Countries became very wealthy from trading in spices.

As Venice was demanding exorbitant prices, Portugal and Spain looked eastward for new routes and then began to search westward. On his first voyage, in 1492, Christopher Columbus was looking not for a new land but for a shorter ocean route to India to gain access to its spices. His expedition received the majority of its financial backing from spice traders. In commerce, spices were considered more valuable than gold.

The great value that was placed on obtaining herbs and spices is recorded in history. Each region had plants and herbs that were specific to that particular area and climate. Countries were motivated to discover and control new routes for spice trade because these herbs were precious. Spices were big business.

A large part of their value lay not in their uses in food preparation but in their medicinal uses. The phrase "the spice of life" can be taken literally. With few exceptions, the spices known today were used very early in human history and played important, sometimes magical, roles in medicine. Before the advent of industrially prepared medicines, herbal remedies were commonly prescribed. In this chapter we will rediscover some of this ancient herbal lore and learn how to use it to improve our dogs' health.

> **HERBS AND SPICES:** The term *spice* includes herbs, which are the fragrant leaves of herbaceous plants, many of which are native to particular temperate regions.

A World of Herbal Medicine

Herbal medicine is probably as old as humanity itself; the discovery of many spices predates the founding of the earliest civilizations. The first humans learned about herbs by trial and error and passed that knowledge from one generation to the next.

The ancient Arabs, Babylonians, Chinese, Greeks, Romans, Hebrews, and Persians were all familiar with the practice of herbal medicine. The Chinese developed a systematic methodology of prescribing herbal medicines. In their view, the body is a reflection of nature, filled with a life energy called *Qi* (pronounced "chi"). Illness is a sign that a person's flow of the Qi is out of balance. Healers use herbs to rebalance the Qi and return the person to health. Combinations of Chinese herbs are formulated to have a deep and powerful healing effect. In these formulations, herbs that complement each other are combined, resulting in a synergistic effect and more potent healing. It's a magnified version of the synergistic effects of the whole leaf or the whole plant. Chinese herbal combinations have a powerful ability to heal illness and deserve a great deal of recognition and respect.

India, too, developed a sophisticated knowledge of botanical medicine. The Indian system of Ayurvedic medicine is one of the most ancient and complete systems of holistic healing. This form of medicine recognizes that there are different metabolic types. A practitioner observes whether his patient has an excess or deficiency in a specific area and uses diet and herbs to bring back a balance.

European proponents of a system known as the doctrine of signatures believed that the configuration and structure of a plant could help them understand what problem that plant could be used for. According to the doctrine, plants with a yellow signature, such as dandelions, can treat liver conditions like jaundice (a condition in which the whites of the eyes and the skin become yellow due to liver failure). The leafy greens of the beet top with red veins are considered good for cleansing the blood. Hawthorne berries *(Crataegus)* are bright red berries shaped like hearts, and they prove to be very helpful in heart conditions. Ginseng root resembles the trunk, arms, and legs of a man and therefore has been used as a tonic for the entire body. The leaves and the cross-section of the fruit of the *Ginkgo biloba* resemble a brain; this herb is used for memory loss.

An Ancient Payment Plan

In ancient China, a doctor was paid when the patient was healthy. When the patient became ill, the patient stopped paying the fee, but the doctor was expected to spend his time and use his knowledge to return the patient to health. Imagine how this payment plan would change the practice of medicine in modern times!

Western herbal use stems from the ancient uses of medicinal plants in Europe. The herbs used by the Native Americans are also incorporated into Western herb lore. The Western approach tends to view the body as a system of organs and cells that must be kept in balance.

Each culture had its particular sacred and common herbs. Over time, just about all have been shared throughout the world. We can now go into a health food store and buy herbs that were considered more precious than gold hundreds of years ago.

In all forms of herbal practice, the restoration of balance and harmony in the body is the primary goal, for this balance is the key to maintaining and restoring health. The World Health Organization estimates that about 80 percent of the world's people now rely on herbs for health care.

The Necessity of Herbs

For many centuries, in all ancient cultures, healing herbs were simply part of the daily diet. Turmeric, the main ingredient in Indian curry, contains a natural antioxidant and anti-inflammatory called curcumin, which helps relieve the pain of arthritis. One of the most valuable spices traded from ancient India was cinnamon, another common ingredient in Indian food. Today cinnamon has been shown to help regulate blood sugar in diabetics, while caraway and fennel seeds, Indian spices as well, promote digestion.

Mediterranean cultures also routinely used healing herbs as spices in their food. Wild oregano and rosemary act as antiseptics. Rosemary also supports endocrine balance and, in our dogs, promotes a lovely coat.

Animals have instincts that draw them to graze on a particular plant to mend their ills. In the spring, horses and sheep will eat certain herbs from the fields that kill intestinal parasites. Wildlife documentaries often show animals deliberately choosing certain plants to eat.

Your dog's body has a built-in system to maintain good health. This system works in a powerful, almost miraculous way to heal your dog of disease and illness. It is more efficient and effective than any computer could design. This multifaceted system needs certain enzymes, minerals, and vitamins to do its job well. Our domesticated dogs need supplements because dogs are not part of the wild food chain that would supply them with fresh food all of the time. Many dogs suffer from the same diseases as humans do, and they can benefit from herbs in their diet. Every body, human and canine alike, must have the fuel it needs for its systems to make repairs.

Our First Medicines

Herbs are really concentrated food sources. Since herbs are foods, the body recognizes their nutrients and utilizes them in ways that naturally promote health. An herb provides a multitude of nutrients that are balanced and easily absorbed. Today we need herbs even more because the majority of our food sources are grown on depleted topsoil. To sustain a good crop, farmers have resorted to mass-produced agriculture, which employs fungicides, pesticides, and tons of fertilizer. This results in an "empty harvest." The produce on the supermarket shelves lacks the nutrients that the cells need to thrive. Herbs in the diet help replace and balance this (as does organic produce).

Herbs contain usable forms of vitamins and minerals from nature. Herbal medicines help replenish the building blocks that a body needs in order to heal.

Partners in Health

Personal philosophy about the body determines whether a user chooses herbs over prescription drugs for healing. Those who choose herbs trust the body's innate intelligence to heal and regenerate and believe that herbs help the body do so by providing the missing ingredients needed to heal. Herbs are part of nature, and our bodies have long known how to utilize their gifts.

Herbs can help stimulate the immune system and adjust the balance of the body for good health. This is vastly different from how an antibiotic works. The antibiotic, which enters the bloodstream, kills off the bacteria in the body and leaves toxic debris behind. The end result of this therapy is a weakened immune system. Herbal medicine increases the immune system's ability, and, most important, the body itself becomes stronger and smarter. Herbs nourish the body and entice tissues to heal.

You may be familiar with the widespread use of an herb called echinacea, commonly used for nipping a cold or flu in the bud by giving a big boost to the immune system. It's important to understand the difference between how antibiotics and herbal medicine works.

The therapeutic effect of herbal medicine stems from its inherent ability to support the functions of the body so the body can more effectively correct the problem. Herbs are often touted for their use as drug alternatives. This is good, because when they are used instead of drugs, they heighten your or your dog's ability to heal. Of course, this also improves general health in the long run, for a wiser body system is a better body system.

It is important to understand that herbs act as assistants. The body will use the nutrients it needs from them. Herbs should not be thought of as miracle drugs.

The Whole Pie, Not Just a Piece

Once the pharmaceutical company extracts and purifies what is considered the "active ingredient," they then own that singular product and are able to charge extraordinary prices for it. Often, the "active ingredient" in the drug now comes with a plethora of side effects. Have you ever listened to the side effects listed at the end of pharmaceutical drug commercials on the television with amazement?

Each herb has a unique combination of ingredients that work synergistically to produce their effect. Once the healthy cocktail of the herb is disassembled, each isolated ingredient is imbalanced. Without the other ingredients present, and in its altered state, it now causes side effects. The synergistic quality of the whole herb has been lost. Of course, pharmaceutical companies would not have any interest in the whole herb because they are unable to patent it and own it, and thus they cannot profit from it. Noticeably, pharmaceutical drugs do not appear to cure, as plenty of folks who continually renew their prescriptions month after month after month well know.

How Safe Are Herbs?

Of course, some herbs are highly poisonous. Socrates was made to drink a preparation of poison hemlock to end his life. However, when used intelligently for beneficial purposes, herbal preparations are very safe. In fact, most herbal preparations are actually much safer than pharmaceutical drugs. Adverse drug reactions are the fourth leading cause of death in hospitalized patients in the United States.

While pharmaceutical companies search for the active ingredient in an herbal plant, herbalists use the entire leaf, the root, or the whole plant. Side effects are rarely seen with herbal preparations, although too many herbs used at once can cause diarrhea in dogs. The herbs you will learn how to use in this chapter, however, are very safe. Herbs definitely have a pharmacological power, and we will be portraying only herbs that can safely and easily be incorporated into your dog's diet.

Many herbal preparations are available from health food stores. Liquid extracts of the herbs are usually easy to administer to your pet. Try to find extracts that have the alcohol solvent removed, because most dogs do not like the taste of alcohol. Herbs and herbal combinations also come in tablets, which can be hidden in tasty cheese or butter if you wish.

Fennel

Purifying and Preventing

Research has shown that dogs do not particularly like the taste of salt. Yet they do appreciate the taste of many of our culinary herbs when these herbs are added to their cooked food. (Simply sprinkling them on dry kibble has never been a hit with my dogs.) My husband and I make stews, casseroles, and puddings for our dogs and, as I've mentioned, we routinely add rosemary and lots of olive oil. I credit my dogs' shining coats to these two ingredients. The rosemary makes their food smell so good, and when added to the mix, it only makes it better.

Many of the herbs you can purchase at grocery stores can be added to your dog's cooked meals. These herbs add a wonderful fragrance to home-cooked food and impart a special touch. They can also help ease physical symptoms and problems.

Both caraway and fennel seeds are digestive aids. They help eliminate flatulence and intestinal cramping. Fennel stimulates lactation as well. (Tip: Guinness and other dark beers also stimulate milk production. This tip has never failed to get results and raise some eyebrows when I suggest it!) Asparagus and parsley are both good for the urinary tract. Parsley also acts as a diuretic and as an aid in kidney inflammation. Sage has been credited with soothing skin conditions and acting as an antibacterial with oral infections.

Basil works on the lungs and is a decongestant, along with having an antiviral and antibacterial effect. Dill acts as an expectorant and is antibacterial. Oregano helps with respiratory problems. Tarragon is indicated in use against colitis, sciatica, and parasites. In general, most of these herbs are simply healthy and tasty and well deserve to be added to your dog's meals.

While we are on the subject of cures in the cupboard, we can go over some common household foods that may be useful. Cucumbers can be peeled and sliced, with one slice held on each eyelid to reduce eye inflammation. Green cabbage leaves are good to wrap around itchy areas on the skin, sometimes called hot spots. To do this, beat the cabbage leaf with a wooden meat mallet and then, when the juices are freed, wrap the leaf around the inflamed area. The cabbage will get warm—you'll be amazed—and the inflamed area will cool down. Witch hazel is made from the witch hazel plant and is also good to spray or dab onto inflamed skin or feet. Applying a paste of baking soda mixed with water will also help soothe an irritated area.

Garlic

Garlic, a member of the lily family, is one of the few herbs with worldwide recognition and use. Among the oldest cultivated plants, garlic has long been renowned for its ability to ward off disease. In 1858, Louis Pasteur proved that garlic was able to kill fungi and bacteria. Modern research has shown that garlic has antifungal, antibiotic, antiviral, antiparasitic, and anticancer effects.

Daily usage of garlic supports the body in ways that no other herb does. It supports the digestive tract, helping support and revive those good bacteria in the gut, and wards off worms. It can be useful as well for the treatment of ringworm. Garlic also helps regulate blood sugar levels.

The odor of garlic comes from the sulfur-containing compounds that account for most of its medicinal properties. We've already discussed how garlic helps prevent flea infestation, as the essence of the garlic will mix in with the oil produced by your dog's oil glands and comes out in the coat's natural oil.

Garlic is best used fresh, and your dog will enjoy fresh garlic in his food. Garlic is also available in health food stores in tablets or capsules. Supermarkets carry powdered garlic, but this form has lost most of its "oomph."

The old adage "if a little is good, more is better" is not true with garlic. If using fresh garlic, half a clove for a small dog and one clove for a medium or large dog is just enough each day.

You can give garlic to your dog whole or you may chop it up and mix the pieces into his food. If you cook for your dog, add garlic to your recipes; it will still be of benefit to his health. Garlic can be used as a flavoring in many of the recipes listed in this book.

WART REMOVAL: To use garlic for wart removal, mash the garlic and tape it onto the wart for a few hours. In some cases, the warts will decrease in size or disappear.

Aloe Vera

For centuries, many cultures have used the aloe vera plant to treat burns and heal wounds. Aloe originated in tropical Africa, where it was used as an antidote for poison arrow wounds. Historically, it was used by the peoples of Greece, Rome, China, and India.

Each leaf contains a gel-like substance that works toward rapid regeneration of tissue on wounds and burns. This gel appears to increase the rate of healing in the cellular matrix and decrease inflammation. It also contains antibiotic and coagulating agents. It is useful for treating fungal

ITCH RELIEF: Aloe gel can be used topically on itchy areas of your dog's skin. It is excellent to use on allergic dogs with hot spots.

infections of the skin and can stop the itch of insect bites. Additionally, taking one to two tablespoons orally three times a day acts as a tonic for the intestinal tract.

Aloe plants can be easily found in the local nursery or garden center and require little care to maintain in a home. Place a terra-cotta pot with an aloe vera plant on your window ledge and watch it grow. The gel from the plant is much more effective than the gel available at stores. The active ingredients remain active for less than three days after cutting off a leaf.

Fresh gel can be obtained by removing a leaf and splitting it. Apply the green-tinged clear jellylike inside of the split leaf to burns, wounds, fungal infections, and insect bites. If you cut a leaf and use part of it, the remaining parts of the leaf need to be stored in the refrigerator.

Dandelion

Rather than being troubled by all those dandelions on your lawn, you can use them to make a healthy tea infusion and detoxify your dog's liver. Dandelion is a somewhat recent addition to the field of herbal medicine, first appearing in Europe in the mid-fifteenth century. The earliest known mention of dandelion as medicine was in seventh-century China. The Chinese use the entire plant, while Western herbal medicine tends to use either the root or the leaf.

Dandelion is a powerful diuretic and is one of the best sources of potassium. Pharmaceutical diuretics drain potassium out of the body and deplete potassium reserves. The dandelion root works as a very effective diuretic, removing excess fluid from the body, and it replaces potassium lost in the process, serving as a wonderful example of how a complete herb works. Dandelion can be used for easing fluid retention, especially with heart problems.

Dandelion reduces congestion in the liver and can even help with jaundice. Both the roots and the leaves can be used for medicinal purposes. The leaves work as a digestive and liver tonic. The root is used as a cleansing tonic for gallstones, jaundice, and constipation and for liver detoxification. Dandelion also increases gastric secretions to aid in digestion.

The nice thing about these herbs is that they can be used preventatively. Some chopped dandelion in a meal works to clean a relatively healthy liver and make it even healthier.

A few fresh leaves can be chopped and added to a tasty meal for your dog. They can taste bitter, so add them sparingly at first. Dandelion-leaf

More Dandelion Ideas

Place 2 to 3 tablespoons of dandelion leaves into 1 cup of water and bring to a boil. Simmer gently for fifteen minutes and let cool. Give a tablespoon of the liquid three times a day to a medium-size dog. An infusion or tea can also be made by pouring hot water over the leaves and allowing the mixture to steep for five to thirty minutes.

juice can be made in a juicer, and a quarter of a teaspoon can be given three times a day for a medium-size dog. The fresh juice is a more powerful diuretic than an infusion, which is prepared from dried leaves. A tincture can be purchased in liquid form in health food stores. A few drops given a few times a day can aid in removing excess fluid in dogs with heart conditions. Dandelion capsules and extracts also can be found in health food stores.

Do not use dandelions from lawns that have been sprayed with herbicides. That would counter our goal of healing the body. Unsprayed leaves can be harvested at any time during the growing season. The fresh leaves are often sold in supermarkets in the produce department. Commercially available dandelion is less bitter than what grows on your lawn.

Cranberries

Cranberries are much more than a traditional food served during the holiday season. Recent studies prove cranberries' efficacy in treating urinary tract infections. It has been known for a long time that cranberries acidify the urine. Bacteria cannot survive when the pH changes. But there is another way that cranberry fights urinary tract infections. It contains a polysaccharide called mannose, which decreases the ability of the bacteria to adhere to the cells lining the urinary tract. The bacteria will adhere to the mannose from the cranberry rather than to the surface of the cells. These bacteria then get flushed out with the urine. Both cranberries and blueberries, which are in the same genus, prevent bacteria from adhering to the cells on the bladder wall.

Additionally, cranberries are excellent as a general health tonic, balancing the acid-base in the body. Many dogs eat far too much protein and grain, causing an increase in the body's acidity. Cranberry makes the body a healthy alkaline and the urine a healthier acid. Adding some stewed cranberries to a meal helps promote a healthier, more alkaline state. Fresh and frozen cranberries are four times as potent as cranberry juice cocktail, while cranberry juice concentrate is twenty-seven times as potent.

The Herbal Garden

In the Middle Ages, almost every monastery had a physic garden, which contained the herbs they needed for cooking and healing. At that time, *physic* was defined as "medicine or healing as an art or a profession." Nowadays it means "something that lifts the spirits or energizes." A healing herb (physic) garden can now do both for you and your dogs.

I love working in my herb garden. When I run my hands gently along the plants and rejoice in their fragrance, it's a healthy feeling. Just the smell of the garden puts me in a better state of mind.

How exciting your herb garden will be! Working in your herb garden is a good excuse to get back in touch with nature while getting some fresh air. Your dog will love the time outdoors, too. You may want to place some sort of relaxing seating arrangement near the garden so that you can enjoy the fragrance during the summer months as you sit and sip a cup of herbal tea.

Fresh herbs have a much higher concentration of phytochemicals (compounds found in plants that are used by our bodies for nourishment when we eat the plants) than do dried-up herbs sitting in a jar on a super-market shelf. When freshly picked, herbs are a joy to use in cooking. I find it extremely enjoyable to go outside in the summer and snip bits of fresh herbs to use in cooking.

It is also fun to dry garden herbs at the end of the season. Gather the herbs when the growing season comes to a close, when the herbs are in their prime and before they begin to fade. Hang small bunches of each herb upside down until dry. You'll then have dried herbs to make into teas and to add to your and your dog's meals during the winter months. You can also make potpourri and rinses and enjoy your bounty in a variety of other ways.

Using plants as medicine brings us back to an understanding of how we fit into the cycle of nature. It may surprise you to learn that some of the plants you may typically purchase for your perennial garden are medicinal plants. The coneflower, also called purple coneflower or echinacea, for example, is a common garden plant. It gives a powerful boost to the immune system and is commonly taken when a person feels the onset of a cold or flu. Another example of a common healing plant is *Hypericum*, or Saint-John's-wort; a pale green plant that produces delicate yellow flowers. This plant can help with depression and has an antiviral property.

In this next section, we will make it easy for you to plant a garden that will provide you with healing herbs throughout the growing season in a

 PERENNIALS are plants that have a life span of more than two years and, if the climate is right, will return year after year.

4-foot by 4-foot space. The seeds and plants are easy to obtain; I usually go for the plants. It's a group effort to run this garden, for you maintain it and your dogs eat the herbs. Of course, you and your human family members can join in and enjoy these herbs yourselves.

The herbs that we will discuss have been used for centuries as natural cures and to help maintain good health. They are safe and easy to use, and they were often used in the diet as spices. As well as making the food taste better, they have healing powers. Fresh herbs are always the best to use, but use them sparingly in the food because they do provide a strong presence.

Many herbs return year after year. In very cold climates, a covering of hay or burlap may protect the more fragile ones. Some, such as chamomile, spread quickly, but they can usually be easily controlled.

Chamomile

German and French varieties of chamomile are often available at garden stores. Chamomile has a calming effect. Add this herb to your dog's diet when he is at that nervous adolescent stage. It also helps ease the pain of teething when prepared as a tea and can promote sleep in elderly animals who pace around at night. In the latter case, the animal would take it just before bedtime.

Chamomile supports the digestive functions and the liver. It will help ease flatulence, dyspepsia, and irritable bowel problems and will settle the stomach. It can also boost the appetite. This herb helps cleanse the blood and supports pancreatic function.

A strong tea of chamomile can help heal skin rashes and soothe irritated skin; this is very useful for allergic, itchy dogs. It also increases the speed of wound healing and acts to reduce inflammation and swelling. You can add it to the diet and use it on the skin. Fresh chamomile is also an excellent insect repellent.

Chamomile Recipe

Chopped bits of chamomile—one to three teaspoons is plenty—may be added to home-cooked meals. The flowers and leaves are the best parts of the plants to use. To make a tea, pour 2 cups of boiling water onto 2 teaspoons of the dried or fresh leaves and flowers and let steep for 10 minutes. For digestive problems, this tea can be given with or after meals.

Your dog is not the only one who can benefit from chamomile tea. Why don't you enjoy a cup yourself and relax?

Chamomile can be harvested throughout the summer. Pick the flowers and leaves when they are free of dew. Dry the herb quickly so the flowers retain their rich pungent scent, but do not dry them at too high a temperature. One home-dried flower can give more flavor than a commercial chamomile tea bag.

Calendula

The vivid colors of its flowers are reason enough to plant calendula. This herb also earns a spot in the garden for its medicinal properties, which were recognized as far back as ancient Roman times. This herb is a favorite among herbalists, and for good reason. It has an almost magical

Calendula—An Ancient Herb

The Romans dubbed what we call the common pot marigold *Calendula officinalis*. *Calendula* refers to the herb's blooming schedule, for it would flower on the *calends*, or new moon, of every month. *Officinalis* refers to its "official" medicinal value.

Calendula Infusion

When making your own calendula infusion, it is best to use the petals alone, for this makes a better product. You can harvest the petals from early summer through late fall. The petals can also be dried and used in a tea later in the season. The flowers can be mixed into handmade soap or mixed with olive oil.

To make a tea, pour 1 cup of boiling water onto 1 to 2 tablespoons of the petals and steep for 15 minutes. The tea can be taken internally for gastritis or mouth ulcers and gum disease. Externally, as a compress, it acts as an antiseptic and has a healing effect on the skin. It also greatly helps stop itching.

effect in healing wounds. Calendula has a more powerful ability to hinder bacteria than many antibiotics do, and it has the benefit of having an anti-inflammatory effect while it promotes new healthy cell growth. It also works against fungal infections. It is ideal for first aid treatment and works well as an antiseptic lotion.

In Europe, calendula flowers are common ingredients in ointments and creams used to treat cuts, mild burns, inflammations, sores, and bee stings. Calendula is a long-blooming, easy-to-grow annual that reaches 2 feet in height. The flowers range from 1½ to 4 inches across and range in color from buttery yellow to deep orange.

To understand calendula's healing power, consider the following anecdote. A friend brought her dog in to see me many years ago. The dog's left front leg had been run over by a gravel truck. All of the skin, muscle, and tendon on the lower front part of the leg had been sheared off. To make matters worse, gravel had been ground into the wound. It looked like the best possible scenario would involve skin grafting. My friend did not have the financial wherewithal to do much at all. We decided that I would remove the gravel and clean it up the wound. Every day, under my direction, she placed fresh bandages, well moistened with calendula, on the wound. By the end of the month, the entire wound had healed and the leg appeared normal. No grafting was necessary, and all of the fur grew back.

I have to admit that calendula is my favorite herb, for it can do so much. In addition to acting as an antifungal and antibacterial agent, it is excellent to place on the skin of itching dogs and can sometimes stop a hot spot in a jiff. For hot spots, use a strong infusion made from the leaves and apply it frequently to the area.

Calendula is widely available in salve and ointment form in health food stores. A liquid tincture is also available. A pad soaked in the infusion or diluted tincture can be applied to speed up the healing of wounds.

Echinacea Immune Booster

To boost the immune system, place 1 to 2 teaspoons of the root and one chopped flower in 2 cups of water and bring it slowly to a boil. Let this simmer for ten to fifteen minutes. A medium-size dog can have one tablespoon per dose, given three times a day. Do not worry about adjusting for size.

The root is the most commonly used part of the plant for infections and inflammation. It can be especially helpful for recurring kidney and bladder infections.

Purple Coneflower—Echinacea

The Native Americans used this herb to treat fevers, wounds, and even snakebites. It was commonly used by the Native Americans of the Great Plains region of North America for its powers of healing wounds and boosting the immune system.

Of course, the early settlers caught on and used echinacea for colds and infections. Later a German researcher, Dr. Gerhard Madaus, brought some seeds over to Europe and conducted scientific research on the herb, which proved its immune-stimulating properties. Today echinacea is the most important over-the-counter remedy in Germany.

Echinacea is the well-known herbal remedy that many start to take the minute they feel a cold coming on because it is effective against both bacterial and viral attacks. Many people have the purple coneflower, from which echinacea is made, as a decorative plant in their gardens, completely unaware of its healing properties. You may very well have admired this common long-stemmed purple flower in a garden without knowing it was the source of the popular herb.

While some people take echinacea all winter with the intent of warding off the flu, its best use is at the very start of a fever or infection. When my twin boys were babies and a fever or cold came on, I would go to my garden and pick one coneflower plant, root and all. After simmering both the root and flower for ten to fifteen minutes, I would cool it a little and add some honey. Each of the boys would drink a cup and go to sleep. When they awoke, their fevers would be gone.

Echinacea can also be used topically, as demonstrated in studies with guinea pigs that showed an increased rate of healing. An infusion made with the root can be applied to minor scrapes and cuts.

Some say the fresh plant is much more effective than the dried herb, and I would fully agree. That is why it is so nice to have it growing in your garden. Of course, echinacea comes in all forms in the health food store: liquid tinctures, tablets, and capsules.

FENNEL TEA: To make a tea, pour 2 cups of boiling water over 2 teaspoons of fennel seeds. Let steep for 15 minutes, then add ¼ to ½ cup of the cooled mixture to your dog's meal. Refrigerate the leftover tea and use for future meals.

Fennel

Fennel is a wonderful digestive aid and has been used for this purpose in Australia and Spain for hundreds of years. Fennel seeds, when taken after a meal, assist in digestion. The seeds have also been used for years to expel intestinal parasites. Tea made from fennel helps rid the body of toxins and helps cleanse the body's cells and tissues. The plant itself can be chopped finely and added to a home-cooked stew for your dog. The seeds can be made into a tea or added to the meal.

Parsley

Parsley is an herb rich in minerals and is an aid to digestion. Its use in meals helps maintain a good pH level that your dog needs for disease prevention. It also freshens the breath, and we all know one or two dogs who could really use that!

Parsley works to detoxify the body and is excellent for the urinary system—the kidneys and bladder. It works as a diuretic to remove water retention in the body and is a good addition to each meal for dogs with heart conditions and fluid retention. Parsley is easy to add routinely to each meal; a teaspoon or more can be finely chopped and added to home-cooked food. Parsley adds that chlorophyll that is so healthy.

Parsley has more vitamin C than oranges do!

More Rosemary Ideas

Throw some bits of rosemary and lavender on your floor and vacuum them up as you clean. They will, as they sit in the bag, give off a pleasant scent as you vacuum.

Rosemary is excellent to add to a rinse for your dog's coat because it promotes hair growth and brings out the luster and color tones in the fur. Rosemary rinses are also great for dogs with flaking, dry skin.

To make a tea, pour 2 cups of water over 2 teaspoons of finely chopped rosemary. Let steep for fifteen minutes and use as a rinse for the coat.

Rosemary

Rosemary originated in France and the United States. A small amount of fresh rosemary can go a long way. This herb has an absolutely beautiful aroma and it is lovely to sit near in the summer months. It would be great to place a bench or a table and chairs next to your herb garden because the aroma in itself has a healing effect on the body and soul.

Rosemary, used topically, has an antifungal, antibacterial, and antiseptic effect. Inhaling the steam from a tea made of rosemary is good for sinus infections. Adding ¼ teaspoon of rosemary to 2 cups of home-cooked food is adequate for flavoring. This herb also helps digestion.

Sage

Sage is another herb that has a wonderful, healing fragrance. It can be used as an addition to the everyday diet by adding a ½ teaspoon of chopped fresh sage to a stew or casserole. It can also be used as a tea to rinse the mouth because of its healing effect on gingivitis. To make a tea, pour 2 cups of water over 2 teaspoons of chopped sage, let it steep for 15 minutes, and refrigerate. You can even add some of the tea to your dog's water bowl and simply allow him to drink it. Start out with small amounts in the water and, if he likes it, gradually increase the amount of tea.

Sage works to strengthen the body in general and has the effect of balancing estrogen levels. It would be good to add this herb to the food of a spayed female who is experiencing urinary leakage while sleeping.

Thyme

Thyme

Myths, legends, and rhymes all seem to have been inspired by the humble thyme plant. The ancient Egyptians used it when embalming their dead. Even today, the oil of thyme, thymol, is an ingredient in embalming fluids. Thyme began in the Mediterranean, but it has spread all over the world and is used by many diverse cultures in their cuisine. Thyme comes in an amazing diversity of flavors, ranging from oregano to cinnamon, lemon, and caraway. Common thyme or any other cooking thyme is excellent to use to flavor stews and casseroles for your dog.

Thyme has antibacterial effects. Thyme oil and its components have been suggested as food additives to more naturally extend the lives of processed foods. Vapor that contains the essential oil has been shown to inhibit airborne fungus and bacteria. Thyme has proven antispasmodic and respiratory effects and has historically been used for bronchitis, as an expectorant, and for laryngitis.

You can dry thyme by hanging it upside down for a week. The leaves can be saved for seasoning your dog's food, or you can mix it with dried rose petals for a lovely potpourri.

Lavender

The lavender plant is known for its relaxing and soothing effects on the spirit. An important use for lavender with dogs is for reducing the buildup of excess sebum, that is, skin oil, on the animals. Lavender works like a charm for some of those lovable yet greasy and smelly dogs. You see, bacteria begin to grow in the excess sebum, and the bacterial growth in a greasy coat is responsible for that musty old-shoe odor that some of our dogs seem to have.

A lavender rinse after a bath, or spraying some lavender tea on the coat, reduces the sebum, works to decrease the bacteria, and keeps that odor at bay. As an added benefit, it is an anti-inflammatory and analgesic, so it decreases itchiness as well. It is beneficial for skin irritations or wounds because it promotes tissue regeneration and speeds wound healing. As an added benefit, the delicate purple or white flowers are beautiful to look at and smell great!

Lavender Rinse

Add a ½ cup of chopped lavender to 4 cups of boiling water to make a rinse. Let it steep for 30 minutes; then strain and place in a clean jar or spray bottle. Refrigerate any that you will not use within five days. Rinse your dog with the tea after his bath, and use the spray bottle to keep him fresh in between.

Herbs for Healthy Skin

The herbs from your garden can be used in healing rinses that can be applied after a bath or sprayed on to keep the skin and coat healthy and to reduce irritation or inflammation. Herbs can be used as treats in your bath, too.

ALLERGY RINSE OR SPRAY

2 tablespoons chopped lavender leaves
2 tablespoons chopped echinacea root
2 tablespoons chopped chamomile flowers and leaves
2 tablespoons chopped calendula (marigold) florets (flower petals)

Place all of these ingredients in an enamel or glass pot. Pour 8 cups of boiling water over them. Let the pot sit on the stove on very low heat for 15 minutes. Remove from heat and let the mix sit and cool for another 45 minutes. Strain and use as rinse, or fill a spray bottle with the mixture and apply as desired.

The type of coat your dog has will decide the best way to use this rinse. Dobermans, Dalmatians, Dachshunds, and other dogs with short coats would benefit from both the after-bath rinse and regular "freshen-ups" with the spray. Collies, Newfoundlands, and other long-coated dogs would benefit from the after-bath rinse and the spraying of any problem areas after the fur has been parted.

OIL-CONTROLLING RINSE AND SPRAY

1 whole sliced lemon, including skin and rind
4 tablespoons coarsely chopped lavender leaves
1 tablespoon chopped calendula (marigold florets)

Pour 6 cups of water onto all ingredients in an enamel or glass pot. Bring to a boil and simmer for 20 minutes. Remove from heat and allow the entire mixture to sit overnight. Strain the liquid and store in a clean glass jar in the refrigerator. Use as rinse after shampooing, and spray on coat as needed.

HEALTHY SHINY FUR RINSE AND SPRAY

2 tablespoons chopped rosemary leaves
2 tablespoons chopped lavender leaves
2 tablespoons apple cider vinegar

Place ingredients in glass or enamel pot and add 6 cups of water. Bring to a boil and, after a brisk boil is achieved, immediately remove from heat. Let mixture sit for a few hours, then strain and store. Use as rinse after shampooing.

A RELAXING BATH FOR YOU

Finally, for you—an after-gardening treat. Take ½ cup of chopped lavender leaves and flowers and add to 2 cups of boiling water. Let this boil for a minute or so. Remove from heat and let sit for 20 minutes. When ready, strain the lavender from the water. You will be using the scented water in your bath.

While the lavender is steeping, make yourself a relaxing tea. Pour one cup of boiling water onto one tablespoon of chamomile flowers. Let this sit for 3 to 5 minutes, strain, and add a scented honey to sweeten.

Put on some of your favorite music. Pour the lavender water into the bath you have drawn, place your chamomile tea on the side of the tub, and relax in the scented warmth, sipping your tea and listening to your music. You deserve it!

AN INVIGORATING BATH FOR YOU

For a more invigorating bath, use rosemary in place of lavender. Take 1 cup of chopped rosemary leaves and add 2 cups of boiling water. Let this boil for about a minute and remove from heat. Allow to steep for 20 minutes.

While the rosemary is steeping, make yourself an invigorating tea. Put 1 teaspoon of grated fresh ginger, the juice of 1 lemon, and 1 teaspoon of honey into a mug or cup. Fill the cup with boiling water.

Put on your favorite music. Strain the rosemary from the water and pour the scented water into the bath you have drawn. Place your tea on the side of the tub and relax into the water. This combination will invigorate you.

ADDITIONS TO THE RECIPES

Garlic, chamomile, fennel, parsley, rosemary, and sage can all be added to the home-cooked recipes that you make for your dog. Add from ¼ to ½ of a teaspoon to a full recipe, as the fresh herbs go a long way. If the herbs are dried, you can double the amount. Parsley can be added more freely, as it is bland and so good for the body's pH. Garlic can be either fresh and chopped or cooked with the meal. Fresh chopped garlic would be added in a smaller amount than cooked garlic. One clove of raw garlic per day is plenty for a medium-size or large dog; give a small dog no more than half a clove per day.

Chapter 7

The Benefits of "Supplemental" Health Insurance

In a perfect world, dogs and their human friends would get all the nutrients needed for a healthy life from a balanced diet of good food. Although no supplements can take the place of real food (no, you can't just pop a pill every day and be healthy), the truth is that our food supply just ain't what it used to be. Some recent studies in both the United States and Britain have revealed how commercially grown foods have been stripped of much of their nutrient value, apparently due to factory farming techniques that rely on agricultural chemicals and nitrogen-based fertilizers. These practices have largely succeeded in wearing out the soil used for crop cultivation. The depleted soil lacks nutrients, both vitamins and minerals, for plants to pull in. The result is produce that might look beautiful as well as being bountiful but contains fewer vitamins and minerals than the fruits and vegetables grown years ago.

That's why I strongly recommend that your dog be given supplements. I like to think of them, in fact, as a form of "supplemental health insurance" for pets, providing whatever extra nutrients your dog needs to maintain optimal health. They become especially important at this time of shrinking food value. If you refer back to chapter 3, you'll see how important these tools and ingredients are to maintaining health.

Vitamins and Minerals: Ounces of Prevention

The more we learn about the benefits of vitamin C, the more we have come to appreciate how important it is in helping keep us alive and well. Besides boosting the immune system, this vital antioxidant plays a powerful role in detoxification, ridding the body of all of sorts of heavy metals, pesticides, and toxins to which we're exposed daily. Vitamin C helps keep our metabolic innards clean and sparkly, prevents disease, dramatically boosts our immune systems, and retards the aging of cells. Those are enormous health benefits from one easy-to-obtain and inexpensive vitamin.

The amount of daily vitamin C that our government recommends is nowhere near what researchers, such as Nobel Prize winner Dr. Linus Pauling, recommended. Rather, it is based on the amount necessary to prevent scurvy, a condition that long ago afflicted sailors who ate absolutely no vegetables or fruits for months, even years, while out at sea. After it was discovered that the tiniest bit of vitamin C would remedy their situation, sailors would pack some limes and lemons for their journeys—which is how British sailors came to be called "limeys."

The government's recommended daily allowance (RDA) of vitamin C is not designed to provide you with enough of this essential vitamin to prevent chronic diseases, to keep your body from degenerating, to ensure optimal functioning of your enzyme pathways and biochemical processes, or to enable you to feel healthy and alert. It is also not enough to allow your system and organs to meet the increased demands placed on them by environmental toxins and stress or to promote longevity.

Although vitamin C can benefit your dog in the same ways it benefits you, dogs are typically given none. Because, unlike humans, dogs manufacture their own vitamin C, it is assumed that the amount their bodies make is sufficient to meet their requirements. Yet that assumption, too, is obsolete, since dogs are routinely exposed to a toxic overload that Mother Nature never anticipated from such factors as dog food, lawn treatments, flea and tick prevention, heartworm medication, heavy metals in the diet, and excessive vaccinations.

If you've ever wondered why it is that a "health care crisis" should exist in a nation as supposedly advanced and affluent as the United States, perhaps one answer can be found in the United States Food and Nutrition Board's recommended daily allowances for various nutrients. These, as it turns out, have been set at levels only high enough to prevent the clinical manifestations of certain known deficiency disease, such as the afore-mentioned scurvy. The same holds true regarding the vitamin and mineral intake of your pets, who have also become the victims of nutritional standards and requirements that are grossly inadequate. This is borne out by the fact that many dogs' coats and energy levels improve whenever even a poor-quality vitamin supplement is administered to them. Even though the owners may think their dogs are receiving good basic nutrition from the food they consume, what they're really getting is a diet so deficient that the addition of anything with some extra nutrient value is enough to make a noticeable difference.

If we hope to keep ourselves and our pets healthy and free from disease, we simply can't rely on government "subsistence requirements" for vitamins and minerals. Nothing better exemplifies the old adage about an ounce of prevention being worth a pound of cure than the need for such nutrients above and beyond what we derive from dietary sources. But before you buy the first vitamin supplement you see, you should be aware that all vitamin supplements are not created equal.

How to Find a Superior Supplement

Unfortunately, many vitamins prepared especially for dogs are similar in quality to commercial dog food. Typical of this kind of supplement is the poor-quality vitamin mixture thrown together with ingredients such as powdered bone meal, nutritional yeast, and liver. Although the taste may appeal to your dog, the bone meal likely contains toxic heavy metals that are easily assimilated, while the calcium it provides isn't assimilated at all. Calcium that can be readily utilized comes either in a water-soluble form produced by plant cells or is attached to amino-acid chains that can be absorbed by the gut. Organic plant-cell calcium is readily available, yet canine vitamin manufacturers and even many veterinarians have continued to recommend bone meal as a healthy additive. To be properly utilized, calcium also needs supportive minerals in specific proportions as well as an acid medium—important details that are neglected by many dog-vitamin manufacturers.

Many vitamin and mineral supplements intended for human consumption are also poorly formulated and derived from inferior sources. Such products can vary substantially in quality and composition and are likely to consist of synthetic ingredients that are cheaper to manufacture and that lack potency or are less easily absorbed by the body. Then, too, many vitamin and mineral supplements, both those intended for pets and those intended for humans, contain binders, fillers, sugars, coloring agents, and flavorings that can compromise their ability to be utilized. Even something as simple as an enteric coating can prevent an elderly person or an individual with decreased digestive enzymes from being able to properly assimilate the ingredients. Such ingredients may even cause allergic reactions in sensitive individuals, human and dog alike.

Reading labels on supplement bottles to ascertain how many milligrams of vitamin C or International Units (IU) of vitamin E they contain can be of little help unless you're familiar with the sources of the vitamins. A good-quality vitamin that is easy to assimilate may actually have less of the key ingredient, yet be more beneficial. It's also likely to be more expensive. When it comes to vitamin supplements, comparing things such as the number of milligrams and pills per bottle isn't really a meaningful way to determine the best value. In this instance, you usually get what you pay for. Again, vitamins are not all created equal. And while higher cost doesn't necessarily ensure better-quality vitamins, the very cheap ones are most likely to be of inferior quality. A good rule of thumb is to go with a known, established, reliable vitamin company whose products are found in health food stores. The vitamins that I often find in commercial pharmacies do not impress me.

The best forms of vitamins are those that are closest to what occurs in nature. They may be available from alternative practitioners as well as in health food stores. And, unlike in the old days when different vitamins and minerals had to be taken at different times of the day to avoid conflicting characteristics, many excellent multivitamin supplements today contain all of the necessary vitamins and minerals in forms that will not interfere with each other. They are also from good sources and are easily absorbed. Now, that's real progress!

There are more inherent problems with the quality of doggy vitamins because most vitamins don't taste very good. Therefore, the average vitamin or mineral supplement for dogs contains large quantities of nutritional yeast and powdered liver to improve its flavor and small, if not negligible, quantities of vitamins and minerals. It is also a fact that pet vitamins usually come from poor-quality sources and preparations.

Some companies are now creating pet vitamins composed of high-grade human-quality ingredients prepared in ways that are extremely appealing to your pets. For example, Deserving Pets prepares an excellent palatable vitamin made from quality ingredients. I have also used human vitamin supplements in the form of tablets hidden in cream cheese.

When a first-rate supplement is given, the difference in coat, energy level, and health is readily apparent. The simplest formula for supplementing your dog's diet is to add the following:

- A multivitamin-and-mineral supplement, given once a day with food.
- A green supplement containing chlorophyll.
- Olive oil and/or flaxseed oil or ground flax seeds, hemp or coconut oil, or an omega-3 fatty acid supplement.

The ABCs of Vitamins

What exactly is a vitamin? My dictionary defines a vitamin as "any of a group of organic substances essential in small quantities to normal metabolism and health, found in natural foodstuffs and also produced synthetically." Both your body and your dog's body work via "metabolic pathways" consisting of all of the tiny biochemical processes that, when taken together, make the whole body work efficiently and, more important, stay healthy and free of disease. Vitamins and minerals keep

> TASTE TEST: Supplements that are concentrated for maximum effect and added to food in a way that does not sufficiently disguise their taste tend to defeat their own purpose. It really doesn't matter how beneficial a vitamin and mineral supplement is if you can't get your dog to eat it.

your dog's many and varied metabolic pathways working well and that fuzzy body functioning at optimal health.

You and your dog share the need for a variety of vitamins, as different vitamins perform different functions to help promote overall health and keep the body's metabolism running smoothly. The basic vitamins include A, B, C, D, and E.

Vitamin A

Vitamin A is good for your dog's coat and eyes, possibly reducing the risk of cataracts. It has antioxidant properties and helps protect against cancer. It is naturally assimilated from animal fats, egg yolks, and cod-liver oil.

A word of caution: a fat-soluble vitamin A supplement should never be taken at doses exceeding 20,000 IU daily. You need not worry about that, however, with *water-soluble* vitamin A, as you cannot overdose on a water-soluble supplement. And while it's true that extremely high doses can be damaging to the liver if taken over long periods of time, taking that high a dose on a day-to-day basis is hard to do and needn't be of concern to most of us.

Carotenes are the water-soluble and therefore safer forms of vitamin A. Beta-carotene consists of a double molecule of the vitamin that is converted into vitamin A in your dog's body, which then eliminates whatever part the dog can't use. It is found naturally in orange and yellow fruits and vegetables.

The B Vitamins

These vitamins, which include B-1, B-2, B-3, B-5, B-6, B-12, folic acid, biotin, choline, inositol, and PABA, are often referred to as stress vitamins because they help alleviate the effects of stress on the body. Each has specific functions, such as aiding red-blood-cell production and muscle functions and helping support the nervous and cardiovascular systems. B vitamins are found naturally in grains, leafy vegetables, beans, molasses, yeast, eggs, fish, and organ meats.

B-12, to cite just one example, is utilized by cells to promote growth and remove waste products and, in your dog, to help build new nerve, muscle, intestinal, and immune-system tissue. But the B-12 content in even healthy food may no longer be adequate for this purpose, having decreased dramatically in the past forty years (in some foods, by as much as 80 to 100 percent). This is largely due to the decrease of certain B-12-producing bacteria in soil, water, and food and the fact that the soil has also been depleted of the cobalt needed to synthesize this important vitamin.

Because of this decrease in naturally occurring B vitamins, it is especially important to include them in any supplements for dogs. Because they dissolve easily in water, excessive amounts are excreted from the body—something that may be indicated by your dog's urine being more yellow than normal. Some people might call this expensive urine, but I call it good insurance. In any event, your dog will not be harmed by taking too many B vitamins.

Vitamin C

Perhaps the best known of antioxidants, vitamin C can help ward off or shorten the duration of viral infections, reduce the risk of cancer, and protect the cells of your dog's body from toxic overload. It can also help alleviate canine allergies, chronic infections, and periodontal disease. Like the B vitamins, it is water soluble and nontoxic, with any excessive amounts being eliminated from the body (although a higher-than-recommended dose can bring on diarrhea). Dietary sources of vitamin C include many fresh fruits and vegetables, and supplements are often derived from rose hips.

Extra vitamin C is especially important for a dog suffering from an illness, since the body requires more of it than usual to help fight off infection, and it becomes rapidly depleted. Even an allergy can quickly use up your dog's supply of vitamin C. That's why dogs who suffer from allergies should get higher doses of vitamin C every day to help their condition. Repeatedly dosing a dog with this vitamin during a viral infection can do a great deal to bolster the animal's immune system, increasing both interferon and white blood cell function. Giving your dog extra vitamin C before and after a vaccination can help prevent vaccine-related reactions and health problems.

Some canine health foods use vitamin C as a preservative, but it is not in any amount remotely sufficient for supplementation. I recommend a buffered vitamin C ascorbate that uses calcium, potassium, sodium, magnesium, or zinc as a buffering agent. (The Ester-C form of the vitamin is generally less palatable and more expensive.) The dose you should administer depends on the dog's size and general state of health. Small dogs can receive up to 250 mg once or twice a day, while larger breeds can be given up to 1,000 mg a day. To keep the dog from developing diarrhea, doses should be increased gradually.

Vitamin D

Found in fish, egg yolks, and butter as well as cod-liver oil, vitamin D is commonly referred to as "the sunshine vitamin" because exposure to sunlight's ultraviolet-B radiation tends to produce it in the body. Considered a hormone—a unique distinction in the vitamin world—it helps your dog's body to absorb and use calcium and is necessary for good bone development. There is also evidence that vitamin D might help to reduce the risk of colon, breast, ovarian, and prostate cancers, research having shown that statistics for such cancers are lower among people who live in sunnier climes. It is also a fat-soluble vitamin that is stored in the liver.

Although most dogs are exposed to sunlight during walks, their fur likely serves as an inhibiting factor in its absorption. That's why most multivitamins for dogs include vitamin D.

Vitamin E

This vitamin, which occurs naturally in grains, nut oils, and leafy dark green vegetables, is an important antioxidant that protects your dog's cells and tissues. From 100 to 200 mg of vitamin E can be given daily, depending on the size of your dog, and it can be combined with vitamin C for extra effect. Vitamin E gets an important boost from vitamin C, creating a powerful one-two preemptive punch against cancer and other chronic diseases. The natural form of vitamin E works far better than the less expensive synthetic versions.

Mineral Wealth for Your Dog's Health

Besides serving as a buffer for acids in the body, minerals carry the electrical charges that implement nerve impulses. Since there are almost twenty minerals that aid and promote your dog's metabolic processes, we will cover only the most important ones, the macro-minerals.

Calcium

Although you may be aware of calcium's importance in strengthening bones and teeth, you may not know of its crucial role in nerve conduction and the ability of muscles to contract. It can be derived from foods such as dairy products, salmon, sardines, and tofu.

Calcium, however, requires an acidic environment to be properly assimilated and is not absorbed well from bone meal or powdered oyster shell supplements. Far more useful is calcium that is derived from plant cells or that has been attached to an amino acid chain. Your dog's body will absorb the organic forms of calcium (calcium citrate, calcium lactate, and calcium orotate) far better than it will the calcium carbonate found in oyster shells.

To work effectively, calcium supplements should also contain the mineral magnesium and vitamin D, both important in promoting calcium utilization. Calcium and magnesium should be served up in a 2:1 ratio.

Magnesium

A calming anti-stress mineral, magnesium, along with calcium, has a sedative effect that is helpful in promoting restful sleep. It is also needed by the nervous system to regulate nerve impulses and conduction. Food sources include nuts, legumes, whole grains, dark green vegetables, meats, seafood, and dairy products.

Potassium

Potassium, which is found in a variety of foods, including turkey, chicken, salmon, cod, sardines, many fruits and vegetables, and dairy products, helps regulate the acid-alkaline balance in your dog's body. It is contained within cells and can be depleted in cases of severe vomiting and diarrhea, causing your dog to become weak and lethargic.

Selenium

Selenium, a trace mineral, is essential to good health but is required in only small amounts. Selenium is incorporated into proteins to make selenoproteins, important antioxidant enzymes. The antioxidant properties of selenoproteins help prevent cellular damage from free radicals, which in turn helps prevent the development of chronic diseases such as cancer and heart disease. Other selenoproteins help regulate thyroid function and play a role in the immune system.

This mineral is very important for your dog's thyroid and heart health and for cancer prevention. The selenite form, called sodium selenite, is the only form that has been shown to directly stop tumor growth. The more common form, selenomethionine, is stored in the liver, whereas sodium selenite goes directly to the tumor.

Plant foods are the major dietary sources of selenium in most countries. Selenium also can be found in some meats, seafood, and grains or in plants grown in selenium-rich soil.

Antioxidants: Preventing Internal Wear and Tear

Antioxidants, which include some of the vitamins previously discussed, are substances that inhibit the destructive effects of oxidation—a form of internal wear and tear that affects you and your dog. Oxidation is a process that begins when toxic substances cause damage to cells, producing unstable molecules with loose electrons called free radicals, which seek to bind themselves to other molecules. A buildup of free radicals speeds the effects of aging, altering cellular DNA codes and damaging internal organs, skin, and collagen. Antioxidants latch on to the loose electrons carried by free radicals and neutralize them before they can cause any damage. (Certain enzymes, such as dismutase [SOD], bromelain, and catalase, also act to protect the body from free radicals.)

Antioxidants

VITAMINS	MINERALS	HERBS	NUTRIENTS
Vitamin C	Zinc	Ginkgo	SOD
Vitamin E	Selenium	Hawthorn	Bromelain
Vitamin A		Rosemary	Pycnogenol
Beta carotene			Quercetin

In addition, many other nutritional components serve as cofactors to help these antioxidants do their jobs and eradicate those free radicals. Coenzyme Q10 (also called CoQ10), for instance, is a very important antioxidant that also plays a key role in the production of ATP—the energy molecule that runs the body.

The fact that our pets' bodies (as well as our own) are exposed to so many more environmental toxins and pollutants these days—just think of all those pesticides and herbicides on grass that dogs are likely to come in contact with—greatly increases the need for regular antioxidants as part of your dog's supplement program. Just think of them as a "first line of defense" against an increasingly toxic world.

The Necessity of Supplementation

By now, you've come quite a way from the commercial dog-food diet that today's conventional wisdom mistakenly assures you is sufficient to meet your pet's nutritional requirements. In today's world of toxic overload and depleted soil, even the best of diets might not be good enough to do the entire job of keeping all systems running at peak performance. That's why my recommendation for "supplemental health insurance" for your best friend and companion is to help him enjoy as long and healthy a life as possible.

Part 2

THE NATURE OF HEALTH

One can think of the dog's body as a sort of biological or inner terrain, akin to soil. Good soil will grow strong, healthy plants; poor, depleted, or undernourished soil will not. That's the way it is with your dog's biological terrain, and that's why I have placed such emphasis on good diet and good supplements in this book. The terrain of every body needs healthy supplies to fuel the healing machine. When properly applied, holistic medicine can be a powerful healer, providing gentle but effective guidance that can remedy many diseases and health problems—without the side effects so often associated with more conventional forms of medicine.

Your dog's body has a system of multifaceted built-in protective mechanisms designed to ward off pathogens and other internal threats and repair any damage. Unfortunately, although the immune system works in powerful, even miraculous, ways to promote healing, it is often unwittingly sabotaged by a lack of support. Not only does poor-quality nutrition frequently deprive the immune system of the vitamins, minerals, and enzymes it needs to perform at peak capacity, but the reliance on drugs, often reflecting our lack of trust in the body's remarkable capabilities, also tends to weaken it.

When your dog's body is given the ammunition needed to run its systems and the guidance needed to correct the "programming errors" that cause disease, it moves rapidly to heal itself. There are many holistic modalities and techniques available, but they all have the same common denominator in that they greatly increase the body's ability to heal and cure itself. It's that simple. Holistic health works with the nature of healing.

Chapter 8

Rediscovering the Natural Path

Brilliant discoveries invented over the span of many millennia afforded humankind many workable approaches to healing. For instance, as far back as 6,000 years ago, the Egyptians were using herbs to heal infections and treat disease. Acupuncture has been practiced in the Far East for 5,000 years. But depending on the place and period in which they were practiced, the various styles of healing might have been considered either fashionable or treacherous.

Nostradamus, the famous French physician and astrologer, practiced medicine in the sixteenth century. He began treating plague victims with a new and unusual medicine—ground rose hips. Rose hips happen to have a high vitamin C content, but vitamin C was yet undiscovered in the Middle Ages. Nostradamus read books banned by the Church, and from them and his own experience learned how to use natural products to successfully cure diseases. This very success put his life in danger, however, for curing a disease known to be fatal put one in league with the devil. Only his close relationship with Catherine de Medici, the queen of France, kept him safe. Catherine's son, King Charles IX of France, appointed Nostradamus as his court physician in 1560.

Healing in America has traveled a varied path. The ways and methods for healing have changed greatly over the centuries, as herbs and homeopathic remedies gave way to pharmaceutical drugs and aggressive treatment of disease symptoms rather than a more naturalistic approach. Then, toward the end of the twentieth century, people began to realize that so-called conventional medicine was creating as many problems as it claimed to fix. People once again sought medicines grown by nature rather than manufactured by man and looked to other cultures and times for treatment options.

Holistic Therapies and the Body's Wisdom

Today terms such as *conventional, holistic, alternative, homeopathic, allopathic,* and *complementary* abound when reading about, writing about, or discussing medicine. *Conventional* clearly refers to the use of surgery and pharmaceutical drugs. By contrast, *holistic* is used almost too broadly, for it portrays a range of approaches from sophisticated and learned modes of healing such as acupuncture and homeopathy to simpler methods such as eating organic foods, exercising, and getting massages. In its most basic sense, *holistic* means choosing to work with the body's innate intelligence to promote balance, strength, and restoration. Sometimes that simply means choosing a healthier diet and taking daily vitamins. Sometimes it means the approach that an owner takes in an effort to save his beloved dog from a deadly disease such as cancer.

Alternative means not using the conventional approach of surgery and drugs. Ironically, although pharmacological drugs are dubbed *conventional* medicine, medical practices such as homeopathy, acupuncture, and herbs were around long before these drugs were and are employed widely in many parts of the world.

Homeopathy refers to a method of healing in which very small amounts of substances that have no side effects are given to create a cure. At the very popular advent of homeopathy, most of the medical schools were homeopathic, thus the term *allopathic* was coined to refer to treatment that differed from the popular and common homeopathic protocols.

My favorite word, by far, is *complementary.* I hope we have approached a time in history when this term can fully describe the nature of medicine. *Complementary* means that the wonderful medley of styles of healing, both new and ancient, can be used together to treat people. There is a time and place for each and every one of them.

The ability to combine the best options from different healing disciplines is known as *integrative health care* and *complementary medicine.* Although the holistic aspect of this is commonly referred to as *alternative medicine*, I believe that both treatment and prevention of disease should begin with holistic care and that the so-called conventional techniques should be used as alternative methods. This approach is often difficult to implement, however, because many of my clients come to me in desperation, after all else has failed. That's when things get tricky. It becomes my job to balance the holistic with the conventional in an already compromised and drug-dependent dog. If the owner had opted for holistic treatment when the dog's problem first developed, it might never have turned into a monster illness.

 TREATING THE WHOLE: Holistic medicine describes a system of diagnostics and treatments for the whole patient, not just a patient's particular disease.

> **MODALITIES:** *Modality* refers to a specific system of holistic medicine, such as homeopathy, chiropractic, acupuncture, herbs, and energy healing.

All holistic therapies work synergistically. Of course, pharmaceutical drugs may be needed on occasion. A critically ill patient may need them to stabilize him, after which holistic products are quickly brought into play. I still find it amazing how much holistic therapies can do to alleviate illness. There is just so much available in the holistic realm, with more surfacing all the time. I see holistic medicine as a vast rain forest teeming with green healing plant life. By contrast, conventional medicine is a tiny weed-filled lot in New York City. That tiny lot offers you steroids, antibiotics, and a few more things. The rain forest offers a vast array of holistic options, with more and more incredible holistic products becoming available all the time.

In deciding what approach to use on my canine patients, I have never excluded any option that I thought would help them obtain better health. I like to think of all of these techniques as composing a literal body of knowledge about how to heal disease. While some are time honored and others relatively recent discoveries, all utilize the inborn knowledge within the body and work with that innate intelligence to create good health.

I use pharmacological drugs when I deem it necessary and have saved lives with them. If symptoms such as an erratic heartbeat or high blood sugar call for it, the correct drug should be used to help the sick individual compensate. Conventional medicine has come up with some impressive techniques and technologies for detecting and diagnosing disease.

Pharmaceutical drugs work differently from holistic products, however. Pharmaceutical drugs typically alleviate symptoms; they rarely cure. At best, they buy time while the body heals. Taking an analgesic for a headache kills the pain while the body works to heal itself. Someone suffering from migraine headaches truly appreciates the relief, but the drug does not correct the actual problem. In all too many cases, the illness becomes chronic because the real source of the problem has not been found and corrected.

In fact, treating only the symptoms can curtail the body's ability to completely heal. When a dog injures a knee, the pain forces him to rest it. When we give our dog a pain-killing anti-inflammatory drug, his knee will feel better, and he will run on that knee and injure it further when instead he should be resting it. The dog's owner thinks that things are just fine because the dog is running around and is not in pain. The consequence, however, may be expensive knee surgery. In addition, both steroids and nonsteroidal anti-inflammatory drugs (NSAIDs) have been irrefutably proven to retard healing.

A Holistic Return

How, you might ask, did such long-recognized therapies as homeopathy, which has remained popular in Europe and India over the centuries, and acupuncture, the value of which has been known for many centuries in the Far East, disappear from the face of healing in the United States? The answer is that when antibiotics took center stage, all other treatment options were dismissed as obsolete or unnecessary—even though many of these new "wonder drugs" would themselves end up fitting that description.

Initially, the effect that antibiotics had in halting the progress of certain all-too-common diseases was so profound that it seemed as though the panacea for all ills of man and beast had been found. During World War I, soldiers suffering from wounds and a variety of infections were effectively treated with these new drugs, as were civilians afflicted with once life-threatening ailments. Before long, the fields of human and veterinary medicine began putting all their eggs into one basket, with antibiotics becoming a newfound source of wealth for both doctors and drug companies.

As a result, antibiotics became overused, prescribed for ailments they could not relieve (such as viruses), which eventually led to the creation of more and more strains of antibiotic-resistant bacteria. Infections from resistant bacteria that do not respond to familiar antibiotics are becoming more and more common. In addition, these drugs, while valuable in certain applications, tended to weaken or to destroy, by their mode of action, the immune system, the body's first line of defense.

Many of our most feared, crippling, and lethal diseases are those that don't respond to antibiotics—not only viral infections but also cancer, heart disease, and autoimmune disease. Such chronic and debilitating ailments have become rampant in both the human and pet populations. One out of two dogs now gets cancer.

That's why our rediscovery of holistic products and procedures is such an important development. While conventional therapies tend to take over the healing function and decrease the body's ability to heal itself, holistic treatments work with the body to fortify and encourage its own healing powers. The holistic experience creates a wiser and stronger body, more able to maintain and retain health. The end result is a healthier patient with a stronger immune system. The most important thing we can do for our dog's health is keep his body strong with inherent health.

Natural medications promote healing, so the pain is relieved *as* the joint heals. Allowing the body to heal at its own pace is the best insurance against chronic disease. The holistic approach assumes that the body is intelligent and that symptoms occur for a reason. This is not to say that an illness or disease should be left untreated or that you can assume your dog will just heal on his own. Rather, holistic treatments can be powerful tools that complement and enforce the body's innate ability to rebalance and restore itself, allowing the body to overcome the disease or injury. Too many of us have forgotten that the body's inherent wisdom, along with a little help from some holistic friends, can re-create true health.

Typically, many patients with chronic problems refill their pharmaceutical prescriptions over and over again, month after month. Patients depend on their medications, and this is very good for the pharmaceutical companies' bottom line. Dispensing a pill that would actually cure your high blood pressure or arthritis would be very bad for business.

As already mentioned, holistic medical treatments can be used together and can be used along with conventional medical treatments and drugs. Oftentimes I see animals with such severe diseases that they may need some of both. Sometimes, they are already on conventional drugs and cannot be taken off them until we can get the holistic modalities working.

If you are fixing a house that has structural damage, you'll need to put in place new beams to hold up the roof before you remove the old, faulty beams. In the same manner, it's necessary to get a dog's body back working on its own steam before removing the crutches provided by pharmaceuticals. This requires a good working knowledge of the healing capabilities of various holistic options and their synergistic effects—how they interact with each other and with whatever conventional medication the animal is receiving. Just as important is the knowledge of how our dogs' bodies change in response to different therapies.

There is an innate wisdom always at work within our bodies and those of our dogs. Without any conscious thought, the cells work at a furious pace toward order and health. They are well acquainted with the actions necessary to continue in their pursuit of life. For thousands of years, humankind has worked to support the inherent objectives of these cells, augmenting and supporting their ability to heal.

Pharmaceutical drugs, while they have their most definite place, cannot compete with thousands of years of documented natural supportive methods of healing. These age-old discoveries are even more important now, as they are needed desperately to help our dogs and us deal with all the toxins in our environment. In many situations, pharmaceutical drugs should be sought if natural therapies, taken in a timely fashion, fail and when truly necessary. In this scenario, conventional drugs become the "alternative medicine."

In this chapter, you'll get a primer in each of the techniques that holistic medicine uses to root out the underlying causes of many chronic health problems, rather than simply addressing the symptoms. As I've said, I like to think of these techniques as a literal "body of knowledge"—that is to say, the body's innate knowledge about self-healing, with the role of holistic medicine being to reawaken the body

The Story of Max the Dachshund

Before introducing you to some new ways of helping and healing your dog, allow me to tell you a real-life story to help put this all together. This short story is about a short dog named Max, a Dachshund.

As is true for many Dachshunds, Max had back trouble. He had a very long back and very short legs. And he liked to jump. While playing with his brother, Max got bumped, and he yelped. One of his discs bulged out, putting pressure on the large nerve that forms the spinal cord.

After Max hurt his back, his owner took him to her local veterinarian, who gave Max steroids (prednisolone) to relieve the pain and swelling. Strict crate rest for a month was also recommended. Max would seem to feel better for a while, but the problem would return. Then his back legs became paralyzed, and he could not urinate on his own. His veterinarian discussed expensive back surgery but said that it was probably too late for that to help. Fortunately for Max, he still had some feeling in the tips of his back toes, but just a little.

Max had a bulging disc in his back. The pressure from the swollen disc had destroyed some of the nerve tissue in his spine, which is why he couldn't walk. He had been taking steroids because they suppress the inflammation in the spine, helping keep the nerve tissue from becoming even more damaged. This is the usual treatment for this kind of problem. Once again, the symptoms are suppressed, but the real cause of the problem is not addressed. For Max, steroids were necessary, and they helped keep the swelling down until Max was treated holistically.

A dog's back is like a suspension bridge between his hips and his head. While our spine is a vertical pole, a dog's spine runs parallel to the ground. Imagine placing a dozen dominoes side by side so they make a long column. Now push on each end and watch where it gives. The dominoes toward the middle begin to bulge out. When the pressure between the top and bottom of a dog's spinal column is uneven, the vertebrae (segments of the backbone) can become misaligned. This puts pressure on the discs, which form cushions between the vertebrae. Max's back is extra long and prone to problems. It's just the way Dachshunds are put together. Other breeds with long backs such as the Basset Hound are also prone to back problems.

from a drug-induced slumber. Holistic methods give that "spark of life" more fuel to generate energy and heal while they also balance.

Acupuncture: The Needlework That Restores

The Chinese have practiced the holistic technique of acupuncture for more than 5,000 years. The procedure, which involves inserting very fine needles into specific points on the body to relieve pain and treat disease, was part of a remarkably sophisticated and accurate science of healing

Max's owner brought him to see me, and I began treating him. First, I used a special laser on the affected area to relieve pain and inflammation. Next, I carefully injected some homeopathic remedies into acupuncture points near the injury. As a result, Max's muscle spasms decreased. The muscles on either side of his back had gone into spasms in an attempt to protect his spine, and this had only made his pain worse. Now these muscles were more relaxed, and I was able to adjust his back with a spinal adjustment. I gently moved his vertebrae back into the correct position. Max already looked brighter and more relieved. I carefully placed acupuncture needles along the sides of his spine; I also placed four more tiny needles in some special points on his legs. This relieves blockages and reinstates the harmonious flow of energy along the spine.

Max went home with Chinese herbs and homeopathic remedies, which will work to keep any swelling to a minimum, alleviate pain, and promote rapid healing. He returned for his follow-up spinal adjustments and acupuncture treatments. With each treatment, the mobility and strength in his hind legs improved. Control of his bladder returned, and Max can now urinate on his own. As Max improved, the remedies were changed to those that help rebuild the nerves that lead to his bladder and hind legs. Finally, Max received nutritional supplements to strengthen his spine.

If Max had contracted a bladder infection during his course of treatment, I would have put him on antibiotics or a Chinese herbal preparation because, considering his condition, they would have been necessary. His systems had been weakened by the painful illness and the use of steroids, and I would not want the infection to spread. I would also have dispensed cranberry (see the subhead on cranberries in chapter 6). The antibiotics would have been dispensed with probiotics (friendly bacteria) and followed with holistic preparations to prevent any further bladder infections.

Max is running and playing again. His brother is still bumping him, and Max still likes to jump. But now his owner practices preventive holistic health care. Every few months, she brings Max into my clinic for a checkup. We give him acupuncture and a spinal adjustment. Max loves this treatment. As far as he is concerned, it's his day out at the spa!

developed in ancient China. The principles of Chinese medicine, for instance, which were published in the period from 400 to 200 BC, included a discussion of how the heart controlled blood flow through the body; something accepted by Western medicine when William Harvey made the same "discovery" 2,000 years later.

The practice of acupuncture, in fact, predates the production of metals, the original needles having been made of stone and fish bones. But it wasn't until 1972, when President Nixon paid his historic visit to China, that interest in this ancient art of using needles to treat pain and disease arose in the United States. It came about serendipitously, in fact, when *New York Times* reporter James Reston required an emergency appendectomy while covering the American Ping-Pong team's trip to China that preceded the Nixon visit and subsequently wrote about how acupuncture had been used to relieve his pain.

A particular acupuncture method is employed in China that enables the patient to have surgery without medical anesthesia. The patient may be awake for the surgery because the acupuncture procedure handles any physical pain. As a result, the president's personal physician became interested in observing the procedure. By the following year, acupuncture had been declared an experimental medical procedure by the American Medical Association's Council on Scientific Affairs.

Acupuncture's popularity extended to animals as well, having been used on animals in China for nearly as long as it has been in existence. Today veterinary acupuncture is recognized as a legitimate medical treatment by the American Veterinary Medical Association. Extensive certification courses are available for veterinarians. And while the idea of inserting needles into certain points on an animal's body to induce healing may still sound far-fetched to some skeptics, its results have often proved to be remarkable, even in treating conditions that appeared hopeless.

Acupuncture has shown to be effective in alleviating a whole range of metabolic, traumatic, arthritic, and neurological problems, including infections, immune disorders, heart problems, arthritis, liver disorders, kidney failure, hip dysplasia, anemia, paralysis, back problems, gastrointestinal problems, and asthma. It also has no side effects, since it does not involve introducing anything toxic into the body. Veterinary acupuncture is a healing science that deals with the individual animal as a living energetic being, rather than simply as a catalog of signs and symptoms.

Why Being Punctured Spells Relief

Acupuncture points lie along meridians—series of interconnecting channels through which the body's energy flow is conducted. The flow and balance of the energy that runs the body is referred to as *Qi* (pronounced "chi") in Chinese medicine and is directly influenced by the positioning of the needles so as to promote deep healing.

Modern medicine has come up with a couple of explanations for this phenomenon. The neurophysiological theory holds that the stimulation produced by the needles results in the release of hormones and

POOR MAN'S MEDICINE: The practice of acupuncture is based on both the natural and scientific aspects of healing. In China, acupuncture is sometimes referred to as the "poor man's medicine" because it is so inexpensive to administer.

neurotransmitters, such as serotonin. These chemicals, along with the body's natural opiates, endorphins, and enkephalins, are always found in larger amounts directly after an acupuncture treatment. Their release probably accounts for the euphoric feeling that subjects appear to experience. This includes my canine patients, who usually pull their owners into my clinic after a few such treatments and who seem to find the therapy genuinely relaxing and enjoyable.

Another hypothesis is the bioelectric theory, which suggests that electrical currents run along the body's nerve pathways and that stimulating these currents has an impact on the system as a whole. To better understand such an effect, imagine that your dog's body contains an electrical current that runs into each organ and system. Visualize each of these as a separate room of a house that is lit by electricity. Now imagine that some of these rooms are only dimly lit due to a poor electrical connection. As a result, the immune system can't do as good a job of cleaning these particular rooms as it does in the rest of the house. However, once the electrical system is repaired, rewired, and balanced and the dirt is more easily visible, the system can come in and make a clean sweep of the areas in question. Acupuncture harmonizes the electrical circuits running through your dog's body so its healing mechanisms can function the way they are supposed to.

Certain misconceptions can make dog owners apprehensive about having their pets undergo acupuncture. They worry about the pain that the needles may cause, but they are surprised to see how fine the needles are (a reporter who once visited my clinic had expected them to be the size of knitting needles!) and to learn that inserting them involves very little, if any, discomfort. The actual treatments last from ten to twenty minutes after the needles are in place and can be performed in a variety of ways. The most commonly used method of stimulating acupuncture points involves simply leaving the needles in place and allowing them to do their work.

Variations on the Therapy

There are variations on acupuncture therapy and how it is administered. These variations include electroacupuncture, aquapuncture, moxibustion, laser acupuncture, acupressure, and gold bead implants.

Electroacupuncture: Needles are attached to an electrical acupuncture device that stimulates the points more aggressively with a small amount of current. This method is most often employed on dogs suffering from paralysis or back problems.

Aquapuncture: This involves injecting an aqueous solution, which may contain B vitamins or a special injectable homeopathic preparation, into the acupuncture points. This method demonstrates how holistic therapies can be combined for maximum effect.

Moxibustion: Specific herbs are burned on the acupuncture points. These herbs, through the smoke, penetrate the skin and serve to relax the area being treated. Moxibustion is an especially good technique to use on a dog whose muscles are stiff and rigid, as occurs with arthritis.

Laser acupuncture: When performed with many of the newer lasers, this treatment can prove to be very deep acting and beneficial.

Acupressure: This involves the manual massaging and stimulating of acupressure points. No needles are inserted; rather, a gentle pressure is applied to the acupuncture points.

Gold bead implants: This method effects a more prolonged stimulation of the acupuncture points by implanting them with various metals. In my practice, I commonly use solid gold beads, inserting them into the acupuncture points while the dog is under sedation or anesthesia. This is a procedure that's easy to perform, effective, and very safe. I commonly use this technique to treat young dogs suffering from hip dysplasia. Many young dogs have come to me with such severe hip problems that it had been recommended that they either have hip replacement surgery or be euthanized. These same dogs are now running and playing.

Acupuncture's Fountain of Youth

In whatever form it takes, acupuncture can be especially helpful in reinvigorating older dogs, which is why I often refer to it as the "fountain of youth." I first became aware of its remarkable rejuvenating powers when I became a certified veterinary acupuncturist and began using the technique on many of my regular canine patients. In many cases, it was almost as if they'd started aging in reverse. Ten-year-old dogs began to look and act as if they were six. Their eyes became brighter and their whole demeanor became more youthful. Many times, a dog's owner and I have watched this phenomenon with no small amount of astonishment.

Acupuncture treatments are normally administered once a week for the first few treatments, although dogs suffering from paralysis or back problems need to be treated more often. With each session, the body readjusts itself and heals a little bit more. Cumulatively, this therapy works to restore your best friend to health and harmony, eliminate any pain and discomfort he might be having, tone up his internal organs, and help him live a longer and happier life.

Homeopathy: Helping Your Dog Heal on His Own

Homeopathy is a very individualized therapeutic approach. The same illness causes a different reaction in each different dog. Here's a situation for you to think about. Four different dogs have itchy skin problems. Two go to a conventional veterinarian and receive drugs such as steroids and antibiotics. These drugs work to suppress the symptoms, and both dogs are prescribed the same medications. The other two canines go to a veterinarian who practices homeopathy. Their owners are asked all sorts of questions about their respective dogs. One dog likes the heat, and his itching gets really bad after midnight. The other dog avoids heat, actively seeks the cold, and gets much itchier after his baths. These dogs each get a different remedy. Their individual remedies are chosen for their individual cases.

Homeopathic preparations are easy to obtain for home use, as they are sold in some pharmacies, in most health food stores, and by mail order from homeopathic pharmacies. They are referred to as remedies and can be used to address all kinds of conditions, from sprains and injuries to a variety of chronic health problems. Homeopathic remedies have a long track record of proven effectiveness.

Homeopathic remedies have no toxic side effects. They are inexpensive and, most important, they are very safe. According to the World Health Organization, homeopathy is the second most commonly used method of health care in the world. *The Homeopathic Pharmacopoeia of the United States* is fully recognized by an Act of Congress. *The Homeopathic Pharmacopoeia* has uniform, specific methods of preparation for remedies, and it works in conjunction with the United States Food and Drug Administration to assure quality and consistency. This means that no matter where or from what manufacturer you buy a homeopathic remedy, it will have been made in the same way, with consistent manufacturing procedures.

Let's Start at the Very Beginning

The innovative German physician Samuel Hahnemann founded this powerful and safe system of medicine known as homeopathy over two centuries ago. It all started in 1790 when he was translating a medical text into German. He disagreed on the reasoning put forth to explain the action of an extract of the bark of a Venezuelan tree, the cinchona, which was successfully used to treat malaria. Upon experimentation, Hahnemann discovered that drinking a tea made from the bark would produce, for a short time, the very same symptoms that one would get from malaria. Once again, as so often happens among the twists and turns on the historical road of healing, there was the rediscovery of an old medical principle espoused by Hippocrates: "Like cures like."

THE LAW OF SIMILARS

Called the Law of Similars, "like cures like" is one of the basic principles of homeopathy. It maintains that a substance administered in large doses, provoking specific disease symptoms in a healthy person, will treat those specific symptoms when administered, in minute doses, as a homeopathically prepared remedy. For example, what happens when you slice an onion? Your eyes and nose will run as if you had an allergy or cold. In homeopathy, one of the remedies used for a cold or allergy will be made from—that's right—onions! However, the method of preparation is not as simple as presenting an allergy sufferer with a glass of onion juice. A homeopathic remedy is prepared in a very special and precise way by a method of repeated dilution and shaking (succession). A homeopathic remedy stimulates the *vital force*, the life force, to react vigorously and cure the disease. The remedy has no actual toxicity or effect on the physiology of the organism, as just about all of its physical substance has been eliminated through a process of dilution. The remedy produces a stronger disease picture, although wholly energetic, for the vital force to react to. The remedy has taught the body to handle the disease, and the result is, again, a stronger and wiser body.

In a similar fashion the syrup ipecac, which will induce vomiting, is made into a remedy to treat someone who is nauseous and vomiting. Homeopathic formulas, unlike conventional drugs, do not directly attack the disease or condition. Instead, these highly diluted substances trigger the body's own self-regulating and self-healing mechanisms, enabling the body to handle the illness on its own.

Dr. Hahnemann encompassed the whole philosophy of homeopathy in this simple statement: "The highest ideal of therapy is to restore health rapidly, gently, permanently; to remove and destroy all whole diseases in the shortest, surest, least harmful way, according to clearly comprehensible principles."

In keeping with that description, you can expect homeopathic remedies to be just as safe for your pet. Remember, homeopathic remedies have no toxic side effects. Rather than suppressing symptoms, they are designed to encourage your dog's own defense mechanisms to effect a cure. This will also help your dog's further ability to fight off disease and pathogens.

A homeopathic remedy, then, can be described as one that stimulates the body's natural defense mechanisms by specifically stimulating the body's vital force to heal. This type of healing also serves to ensure improved immunity and health.

AN ENDURING ALTERNATIVE

During the first half of the nineteenth century, homeopathy thrived in both Europe and the United States, earning itself a solid reputation during Europe's cholera epidemic of 1832, when homeopathy's recovery rates proved to be higher than those of the conventional physicians of the day. Homeopathy was endorsed by several renowned nineteenth-century Americans, including poet Henry Wadsworth Longfellow, novelist Nathaniel Hawthorne, and industrialist John D. Rockefeller.

In fact, many notable and famous people have supported homeopathy, including Mahatma Gandhi, who said, "Homeopathy cures a larger percentage of cases than any other method of treatment and is beyond doubt safer and more economical, and is the most complete medical science."

While homeopathy gained converts throughout the world and has remained popular in Europe and India, its following in the United States was eclipsed for a time with the advent of medical politics, which promoted newer, more profit-driven types of treatment at the expense of more natural ones. In recent years, however, the benefits of homeopathy have come to be rediscovered by millions of Americans who have been alarmed by the high risks and side effects of conventional medicine.

But what's in it for your dog? The answer is that homeopathy offers as much to your pet as it does to you. That's because in homeopathy, everything that applies to people applies equally to animals. The 2,000-plus remedies it offers are considered just as effective for humans and animals alike (and the selection criteria are also the same). Here's another point to consider: while homeopathic remedies were developed out of experimentation and research studies, none have ever involved animal testing. Such research was done instead on healthy individuals who volunteered their services.

How Homeopathic Remedies Work

Homeopathic remedies are prepared from a wide range of animal, vegetable, and mineral substances, including insects, poisons, and modern medicines such as antibiotics. Quite frankly, homeopathic remedies can be made from just about anything, although about 80 percent come from plants, some as familiar as lily of the valley and poison ivy, and some as rare as the St. Ignatius bean from the Philippines. No matter what substance may be involved, however, because of the method of preparation, a homeopathic remedy will never have a toxic side effect. For example, some remedies are made from things as toxic as cobra or rattlesnake venom, but because of the method of preparation, they are

Homeopathic Remedy Preparation

A preparation to be used as a homeopathic remedy may be diluted using ratios of either ⅒, known as an X potency, or ⅟₁₀₀, referred to as a C potency. This distinction is important for you to know when you purchase such remedies. A remedy is listed by its name, followed by the number of times it is diluted and potentized and its dilution ratio. To illustrate, the remedy Arnica 6c is composed of the herb arnica, which has been diluted and potentized six times using a factor of ⅟₁₀₀, whereas the remedy Bryonia 30x is made from the herb white bryony, which has been diluted 30 times at a ratio of ⅒.

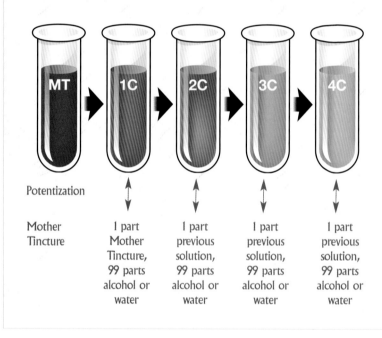

MT	1C	2C	3C	4C
Potentization				
Mother Tincture	1 part Mother Tincture, 99 parts alcohol or water	1 part previous solution, 99 parts alcohol or water	1 part previous solution, 99 parts alcohol or water	1 part previous solution, 99 parts alcohol or water

rendered harmless. As a result, homeopathic preparations are some of the safest and most nontoxic medications available today.

THE DILUTION SOLUTION

When Dr. Hahnemann initially set out to determine the minimum doses required to bring about improvement, he found, much to his surprise, that the more he potentized a remedy, the more powerful it became. He there-after began systematically diluting, then "succusing," or vigorously shaking, each of the substances he wanted to test. After this process was complete, the remedy was considered *potentized,* meaning that the liquid involved had retained the memory, but none of the toxic effects, of the substance it was made from. By stimulating a body's natural defenses without adversely affecting them, the energetic capacity imbued in this memory creates a powerful tool to promote natural healing.

PRESCRIPTIONS FOR THE INDIVIDUAL

There are so many homeopathic remedies currently available that just the commonly used ones fill entire books—and there is quite a collection of books out there that discuss them in detail, should you be up for some reading. To simplify things somewhat, in the section on dogs with special needs (see chapter 11), I'll acquaint you with some of the remedies commonly used for treating certain ailments. But for now, I'd like to touch on what these remedies can accomplish and the factors that go into selecting them.

Homeopathic remedies can be used for a variety of veterinary purposes. Within homeopathy itself, there are many avenues available in addition to the rigid classical approach, in which only one remedy at a time is used. Homeopathic remedies can also be used for treating acute emergencies or first aid situations such as shock, trauma, and bee stings. Interestingly, the homeopathic remedy Apis mellifica, made from the common honeybee, is the remedy of choice for bee stings. Another homeopathic approach is organ drainage, with the aim of eliminating the toxins from organs such as the liver, kidneys, and spleen. Specific remedies work with each organ. There exists yet another, more modern, avenue of homeopathy referred to as homotoxicology. Without denying the basic principles of homeopathy, it uses a more scientific explanation and clinical language that is easily understood by today's doctors. Homotoxicology introduces new classes of homeopathic remedies produced on the basis of the most recent scientific discoveries.

An interesting true story illustrates how homeopaths learned from every avenue and developed many remedies to deal with a plethora of problems. In colonial times, the child of a settler had a disease then known as dropsy. His belly was filled with fluid, and he was dying. Some Native Americans, learning of the child's illness, killed a few honeybees, toasted them on a fire, and had the young boy take them. The fluid passed, and he lived. Today, the remedy Apis, prepared in a standard homeopathic fashion, is commonly used for edema and swelling and to promote urination.

Homeopathic remedies are also used to cure deep-seated chronic diseases, which usually requires extensive study to determine the precise remedy that is indicated. In this situation, the healer takes the patient's full history, including all mental, emotional, and physical symptoms.

Each individual responds differently to an illness, and this is very important in choosing the correct homeopathic remedy. How an individual responds to an illness is just as important as the illness itself in deciding what remedy to take.

Every homeopathic remedy has its own picture of disease, which was carefully recorded during its proving. Each remedy in the *Materia Medica* contains a description of the symptoms and modalities associated with it, set out under the systems of the body. One of the characteristic features of a homeopathic *Materia Medica* is the inclusion of modalities, meaning what things make the patient feel better or worse. These can include cold, heat, movement, rest, and even the amount of attention that the patient seeks when ill or the mood that the patient is in. We also find mental symptoms in the *Materia Medica* relating to the temperament, emotions, and feelings of the patient.

Consider, for example, how two people might respond to being afflicted by the same cold virus. One seems to require constant attention and a lot of fussing and have no thirst, even though suffering from a fever. The other wants to be left alone to lie in a quiet room and, despite being very thirsty, snaps at the person who brings him a drink. The first individual might need the remedy Pulsatilla, which suits individuals who want to be loved and pampered when sick, while the second might be best off with Bryonia, which suits the patient who feels better when lying quietly. (Of course, many more of the symptoms and modalities are often taken into account when choosing the appropriate remedy.)

In another example, a dog with arthritis who is very stiff after lying around and who is especially bothered by damp, cold weather might need the remedy Rhus toxidendron (commonly known as "Rhus tox"). Conversely an arthritic dog whose condition is made worse by exercise and warmth and who prefers to lie on a cool floor might benefit from Bryonia.

As you can see, the remedy Bryonia was prescribed for both a cold and arthritis. What is the common denominator? Both patients who were prescribed Bryonia feel better when they are resting and would rather not move about.

Each remedy has its own personality—a whole "picture" associated with it, including many detailed symptoms for which it can be used. This is why two dogs with the same illness can be given different remedies, and why a particular remedy can be used for different illnesses. Remember the scenario presented at the beginning of this section? The two itchy dogs who visited the homeopathic veterinarian were given different remedies, as one loved the cold and the other craved heat.

The fact that mental and emotional factors need to be assessed in addition to the physical presentation of the disease changed the way I practiced veterinary medicine. I had to notice the dogs more than their owners and open up a true line of communication with my patients. My patients responded in kind. The dogs I treat make it evident that they consider me their friend, and I can tell how much they appreciate the fact that they matter to me and are being recognized as individuals.

COMBINATION REMEDIES

Not all homeopathic remedies are derived from a single substance. Products containing combination remedies are formulated to treat different problems when the best option isn't always evident. These remedies are often sold in health food stores, and while they are geared mainly toward human health, veterinary versions are also available. However, the human products are just fine to use on animals. Dogs and people have a lot of the same problems.

Combination remedies have been designed to treat such ailments as asthma, diarrhea, arthritis, and the like, to improve the health of particular organs such as the liver or kidneys, to detoxify the body of such substances as heavy metals or pesticides, or to alleviate nervousness and other emotional problems. Many of the remedies they contain complement each other and work synergistically for maximum effect.

How to Use Homeopathic Preparations

Doses of homeopathic remedies are not adjusted for size or weight as, let us say, an antibiotic or herb would be. In homeopathy the potency, or number of times the remedy was diluted, and the frequency of the dose are what matter. In most cases, as soon as the symptoms improve, the remedy has done its job and thus is discontinued.

Everything that touches the remedy should be clean and odor free. Remedies may be obtained either in a water-based liquid, which is often preserved with a little alcohol or vinegar, or as small medicated white pellets that are coated with the remedy. Dogs usually do not mind the taste of these preparations, which need to be dissolved directly on the blood vessels—on the gums, in the mouth, or inside the lips. Remedies need to melt on the mucous membranes of the mouth and therefore should not be hidden in food. If using a liquid preparation, the liquid is dropped under the lip, onto the gums. If using the pellets, they are easily inserted into the lip fold and allowed to absorb—which is much easier than having to pry your dog's mouth open to push a pill down his throat!

More About Bryonia

The homeopathic remedy Bryonia is made from a flowering plant called white bryony, which grows in England. Bryonia is indicated for conditions, including cold and flu, in which the patient is tired and irritable and does not want to move. It is also good for arthritis that worsens after exercise and in which the patient feels better after and when resting.

HOMEOPATHIC REMEDIES are easy to administer. Remedies come in the form of tiny white pellets that can be tucked into your dog's lower lip fold to melt. They also come in liquid form in which a few drops can be placed on your dog's gums. Additionally, a few pellets can be placed in a small amount of spring water and stirred, and this water can be given as a remedy.

It requires an open mind to follow a path that is not in complete accordance with the conventional wisdom taught in medical and veterinary schools. I have never excluded anything that I thought might help my canine patients achieve optimal health. Homeopathy, I have found, works beautifully alongside sister therapies such as acupuncture and various other treatment options described in this book. In fact, whether used alone or with other therapies, homeopathy usually works well even when combined with conventional drugs. Many of my new patients, for instance, come to me in very bad condition and would not survive if abruptly taken off the pharmaceuticals that have been prescribed for them. I give them the benefit of appropriate holistic treatments while slowly weaning them off the medications on which they have become dependent. It all works together for the benefit of your pet.

Flower Power: It Really Works

Ask who Bach was, and the answer you're most likely to get is that he was a famous composer. But there was another Bach, a homeopathic physician known for his ability to soothe the emotions of both man and beast, whose works flowed from floral essences rather than from musical notes. I'm referring to Dr. Edward Bach, the British physician, bacteriologist, and immunologist who in the 1930s discovered what have become known as the Bach flower remedies. These are a series of thirty-eight special preparations, all but one derived from the essence of a wildflower or tree blossom, designed to treat different emotional states running the gamut from depression to nervousness to aggression to hyperactivity to apathy.

Having administered these remedies to dogs suffering from emotions such as jealousy, I can vouch for their effectiveness in many cases. The owners of a puppy that whines may find that the Bach flower remedy Chicory makes the house a lot more tranquil. A tendency to bite might be nipped in the bud with a little Bach flower remedy Snapdragon. Bach flower remedies are usually available through health food stores, and books explaining what each remedy treats are interesting to read and easy to find.

The production of flower remedies has grown exponentially. You can find numerous companies in many countries making flower remedies from their indigenous plant life. The real beauty of Bach flower remedies or any other flower remedy is that they're easy to figure out and you can administer them at home. And they have no side effects or undesirable repercussions should the wrong one be used for a particular condition.

The Backbone of Health

Your dog's brain takes in millions of bits of information about what is going on in his body. All of this information is carried on a cable made up of billions of nerve wires that run down a dog's back. This cable is called the spinal cord. This cable sends messages to all of the organs and muscles of your dog's body and acts as a relay center, both sending and receiving data.

Ancient Greeks looked at people's backs and noticed the regular bumps formed by the spinal column. They thought these bumps looked like thorns, so they called them *spina*, which is the Greek word for "thorn."

The delicate spinal nerves are protected by special bones called vertebrae. The vertebrae of the spine are stacked up like a pile of bagels whose holes are all lined up. People have a vertical spinal column, as they stand upright on their legs, and dogs have a horizontal bridge of vertebrae.

The neck vertebrae hold up the head. The vertebrae that sit just under your dog's head are called the atlas because the Greek god Atlas held up the globe of the earth the way the atlas of the spine holds up the globe of the head. Vertebrae are present all the way down your dog's spine; they end at the sacrum, which connects to the hips on either side.

Between each vertebra are pads called discs, which act as little cushions, or shock absorbers, so your dog's vertebrae won't bump into each other when he walks, jumps, and plays. They are, in fact, jellylike fluid-filled sacs. Displacements of the vertebrae that cause discs to bulge into the center of the spine's canal can pinch the spinal cord and the nerves that branch out to the body from the spinal cord.

Disc displacement will alter the flow of the vital communication between your dog's brain and body. If severe, the displacement can also be a very painful experience for a dog and may even cause paralysis. A backache acts as a danger signal for people, alerting them to a possible pinched nerve. A dog's back may hurt him, but he has no way to tell his owner. I have seen many agility dogs and working dogs who stop performing as they used to because of a pinched nerve and spinal pain. After an adjustment or two, they returned to their normal selves.

SACRUM: *Sacrum* is from the Latin word for "sacred" because it was this lower hip portion of an animal that was used for sacrifices to the gods.

A paralyzed dog has experienced a severe injury to his spinal cord. Correcting the positioning of the vertebrae deals with the root of the problem, while drugs or holistic preparations act to minimize swelling and pain. I have seen hundreds and hundreds of dogs with severe disc problems who have recovered through the use of adjustment, acupuncture, homeopathy, and Chinese herbs.

The science of spinal manipulation is based on the fact that the spinal cord and massive nerve network that emanates out from it carry communications essential to health and life from the brain to the organs of the body. It is the unimpeded function of the nerves and nervous system that helps maintain health and alleviate pain and discomfort. The nervous system has dynamic, intelligent impulses that work to impart natural health.

Veterinarians who practice spinal manipulation care are becoming more and more common and are much needed. Life seems to provide many opportunities for injuries. Dogs at play leap and bump each other; agility dogs jump, crawl, and twist; and Dachshunds, well, are just Dachshunds. One very careful Dachshund was tentatively walking on a pile of frozen snow to go potty. The top frozen crust broke, and he fell down into 4-foot deep snow. His owners rescued him and, being "in the know," rushed him in for an adjustment. And did he need it!

Prolotherapy

You may never have heard of this particular therapy, but it is my treatment of choice for dogs with knee injuries. Prolotherapy stimulates the repair process after an injury. It is an effective treatment for chronic back, joint, and musculoskeletal injuries.

Ligaments and tendons are the fibrous tissue that connects bone to bone and bone to muscle in a joint. If you look at a fresh ligament, it appears as a white sheet or band. There is virtually no blood supply to ligaments, so they heal very slowly. When they finally do heal, they are never as strong as they used to be and are more prone to reinjury.

Prolotherapy has been around for a long time. Once again, Hippocrates, the father of medicine, took the first step. He stabilized the shoulders of javelin throwers by inserting hot needles into the joint capsules to provoke scar tissue. In 1835, several medical doctors researched the use of irritating substances to provoke healing. The term *prolotherapy* was coined in 1950. Since then, much research has been done, especially with rabbits, and decades of clinical experience have also been reviewed. It was found that prolotherapy had a profound regenerative effect and that the ligaments of rabbits were stronger and larger than they had been before they were injured.

By 1970, the use of prolotherapy had been fairly well perfected, and by 1980 a great deal of research demonstrating both microscopic and

Prolotherapy Defined

Merriam–Webster's Unabridged Dictionary defines prolotherapy as "the rehabilitations of an incompetent structure (as a ligament or tendon) by the induced proliferation of new cells." It has also been written as Prolo Therapy.

clinical regeneration and improvement had been done. Additionally, many medical doctors have documented years of clinical success with prolotherapy. One important research discovery was that nonsteroidal anti-inflammatory drugs (NSAIDS) cannot be used in conjunction with prolotherapy, as their use seriously slows healing.

With prolotherapy, injections are made into the ligaments around the joint and, if needed, into the joint itself. This stimulates the ligaments to regenerate and stimulates new cartilage growth in the joints. In the hands of a holistic-minded veterinarian, this therapy is key to stimulating the growth and repair of collagen, ligaments, and connective tissue. This treatment causes marked relief of pain from hip dysplasia, back problems, and knee problems. Prolotherapy causes the ligaments and surfaces in these areas to be rebuilt and strengthened.

Once again, as with so many holistic-minded modalities, prolotherapy stimulates the body's own natural healing and repair mechanisms. After the tissues are rebuilt, there is a stronger, more supported area as well as less pain. The bottom line is that it works—and works very well. Prolotherapy speeds healing exponentially, and the result is an even stronger ligament!

For many years, I would treat dogs with anterior cruciate ligament injuries (knee injuries) with numerous acupuncture treatments. The rate of improvement would depend on the severity of the injury. Often, the patient would reinjure the knee by overusing it as soon as his discomfort went away, and then he'd be back to holding his leg up in pain. Owners who were not in the habit of taking their large-breed dogs out on a leash would be pulled around by their dogs for weeks and have to go to all extremes to keep their dogs from jumping and playing, as letting a dog with a knee injury out in the yard to romp or relieve himself off lead was a big no-no. But what could we do? Ligament injuries just took a long time to heal.

Now, I just do a quick prolo treatment and tell the owner to keep the dog quiet for a few days. If the dog is of a sensitive disposition, I will give a little sedative. It is a fast procedure, so the more stoic dogs are done with the treatment in no time. The injections contain a local anesthetic, dextrose, and a few other healthy ingredients. As far as ligament injuries go, I find it the best thing since sliced bread. It's definitely, as the old saying goes, "the bees knees." Veterinarians who practice prolotherapy are rare, but a course to learn it has been made available over the last few years. The American Holistic Veterinary Medical Association (AHVMA) or holistic veterinarian Dr. Roger De Haan, DVM, MTS, CVC in Kings Mountain, North Carolina, may serve as a referral source. The Web site www.getprolo.com also has valuable information on this form of therapy.

Allergy Elimination Techniques

If we look at our immune system and compare it to a computer, we can see how it remembers and reruns a program, recognizing an invading "bug" many years after the original infection and gearing up against it, knowing just what to do. But what if the item to which the immune system is reacting is a simple food or a tree pollen? Where did the body learn to react so ferociously when an allergen is introduced? If the entirety of a body's construction is geared toward survival, then where is the sense in a child dying from eating one piece of a peanut or from one bee sting? Allergies in their mildest forms are merely nuisances. But, for some, contact with an allergen could result in death.

An allergy is an inappropriate and exaggerated response by the immune system toward a substance it has logged into its computer as an enemy. Allergies may present as many different things, among them digestive problems and, of course, the itchy dog. A remarkable technique for eliminating allergies was discovered several years ago by Dr. Devi Nambudripad.

Afflicted all her life with extremely severe allergies, Dr. Nambudripad became both a chiropractor and an acupuncturist in the course of searching for solutions to her problem, all the while surviving on white rice and broccoli, two of the only foods she could tolerate. One day, however, she made the mistake of biting into a carrot and began to develop an immediate severe allergic reaction. Quickly placing needles into some of her own acupuncture points, she passed out while still holding on to the offending carrot. Upon awakening, she had a great feeling of peace and discovered she was no longer allergic to carrots.

From this serendipitous discovery, she subsequently developed and refined a therapy for allergy sufferers that she dubbed the Nambudripad Allergy Elimination Technique (NAET). This noninvasive method uses a special combination of chiropractic treatment, muscle response testing, and acupuncture to reprogram the brain and nervous system.

The technique is one that might be compared to using a virus search program to correct a malfunctioning computer. After first identifying an allergy trigger through muscle response testing, the practitioner goes about correcting the source of a blockage or imbalance in the body that is causing the allergy. This is done by a technique that corrects the immune system's misperception of the allergen. This, in effect, enables the body to heal itself by restoring the unrestricted flow of such energy—a sort of corrective

Working Wonders

As millions of Americans discover the benefits offered by the various types of holistic medicine, it is becoming more and more apparent to them that these same techniques can work wonders for the health and well-being of their companion animals. Unlike conventional medicine, which often uses dogs and other animals for research and testing, holistic therapies are completely "animal friendly." My patients have always seemed to love their treatments. It's a nice change to see dogs rushing their way into a veterinary clinic rather than dragging their owners back to the car.

reprogramming that harmonizes and therefore normalizes the body's reaction to the allergen. Each treatment teaches your dog's body that an allergen, whether it be a food such as beef or pollen, is a friend rather than an enemy.

The substances to which a person is allergic are identified using test vials of allergens, which are evaluated using applied kinesiology. The technique is one that involves using your muscles to ascertain how your body responds to something or, to put it another way, using your muscle strength to measure bioenergy. It's a method widely used by holistic veterinarians, chiropractors, and naturopathic doctors, but you needn't be a professional to learn and practice it. It's a practical, reliable, and effective diagnostic tool that has become increasingly popular over the past three decades or so.

The inventor of applied kinesiology is Dr. George Goodhart, a Detroit chiropractor. After he held his first seminar in 1974, many other practitioners began using the technique with great success to determine the causes of problems that had previously seemed to defy diagnosis. Over the ensuing years, this method of testing for triggers of various conditions blossomed into a major diagnostic art, with many more medical professionals, including veterinarians, adopting it in their practices. (*Your Body Doesn't Lie* by Dr. John Diamond is an excellent source on the subject.)

A few visits are usually sufficient to eliminate food allergies, while follow-ups are generally needed to successfully rid patients of allergies to grass, pollen, weeds, trees, flowers, dust, fabrics, mold, vaccines, and anything else that triggers a response. Other forms of treatment that are based on this technique have since been developed.

Chapter 9

Eliminating Allergies

In this chapter, we'll look at the common problem of allergies in detail. The easiest way to understand allergies is to understand the immune system. In the previous chapter, we discussed comparing the immune system to a computer. Your immune-system computer registers various enemies, never to forget their identities. You probably feel secure that you'll never get measles or mumps as an adult if you had them as a child. You know that your immune system has compiled its own file on these attackers and will never again let them make inroads into your body.

In the case of allergies, however, the immune system also begins to register certain good guys as enemies. Common and innocuous substances become identified by the immune system as threats to the body. Consider the child who is allergic to peanuts. One small bit of peanut in a candy bar or even just breathing in peanut dust is all that it takes to initiate a severe allergic reaction, one so exaggerated that it actually becomes life threatening. Why do peanuts cause this particular child to suffer when all of his friends are eating peanut butter and jelly sandwiches for lunch? Because his internal computer has been corrupted to behave in a self-destructive manner.

A similar, if not quite as severe, situation exists with other typical allergies. The immune systems of some dogs, not unlike virus-corrupted computers, have registered simple foods, vitamins, pollens, molds, and many other substances as threats that call for some type of response. Simply being fed a food allergen may not be enough in itself to get a dog's immune system hopped up to the point at which itching or diarrhea occurs. However, when seasonal pollens and molds are added to the mix, the total number of allergens present will reach concentrations high enough to exceed the dog's threshold and will cause allergic symptoms such as chronic itching. Foods play a big part in the overall allergic reaction when it does occur, with the pollens acting as the straw that broke the camel's back.

Why would a dog's internal computer program go haywire? One likely explanation is that vaccinations have worked to confuse his immune system and cause this exaggerated response. The immune system, you see, was never designed to ward off simultaneous incursions by several different agents. I know of no recorded cases in which a person was exposed to polio, smallpox, measles, mumps, and whooping cough all at one time. The immune system's design is compatible with the laws of statistics, meaning that the immune system isn't set up to handle such a multipronged attack because the chance of one occurring is so low. But such an attack on the immune system is exactly what multivalent combination vaccinations simulate. The immune system is being asked to register and fight off, all at once, all of the vaccine components. For a dog, this means distemper, parvovirus, leptospirosis, adenovirus, hepatitis, bordetella, and perhaps also coronavirus, rabies, and Lyme disease. In addition to antigens and viruses, vaccinations contain formaldehyde and mercury. Neither our nor our dogs' immune systems were designed for having multiple disease organisms, antigens, and toxic substances injected into the body at one time, as is the case with vaccines.

Even more significant in these vaccines are the tiny bits of chicken and cow material left over from the chicken embryo and bovine serum in which the viruses are incubated. Unfortunately, when these food products are introduced to the body with the invaders, that's how the body's internal computer is likely to subsequently identify them. Just imagine yourself living in a house on the prairie and being attacked by a gang of a dozen outlaws. As you prepare to defend yourself from the invaders, would you try to differentiate between them to decide if perhaps some were benign? Or would you register them all as enemies? You'd likely do the latter, and that's exactly what the immune system is prone to do.

It's no coincidence that the first foods usually removed from the animal's diet are chicken and beef, kissing cousins to the egg and bovine serum used to incubate vaccine viruses. A "hypoallergenic diet," typically consisting of lamb and rice, is likely to be substituted. But the proteins in lamb are not so far removed from those in beef, and because the dog is usually fed the same thing every day, he'll soon become allergic to lamb, too. The concerned owner may switch the dog to wild game, such as venison or rabbit, but these foods, too, soon begin to trigger the immune system to put up a fight. After going through a veritable dietary petting zoo, the hypoallergenic food of last resort is a special predigested protein. So palliating the problem by changing the food tends to be only a short-term fix at best.

This canine equivalent of a faulty computer program will find more and more substances to become allergic to. As the years pass, the two-week summer allergy becomes a three-month allergy and finally results in year-round itching as your dog's allergies increase.

Itching to Get to the Root of It

The increased frequency of vaccinations is only part of the explanation for allergies. What else caused the immune system, so brilliantly designed to ward off pernicious invaders, to come to mistake innocuous substances for sources of imminent peril and, in so doing, wreak such havoc inside the body it is supposed to protect?

One thing is apparent: the incidence of allergies and asthma has been on the rise in recent years. Veterinarians of a half-century ago, for instance, encountered far fewer animals suffering from allergic reactions. But then, feeding table scraps to dogs was much more common in those days, and vaccinations were far more limited in scope.

Along with the increase in vaccinations, there has been the increased exposure to environmental toxins, potent pharmaceuticals, and chemical additives in the food supply. Pesticide use, for example, has proliferated in recent years, and both dogs and children are particularly likely to be exposed to toxic residues on lawns, which may also cause far more serious health consequences.

Unfortunately, nature did not design the immune systems of mammals to cope with the array of synthetic poisons to which we and our pets are constantly exposed. Such factors could well account for many of the allergies we see in dogs (and people) today, as well as the fact that an allergic dog is more likely to breed progeny with the same problems. Root causes aside, the fact to remember is that allergies tend to intensify and widen with time unless aggressive measures are taken to nip them in the bud.

One point being overlooked is that the best way for an allergy to develop and grow in intensity is through repeated and frequent exposure to something. Doctors, for instance, commonly become allergic to the powder or the latex in latex surgical gloves. This would not happen if they didn't routinely use them. Or a woman who works in a hair salon may develop allergic lesions on her hands when exposed to hair dye, while someone who works at a newsstand may become similarly sensitive to newsprint and ink. As the immune system increasingly responds to such routine exposures, it also develops allergic responses to other items in the environment, such as dust, molds, fabrics, pollens, weeds, grasses, and trees. So you can see why feeding your dog the same lamb kibble day after day after day because he was allergic to chicken and beef often results in a new allergy to lamb! It should be apparent by now that there's something wrong with the basic approach to treating allergies.

It All Adds Up

Conventional kibble, in particular, can perpetuate the allergy cycle because, in addition to being consumed on a daily basis, it contains various dyes, preservatives, and poor-quality proteins that can serve as red flags to a malfunctioning immune system. By varying your dog's diet

The Allergen Equation

The intensity of an allergy might be the result of a synergistic effect of two or more allergens combining. Your dog might have a severe allergic reaction to yeast, for instance, and mild reactions to corn, wheat, and soy. And while you might make a point of not feeding him anything that contains yeast, a food with a combination of the latter items might produce a reaction just as severe, if not more so. The fact that these three ingredients are present together will increase the allergic response, even though the allergy to each of them individually is not nearly as severe as the one triggered by yeast. The number of allergens in your dog's environment plus the intensity of the allergy to each substance equals the total allergic reaction.

Another factor that influences the occurrence of allergic reactions is seasonal change. During the winter in some northern climes—when grass, weeds, trees, and pollen become dormant and covered over—many allergy-prone animals may experience some relief, while others may actually suffer an increase in allergic reactions to dust, molds, and debris from heating systems. In autumn, romping in fallen leaves increases a dog's exposure to such potential allergens as fungus, mold, and mildew.

Every season has its own allergy triggers, which affect different dogs in different ways. Whereas an allergy trigger might cause our eyes to itch and water, the same trigger is more likely to affect a dog by irritating the area above the tail, along with other areas of his body. If we experienced allergies as dogs do, we'd probably be going around scratching *our* butts while complaining about how bad the ragweed is this year!

and not feeding him the same food day in and day out, you'll not only provide him with more balanced nutrition and make him a happier camper, but you'll also reduce the opportunity for food allergies to develop. Variety in your dog's diet—for example, fish one day, lamb the next, and dairy the third day—will also allow you to isolate, and then remove, those food items to which your dog might be allergic.

Skin Allergies

A dog afflicted with skin allergies may develop itching anywhere from his head to his tail. That's because he has more mast cells than a human has. These mast cells release compounds that cause itching and are distributed over a dog's entire body. Mast cells release histamines in response to certain triggers, and this starts the actual irritation and itching. Just as your mother told you in the case of mosquito bites, "The more you scratch, the more you itch." I've tried telling this to my allergic patients, but they just don't seem to get the message, preferring to literally chew holes in themselves!

When the immune system begins acting like a fire department responding to a bunch of false alarms, it is diverted from its intended task, which is to fight bacterial infections, viruses, cancers, and other alien invaders. What allergies do is exhaust the body's inherent defenses, cause imbalance and disharmony, and lead to the production and retention of toxins.

What Doesn't Work

To make matters worse, the drugs routinely used to treat allergic reactions act to suppress the overburdened immune system. The use of corticosteroids, for instance, can send that devoted but confused immune system sprawling. In addition to being toxic to your dog's liver, these drugs throw the body's pH balance out of kilter, with all of the resulting problems. Steroids, while relieving the symptoms, only entrench the problem more deeply in your dog's body, making it more toxic. Typically, if the allergens are still present after a few days to weeks off the steroids, your dog will need to go on them again. Steroids do not cure the problem; rather, they simply suppress the immune system's ability to function. Antihistamines are the least toxic of the pharmaceutical options, but they are also the least effective when it comes to reducing itching and may not help severely allergic dogs at all.

To complicate the problem, conventional allergy testing methods, which consist of either injecting allergens into the skin or a blood analysis, are likely to prove inadequate. One reason is that the actual number of allergens for which testing is done tends to be rather paltry, especially when compared with the thousands of potential allergy triggers in food and the environment. While efforts are being made to improve the reliability of these tests, they now stand at less than 50 percent accurate. This means that, basically, it's a toss-up as to whether the results are correct. Combine that with the small number of antigens tested, and it's no wonder that allergy vaccines do not work in many cases. It's simply a matter of statistics, and when the dice are thrown right, the hyposensitization therapy (in which vaccinations of antigens that are serially increased in concentration are given to decrease sensitivity to an allergen) does afford improvement.

In instances in which allergens are identified and removed from the dog's environment, diet, or both, relief is likely to be only temporary.

EFFECTS OF STEROIDS: If your dog has been on steroids for a period of time, you will need to wean him off them slowly because the adrenal glands, which produce the body's own natural corticosteroids, tend to atrophy with long-term use of such drugs and need time to learn to become fully active again.

Allergy Symptoms

Signs and symptoms of skin allergies include the following:

✓ Scratching the head, ears, or body incessantly

✓ Rubbing the face and/or body on the carpet and chairs

✓ Chewing and licking the body and paws

✓ Hair loss and red irritated skin

The underlying problem won't be solved because the dog's immune system is on a sort of witch hunt, seeking out and finding new things to respond to with allergic reactions. The dog's internal computer system is often busy finding more and more items to which it will become allergic.

Holistic Treatments

Rather than simply attempting to identify and remove the growing list of substances that trigger your dog's allergies, a much more efficient remedy would be to fix the faulty immune system, the computer that has gone awry in your dog's body. And that's where holistic solutions, especially homeopathy, NAET, and other allergy elimination techniques that have branched out from NAET, can be especially effective. An easy way to understand these methods is to make the parallel example of doing a virus search on your computer to clean up any glitches. The aforementioned techniques work like the computer program you would install to do the virus search.

Methods for treating allergies include adjusting the diet, limiting vaccinations, checking thyroid function, providing vitamins and supplements, using topical preparations, administering remedies, and trying an allergy elimination technique.

ADJUSTING THE DIET

Dogs are often allergic to items present in food. There are certain food items that the majority of allergic dogs react to: nutritional yeast, wheat, beef, chicken, eggs, and corn and fish oils. The by-products in many commercial foods may also promote allergies. Changing the food can help, but if the same diet is given every day, the dog's immune system will eventually recognize the products that the dog eats daily as allergens to react to.

Nellie's Story

Nellie, a wonderful Golden Retriever who is a patient of mine, can testify to the curative powers of holistic healing methods. Here, in her own words (with her owners' help in providing a translation from "caninese") is her story—one dog's odyssey through the medical system in search of allergy relief.

When I was a little over a year old, I began doing things like licking my paws and running my face along the carpets. My owners, who are very attentive, took me right to a veterinarian, who diagnosed my problem as an allergy and started me on the steroid prednisone, which I took every day. But even on a really high dose, I didn't improve. We then tried antihistamines, but they didn't help either. I was then tested for a thyroid condition and put on another drug, called Soloxine, along with more steroids and antibiotics, and I seemed to improve for a while. The steroids I was taking caused me to drink water constantly, so my owners tried to cut back on them, but I would get very itchy again.

A year later, my owners decided to try another veterinarian. I went home with a new steroid and more antibiotics. Soon, my chest hair was gone and my skin had become thick and greasy. My paws didn't look so good either. We then went to a third doctor, who took a blood sample from me and sent it away to determine what exactly I was allergic to. This doctor also gave my owners a serum that they injected under my skin every week. While they were told that it would take at least nine months for the injections to work, I still was no better over a year later.

So the next stop was a veterinary school hospital (my owners were sparing no expense to try to get me better), where this time I was given a skin test for allergies. From this test, another serum was developed. I was put on the new serum and back on my old friends, the antibiotics, along with antihistamines, but I just kept getting worse.

By this time, my owners were getting pretty upset. The fur was gone from my paws, which had developed black skin with red irritated areas. It was the same under my neck, which also had begun to ooze. I still itched all the time, my skin burned, I had no energy, and my owners were getting desperate and disillusioned.

Then, just as it seemed as though I would be doomed to a life of irritation and misery, my owners heard about Dr. Khalsa. Not particularly hopeful, we visited her office, and she immediately started me on homeopathic remedies, a rotating diet so I did not eat the same thing every day, and an allergy elimination technique. The improvement was noticeable after the very first visit! As the treatments progressed, I scratched less and less, the fur grew back under my neck and on my paws, and my skin returned to normal. After a few months, I stopped scratching altogether. My coat is now soft and bright, and I feel like a brand new dog!

To avoid this problem, feed your dog a rotating diet. Usually three different hypoallergenic, typically home-cooked, diets are chosen. Jars of baby-food meat or healthy deli cuts without preservatives can be handy to use in a pinch. Typical proteins include lamb, venison, salmon, and duck. On Day 1 you might feed lamb, white rice, and some chopped parsley and carrots. A sample diet for Day 2 might include venison and cooked white potatoes, along with some chopped kale or greens. The menu for Day 3 could be some cooked oatmeal and salmon. These three diets would be rotated on a regular basis.

LIMITING VACCINATIONS

Routinely giving cocktails of vaccinations containing six or more diseases encourages your dog's immune system to react incorrectly. Read the "Injecting Doubt into Annual Inoculations" section at the end of this chapter to learn more about vaccines, and research what vaccines your dog really needs.

CHECKING THYROID FUNCTION

Thyroid problems may contribute to the allergic symptoms your dog exhibits. Checking the thyroid requires a simple blood test that tests the T4 and free T4. Free T4 is the active tiny fraction of unbound total T4. These two readings will help determine if your dog's thyroid is underactive. If you have a diagnosis of hypothyroidism, your veterinarian will want to prescribe supplemental thyroid medication. Often, after a dog's thyroid problem is corrected, allergies and secondary infections subside. When a thyroid problem is found and corrected, holistic therapies also seem to work more quickly. While this may differ for every dog, every bit helps. The thyroid is a master gland, and it regulates the performance of many important organs as well as the immune system.

I like to send my tests to Dr. Jean Dodds in California, for she has unquestionable expertise in the area of thyroid malfunction, and she reads all of the tests. Her nonprofit organization, Hemopet (www.hemopet.org), is on the cutting edge of advances in treating thyroid problems, and I have always found her advice very valuable.

PROVIDING VITAMINS AND SUPPLEMENTS

Vitamin C is an important vitamin for dogs with allergies. Dogs with allergies rapidly use up their stores of self-made vitamin C. Allergic dogs definitely need extra vitamin C to help decrease their allergic responses and to help remove toxins from the body. Vitamin C is even more important for dogs who are on steroids or who have been on antibiotics. The dose of vitamin C would range from 250 mg to 2,000 mg once or twice a day, depending on the size of your dog.

Too much vitamin C all at once will cause loose stools. Always increase the dose of vitamin C gradually to avoid diarrhea. While some dogs may do well on 2,000 mg of vitamin C twice a day, some may be able to tolerate only 500 mg a day. After the lower dose is well tolerated, the dose can be slowly increased.

Vitamin E works in conjunction with vitamin C. Both vitamins act as antioxidants. A recommended dose of vitamin E is from 200 to 400 IU once a day for any size dog.

Omega-3 fatty acids have been found useful in relieving allergic skin conditions. Flaxseed oil is easily available in health food stores and can be given in a dose of 1 teaspoon to 1 tablespoon a day, depending on the size of your dog. Other sources of omega-3 fatty acids are evening primrose oil, borage seed oil, and black currant seed oil. Hemp oil and olive oil, along with coconut oil, are also good sources of "good fats."

Other helpful supplements include an antioxidant combination containing CoQ10; a dose of 30 mg can be given once a day. Zinc can also be helpful with certain skin conditions. Zinc picolinate is the best form, and 10 mg can be given once a day. Querciten, a neutraceutical found in health food stores, assists in the temporary relief of allergies by reducing the release of histamine from the mast cells, thus minimizing the allergic response.

USING TOPICAL PREPARATIONS

Dogs with allergies often chew at themselves incessantly. The more they chew, the more they itch—just like that mosquito bite. It is very important to put an end to the scratch-itch-scratch-itch cycle that is created. There are many topical preparations that can help soothe the irritated area and decrease the inflammation.

- Black tea or Japanese green tea prepared as a very strong brew is applied to the inflamed area for three to ten minutes to soothe it. The rest of the brew can be stored in refrigerator and used later.
- Calendula tincture can be applied to the irritated areas either full-strength or diluted 1:1.
- A cotton ball soaked in witch hazel can be placed on itchy area a few times a day.
- Aloe vera can be applied to the area one to three times a day. The jelly from the fresh plant works the best.
- Baking soda can work wonders! Mix one teaspoon of baking soda with a little water to make a paste. Place the paste on the areas that are itchy or reddened. Leave the paste on for a few hours and wash off.
- Baking soda spray can be prepared by mixing 1 tablespoon of baking soda with 8 ounces of water. Put the mixture in a spray bottle and use when necessary. Shake before using.
- Oatmeal poultices are easy to make. The powder, mixed well with water, is placed on the area for a short time. Aveeno colloidal

oatmeal, found in pharmacies, can be used as a tub bath or poultice.

- Preparation H cream contains no harmful ingredients and works to stop itching and burning. It can often prove helpful with itchy skin.
- Cabbage leaf is an old-time remedy used to remove heat and inflammation from an area. Pound one cabbage leaf until the surface is broken and the juice oozes out. Hold this leaf on the inflamed area. The leaf will begin to get warm as it soaks the inflammation out. Remove the leaf after several minutes.

ADMINISTERING HOMEOPATHIC REMEDIES

Homeopathic remedies need to be chosen in relation to the symptoms they produce. The type of reaction that occurs in relation to the problem is important when deciding on a remedy. Some dogs itch less and feel better when they are warm. They may sit out on a black driveway and bake in the sun. Some dogs desperately need a cool environment and will lie on the tiled bathroom floor or sit by the air conditioning vent.

You should begin to see results with the following remedies in two to ten days. If no relief is gained or if the dog gets worse, discontinue the remedy.

- *Sulphur 6c.* This remedy is indicated in dogs who prefer a cool environment. The skin can be red and the itching intense. The skin can also have an unhealthy, leathery look to it. This remedy would be given twice a day for one week.
- *Arsenicum album 30c.* This remedy would be used with dogs who prefer the heat. The skin can be dry and flaky, and the coat can appear lusterless and dry. The dog who needs this remedy may also be thirsty and restless. Dose at twice a day for two weeks.
- *Graphites 30c.* This remedy is good for dogs who get hot spots with their allergies. These areas can ooze a sticky yellow or honey-colored substance that causes the fur to stick to the area. Give this remedy four times a day for one week, and use

HOMEOPATHIC REMEDIES are easy to administer. Remedies come in the form of tiny white pellets that can be tucked into your dog's lower lip fold to melt. They also come in liquid form in which a few drops can be placed on your dog's gums. Additionally, a few pellets can be placed in a small amount of spring water and stirred, and this water can be given as a remedy.

Discontinue the remedy after the problem resolves. Homeopathic remedies work to assist the body to heal. When this is accomplished, the remedy is stopped.

calendula tincture topically as well. You may need to shave the fur in this area so that the hot spots can get some air and dry up. Apply the calendula several times a day, reducing the frequency as the area improves.

- *Rhus toxidendron 30c.* This remedy is made from poison ivy, and we all know how itchy a poison ivy infection can be! The dog who needs this remedy will often have a pimply vesicular rash with much itching and redness. Warmth lessens the severity of the symptoms. Dose at three times a day for two to four weeks.
- *Grindelia 30c.* This homeopathic remedy can be given up to three times a day, as needed, to help decrease the intensity of the itching.
- *Psorinum 200c.* This remedy is excellent for conditions in which the skin appears unhealthy. The coat may have a noticeable musty odor, the skin is commonly dry, and the itching is intense. This remedy should be given once a day for one week. If symptoms reappear later, give the remedy again for one week.

EMPLOYING AN ALLERGY ELIMINATION TECHNIQUE

This procedure is covered at the end of chapter 8. It can provide a permanent cure for allergies by reprogramming your dog's body to react to the allergens as harmless and acceptable substances.

Other Complications with Allergies

Dogs with allergies often have concurrent infections. In addition, other conditions, such as fungal infections and sarcoptic mange, can be misdiagnosed as allergies.

Ear Infections

Ear infections are a common medical problem. Allergies and ear infections go hand in hand. Many dogs with allergic skin conditions also have reoccurring ear infections. While any dog can contract an ear infection, dogs with both mild and severe allergies tend to get ear infections more often. These infections can become painful and uncomfortable. The conventional ear ointments typically resolve the symptoms, yet the infections come back over and over again. To really cure a deep chronic ear infection, it is usually necessary to treat the allergies holistically, in addition to treating the ear infection aggressively with conventional medications. If your dog suffers from ear infections and also has allergies, be sure to review the previous section on allergies.

Both yeast and bacteria inhabit a healthy dog's ear. They live in a delicate balance and keep each other in check. When one overgrows, an infection occurs. Typically, the yeasty-smelling dark-brown infection comes first. This yeast infection can go on for a long time and can

Inside the Ear

The dog's ear canal is made up of a long vertical canal and a short horizontal canal. It resembles the letter L. Typically, we can only see about one-third of the way down the vertical section of the ear canal. The top part of the ear canal may look healthy and clean when the conventional ear medication is finished. However, deep in the bottom part of the ear, the infection still festers. Give it a little time and it will reappear—this time with a vengeance.

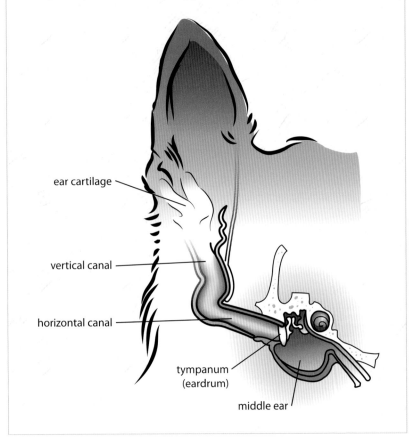

ear cartilage

vertical canal

horizontal canal

tympanum
(eardrum)

middle ear

commonly reoccur. After some time, the yeast infection develops into a bacterial infection. Further down the line, the bacteria that colonize the ear become those that are resistant to most antibiotics. *Proteus* and *Pseudomonas* are the two most common bacteria that become antibiotic resistant. These two bacteria have a very foul odor that is easy to remember.

It is important for you to know that this scenario of reinfection occurs because each infection is never completely cleared up. The yeast or bacteria remain in the lower part of the ear canal. So the infection you thought came back never really went away.

Look for the following signs and symptoms of ear infections:

- Head shaking and whining
- Scratching in and around the ear
- Brown waxy discharge with a sweet, musty, yeasty odor. The brown-colored yeast infection is typically not painful, although it can be itchy
- Purulent foul-smelling yellow or green-tinged discharge, which typically indicates a bacterial infection

YEAST INFECTION TREATMENTS

Yeast infections are the simplest ones to treat. Clean your dog's ears with a simple solution of half hydroxide peroxide and half water. Use warm water so it will be more comfortable in your dog's ear. Clean the ears with this solution about twice a week. This will help bubble up the debris deep in the ear. You can also try using the undiluted hydrogen peroxide in the ear. After the liquid is placed in the ear with a dropper (use about one teaspoon), massage the base of the ear to work the liquid into the ear.

Yeast Infection Miracle Solution

Here's how to make a wonderfully effective treatment for curing yeast infections:

4 ounces of rubbing alcohol
1 tablespoon of boric acid
4 drops of Gentian violet (1 percent solution)

Mix all of the ingredients together and shake well. Place in a dropper bottle. *Make sure that your dog's ears are not inflamed or ulcerated before you use this product.* If your dog exhibits pain or great discomfort after application, discontinue use immediately. Use a half dropperful in the ear twice a day for one week. After the first week, use one dropperful once a day in the ear for one or two more weeks. After this, even if the ear looks great, continue to use the solution twice a week for two or three months. This will handle the infection that persists deep down in the ear.

As a side note, Gentian violet can stain clothing, walls, furniture, and carpet. In this solution, however, it is very dilute and rarely causes a problem. Regardless, I would not treat your dog's ears while wearing your favorite white silk shirt.

Now, let your dog shake his head to dislodge the debris. (Do this in an area where the walls or furniture will not get splattered.) Clean out the rest with cotton balls.

Another effective treatment is the "miracle" solution on page 149, which can be made at home, as it uses old-fashioned yet effective ingredients. All of the ingredients are available at your local pharmacy.

BACTERIAL INFECTION TREATMENTS

Bacterial infections often come along later, as the result of chronic reinfection. Conventional antibiotics, both oral and those applied within the ear, are often necessary to control the infection and to alleviate the severe pain that a dog can experience with a bacterial ear infection. Your veterinarian may have to do a test called a culture and sensitivity to find out what type of bacteria is growing and which antibiotic will work best. Many Chinese herbs and herbal combinations are available to assist in building the immune system, strengthening your dog's ability to fight off this problem.

HOMEOPATHIC REMEDIES

Here are some homeopathic remedies for ear infections:

- *Hepar sulph 30c.* This is a good remedy to give a dog whose ears are infected with pus and are painful. Give this remedy three times a day.
- *Kali mur 6c.* This remedy helps to calm the inflammation and should be given three times a day.
- *Belladonna 6c.* This will help decrease redness and inflammation in the ear. Give this remedy three times a day.
  Note: the three remedies above can be combined and used in cases of painful, infected, and inflamed ears.
- *Mercurius sol 30c.* This remedy is good for infections that have a green-colored discharge and musty smell. Give this remedy twice a day.
- *Mercurius corr 6x.* This remedy may be useful for treating ear infections that have bloody ulcerations. Give this remedy twice a day.

HOMEOPATHIC REMEDIES are easy to administer. Remedies come in the form of tiny white pellets that can be tucked into your dog's lower lip fold to melt. They also come in liquid form in which a few drops can be placed on your dog's gums. Additionally, a few pellets can be placed in a small amount of spring water and stirred, and this water can be given as a remedy.

Discontinue the remedy after the problem resolves. Homeopathic remedies work to assist the body to heal. When this is accomplished, the remedy is stopped.

Fungal Infections

Fungal infections often go hand in hand with allergies. Fungi do not grow well in laboratory conditions, and they are often not identified. Certain breeds, such as the West Highland White Terrier, have a propensity for allergies with concurrent fungal infections. Fungi grow slowly, yet tenaciously. A fungal infection can be difficult to get rid of because once it is established, it is slow to recede.

When a dog has thick, dark, elephant-like skin on the underarms, belly, or feet, he may be infected with a fungus on his skin called Malassezia. This complicates a skin allergy because the fungus causes its own set of symptoms and problems. The presence of the Malassezia alone would make a dog very itchy.

Signs and symptoms of Malassezia include:

- Elephant-like, hairless, thickened, darkened skin
- Off-white, grayish crust that flakes off of the skin
- Symptoms more prevalent in underarm areas and under the neck
- Musty, sweet, yeasty odor
- Itchiness
- May cause persistent itchiness even after allergies begin to improve
- Budding yeast organisms found in skin cytology
- May be accompanied by brown, sweet-smelling ear infection

Malassezia

Malassezia occurs when the organism *Malassezia pachydermatis*, which is normal in the skin and ear canal, overgrows and causes itching and inflammation of the skin. It can also cause a brown, sweet-smelling substance in the ears.

Malassezia is commonly found on the thickened, denuded areas of the skin of dogs with chronic allergies. Often it is found in areas that sunlight cannot reach, such as the belly, lower neck, and underarms. The allergy and the yeast infection play off of each other, each one contributing to the other's ability to cause a problem. Typically, the yeast would not be there if it weren't for the allergy, and its presence makes the itching worse and causes the skin to become thickened and dark.

Hypoallergenic Antiyeast Meal

Here's a good meal to prepare for a dog with yeast problems:

3 cups of diced potatoes
1 cup of beef, chicken, fish, or lamb (for dogs who also have allergies, use tilapia or another bland white fish)
1 cup of mixed vegetables (cauliflower, string beans, broccoli)
2 cloves of garlic
1 tablespoon of apple cider vinegar
⅛ cup olive oil

Chop garlic and let sit while meal is prepared. Place potatoes in saucepan with just enough water to cover, and cook until tender. Add diced meat, vegetables, and olive oil. Heat until meat is done, about 10 minutes. Let cool. Mix in garlic and apple cider vinegar.

While the bacterial infections of the skin are typically recognized and treated, fungal and yeast infections can often go undetected. Antibiotics actually do have some antifungal activity, and dogs who have a yeast or fungal infection can appear better while taking the antibiotic. A few weeks after the antibiotic is stopped, the whole problem returns.

Special shampoos with antifungal ingredients are available at most veterinary offices. Drugs such as Nizoral (ketoconazole) and Sporonox (itraconazole) can be prescribed by your veterinarian to help resolve a fungus problem. There are natural products that also work as an antiseptic for the skin (see chapter 6 for some recipe suggestions for rinses and sprays).

Ringworm

Ringworm is a fungal infection, so named for its appearance. A round area of fur is denuded as the fungus grows in a circular pattern. The far edge of the circle can have a red edge, and often the fur in the very middle of the circle is growing in, so the pattern appears as a ring. This distinct appearance makes ringworm one of the easier fungi to identify.

Signs and symptoms of ringworm include the following:
- Moth-eaten appearance to the fur
- Circular lesions
- Lesions that are predominantly on the underside of the dog—the side that sees no sun
- May be accompanied by secondary bacterial infections within the circular area of the fungus

One homeopathic remedy for ringworm consists of 30c Bacillinum, 30c Chrysarobinum, and 30c Psorinum. Mix all three of these remedies together, and give twice a day for two weeks.

Sarcoptic Mange (Scabies)

The beginning stages of sarcoptic mange (scabies) may look just like an allergy. Mange is caused by mites, and scabies *(Sarcoptes)* mites are very difficult to find in skin scrapings. If your dog starts scratching suddenly and very intensely and he plays with other dogs who may carry the mite, scabies is a possible culprit. If you are getting small clusters of itchy red bumps on your body at the same time, it's a good indicator that the culprit could be scabies.

The mites that cause scabies resemble microscopic crabs, and they tunnel deep into a dog's skin, causing allergic reactions and irritation. This contagious mange travels easily from dog to dog. Foxes also can carry this mite and transmit it to dogs. When the mites jump on people, they can cause the aforementioned clusters of red, itchy bumps on the skin. These bumps can be very itchy, especially after a hot bath or shower.

DETECTING SCABIES

Scabies mites are very hard to detect in the typical skin scrapings done by veterinarians, as they live deep down in the skin. It's important to know that the beginning stages of scabies can look just like a skin allergy. When I'm considering scabies in a dog, I know that the chances of isolating the mite under a microscope are fairly low, so I look for bumps on the owners and ask whether there are any other dogs in the family that are also itching. If it's only one dog out of four that's itching, the possibility of scabies decreases. I also check out how intensely the dog is scratching. Most dogs with skin allergies scratch the most intensely when they're bored, but a dog with scabies will stop in the middle of playing or chasing a squirrel and just go at it. A dog with scabies may have very dry, flaky, itchy areas on the tips of his ears, and this is also an important finding.

Being a good detective is a necessary part of diagnosing scabies. Late-stage scabies has a particular pattern of white thick crusts on the tips of the ears. Many dogs do not have this crust in the initial stages, for it takes quite a while to develop. Loving dog owners can take such good care of their pooch that the typical signs of scabies never surface.

Quite often, a veterinary dermatologist will start the canine patient on a course of treatment for sarcoptic mange in order to make sure it is not being missed. Patient improvement from the treatment indicates that the mange was present.

Signs and symptoms of scabies include the following:
- Ferocious scratching, especially if the dog will stop whatever he's doing to scratch

- Other scratching dogs in the household
- Contact with unknown dogs or a fox
- Red bumps on humans
- Dry crusty areas on tips of ears
- Appearance of something that resembles a skin allergy (allergic dermatitis)

TREATING SCABIES
Your veterinarian will help you choose which of the following treatments is best for your dog:

- *Several oral doses of ivermectin*. This is prescribed by your veterinarian and has the advantages of being quick acting and easy to give. With a healthy animal, it is relatively nontoxic unless it is contraindicated for your breed of dog (as it is for some herding breeds), so it is best to check with your vet.
- *Lymdyp—a lime sulphur solution that smells like rotten eggs*. It is used as a rinse on your dog and left on his coat to dry once a week for several treatments. It is very safe and can be used on a dog of any age, but the odor results in less owner compliance in the winter months.
- *Selsun Blue shampoo*. This can be used to shampoo your dog, twice a week for two weeks, but only is suitable for very mild cases.
- *Revolution* (monthly parasite preventive).

Note: No matter what treatment you use, all bedding should be washed and areas thoroughly vacuumed after each treatment. All dogs who have scabies should be treated simultaneously.

Injecting Doubt into Annual Inoculations
You've received your postcard from the vet's office reminding you that it's vaccination time again. But didn't you just go through this same routine last year? If your dog needs to be vaccinated so often, why, you might wonder, don't you need to have that polio vaccination you received as a tiny baby repeated annually?

Should you dare to query, you will probably be lectured about the validity and importance of vaccines. Who are you to question professionals who do this every day? Folks have been made to feel confused under these circumstances and have ended up being embarrassed into having combination vaccines injected into their pets in spite of their doubts about the vaccines' safety or necessity.

If expert advice is what is needed, be aware that many experts working at prestigious veterinary schools are speaking out against the regime of yearly vaccines as well as questioning the validity of giving certain vaccines at all. Before I get carried away with my own opinions, let's consider some of the official positions taken by various veterinary institutions. *Current Veterinary Therapy IX*, a major reference book for veterinarians, states that the practice of giving annual vaccinations "lacks scientific validity of verification" and goes on to note that "immunity to viruses persists for years or for the life of the animal."

In 2006 the American Animal Hospital Association's Canine Vaccine Task Force recognized that vaccination decisions must always be made on an individual basis, based on risk and lifestyle factors. Updated and new information, including serologic testing, vaccine adverse event reporting, and medical and legal perspectives, was taken into consideration. It was the opinion of the task force that vaccines against canine distemper, canine adenovirus-2, and canine parvovirus produce excellent immune response and can be used in extended interval vaccination programs and at the discretion of the veterinarian.

In 2007 the American Veterinary Medical Association Committee report stated that the annual revaccination recommendation frequently found on many vaccination labels is based on historical precedent, not scientific data. The American Animal Hospital Association's Canine Vaccine Task Force stated in 2003 that "Misunderstanding, misinformation, and the conservative nature of our profession have largely slowed adoption of protocols advocating decreased frequency of vaccination."

Furthermore, serology testing and challenge studies indicate that the duration of immunity for the canine distemper and canine parvovirus vaccines has been demonstrated to be a minimum of seven years. As a result of all of this scientific research, most of the veterinary schools in North America have changed their protocols for vaccinating dogs. These veterinary schools, along with the American Veterinary Medical Association, have looked at studies that show how long vaccines last and have concluded that annual revaccination is unnecessary. Quite simply, there is no scientific documentation to support the supposed need for yearly vaccinations. At the same time, research shows that these same vaccinations subject a dog to the potential risks of allergic reactions and immune-mediated disease.

In 1995, C. A. Smith, in the *Journal of the American Veterinary Medical Association*, explained that vaccination is a potent medical procedure with both benefits and risks for the patient and that revaccination of patients with sufficient immunity does not add measurably to their disease resistance and may increase their risk of adverse post-vaccination events. She also stated that adverse events may be associated with any of the ingredients in the vaccine mix. Possible adverse events include anaphylaxis, immunosuppression, autoimmune disorders, and transient infections.

When your dog receives his DHLPP vaccination, it includes distemper, hepatitis, leptospirosis, parainfluenza, and parvovirus. In many cases, dogs also receive vaccinations for coronavirus, bordetella, Lyme disease, and rabies at the same time, which means that he's getting from five to

Breed~Related Risk

Studies show that some breeds, such as the Akita, American Cocker Spaniel, German Shepherd Dog, Golden Retriever, Irish Setter, Great Dane, Kerry Blue Terrier, Dachshund (especially the longhaired variety), Poodle, Old English Sheepdog, Scottish Terrier, Shetland Sheepdog, Shi Tzu, Vizsla, and Weimaraner, as well as breeds with white or predominantly white coat color, have an increased frequency of immune-mediated disease. A significant number of these animals had been vaccinated within thirty to forty-five days of the onset of their autoimmune disease.

This information comes from an article by W. Jean Dodds, DVM, "Vaccination Protocols for Dogs Predisposed to Vaccine Reactions," which appeared in the Journal of the American Animal Hospital Association. Dr. Dodds is known for her research on animal vaccinations and her *Canine Minimal Vaccine Use Protocol.*

nine inoculations all at once. This is the equivalent of a person's getting immunized for encephalitis, measles, mumps, hepatitis, polio, whooping cough, tetanus, Lyme disease, and flu all at the same time.

The devastating effects of such cocktail vaccinations on humans—in this case, Gulf War troops—were described in H. McManners's article "Scientists Link Gulf War Illness to Vaccines and Drugs," which appeared in the June 22, 1997, edition of the *London Sunday Times*:

> The drug cocktail suppressed one part of the body's immune system, known as Th1, which combats viruses and cancers. At the same time, Th2, a part of the immune system, which normally reacts mildly against pollen or house dust mites, was made hypersensitive to outside irritants. The double effect meant that the soldiers were more likely to succumb to common diseases, while also suffering extreme allergic reactions to harmless elements in the atmosphere.

A further report documenting the relationship between vaccinations and Gulf War Syndrome, published in the British medical journal *Lancet,* opened the door to massive legal claims filed on behalf of the ailing veterans.

There's just not much reason for veterinary drug companies to research vaccine-related problems in pets or the true duration of immunity to vaccinations. But such research has been done with children in numerous countries. Although manufacturers of drugs for humans attempt to isolate cases of vaccine injury as unusual and a tragic consequence of progress, they don't seem to have any interest in attempting to discover whether kids who have received no vaccines at all are healthier than those who do.

A Japanese study done in the year 2000 looked into that question and found asthma cases in vaccinated children to be ten times higher than in those who had not received any shots. In addition, more than 50 percent of the vaccinated kids had either asthma, rashes, or chronic runny noses, compared with less than 10 percent of the unvaccinated children. (H. Yoneyama, M. Suzuki, K. Fujii, Y. Odajima, "The Effect of DPT and BCG Vaccinations on Atopic Disorders," *Arerugi,* 49[7] [2000]: 585–92.)

Fifty years ago, before vaccines became an annual ritual, the incidence of allergies, autoimmune disease, and cancer in the canine population was a mere fraction of what it is today. Since then, vaccine manufacturers have encouraged the veterinary establishment to use their products whenever and wherever possible, and as a result have evolved into multibillion-dollar enterprises. But they've also been successful at something else—evading responsibility for the damage their products cause. In recent years, vaccine companies have become indemnified. This means that you can't sue the manufacturer if your pet becomes severely ill or dies due to a vaccination, although occasionally the medical expenses might be reimbursed to demonstrate the "good will" of the company.

By and large, the public has learned to blindly accept the notion that it is essential for dogs to be inoculated every year with a combined vaccine. Owners who want their dogs to stay healthy are told that is what it takes and are sent regular reminders that these "important" shots are due. Yet veterinary journals, medical textbooks, and veterinary schools have all spoken out against this practice, emphasizing that there is no justification for many of these vaccines to be injected annually.

If you, like myself, have cried during the movie *Old Yeller*, you may be wondering about the rabies vaccine. Rabies is contagious to all mammals, including humans, and is an awfully frightening fatal disease. Research is currently being done to assess the exact duration of immunity following the vaccination. Qualified laboratories also perform vaccine titer tests for rabies that will inform you if your dog has retained immunity from his last vaccine. However, for the time being, owners are obligated to have their pets vaccinated for rabies on a schedule as determined by state and local laws.

While attitudes are gradually changing toward canine vaccinations, especially the necessity of administering so many so often, you have to realize that many people are still trapped in a conventional rut. You must therefore expect to encounter opposition if you express a desire to cut back on your dog's immunization program, and be ready to stand your ground politely but firmly.

Guidelines for Vaccinations

Whenever you choose to vaccinate your dog, follow these guidelines:

1. Make sure your dog is in optimal health at the time of each vaccination.
2. Never administer vaccines to a dog who is on a corticosteroid (e.g., prednisone, prednisolone, and dexamethasone) or any other immunosuppressive drug.
3. Do not allow vaccinations to be given to a dog suffering from cancer or any severe illness such as liver problems or kidney failure.
4. Do not allow your dog to have unnecessary vaccinations.
5. Do not allow ineffective vaccines such as Bordetella (kennel cough) to be administered annually on the assumption that it will provide your dog with twelve months of immunity. The effectiveness of this vaccine is very short lived, so it would need to be given within three months of boarding if it is required by the kennel.
6. Do not allow your dog to have vaccines that have not been proven to be either safe or effective.
7. The dose of vaccine given should correspond with the approximate size of the dog.
8. Do not have your dog inoculated with his first puppy booster until he is at least nine to twelve weeks of age. Just keep him away from public places for a bit longer.
9. The interval between the first vaccine and the booster shot should be three to four weeks; otherwise, the shots can interfere with each other. Upon being infected with the vaccine virus, cells increase their production of interferon; therefore, if the second vaccination is administered too soon (within a week to ten days), it will be less effective. Delays of longer than eight weeks should likewise be avoided. The exception to this rule is the rabies vaccination, which is given once at three to six months (later being better) and then a year later, with subsequent shots administered on whatever schedule your municipality requires.

Veterinary schools are now at the forefront of change. For daring to go against the conventional wisdom when the health of patients is at stake, they deserve to be commended. If they can do it, you can, too. Let your veterinarian know how you feel about vaccines, and make sure it is documented in your dog's records. Get your veterinarian to agree that he will not give your companion any inoculations without your prior consent. Make it clear, also, that you'd like a vaccine titer test (a simple blood test that proves immune memory) done once a year (if that is indeed your preference), and use copies of the titer tests to prove standing immunity for your pet if he is to be boarded or admitted for surgery.

Boarding kennels are slowly learning to accept titers as alternatives to vaccinations. When the people who operate your kennel don't accept titers, educate them. (You might even give them a copy of this book.) If they still insist on requiring shots, maybe you should find another kennel

10. Give your dog the homeopathic remedy Thuja 6x (available at most health food stores) at a dose of twice a day for two weeks following any and all vaccinations. This should help to reduce any chronic damage from the vaccine.

11. If your pet experiences discomfort (swelling, redness, or pain) at the site of the inoculation, give him the homeopathic remedy Ledum 30x and Hypericum 30x (commonly available at health food stores) four times a day for three days.

12. If your dog experiences a mild fever after a vaccination, administer the homeopathic remedy Belladonna 6c four times a day until the temperature returns to normal for an entire day. Also contact your veterinarian.

13. If your dog begins to develop any swelling around the face or muzzle following vaccination, give him the homeopathic remedy Apis 200c every fifteen minutes. You can also give the over-the-counter drug Benadryl; check with your vet for the dosage. If the swelling persists, get him to your veterinarian ASAP, as he may be suffering from anaphylactic shock, which can cause the throat to swell until it constricts the airways, causing death. Your veterinarian can give him an injection of steroids, which usually handles the problem uneventfully.

14. The best vaccination protocol is one combination puppy booster after ten weeks of age and then a booster three to four weeks later. The next booster would be a year later, and this booster, being administered after the age of six months, will most likely provide lifetime immunity to parvovirus and distemper.

15. Instead of having your dog revaccinated for distemper and parvovirus the year after his "one year" vaccine, use blood titer tests to determine whether or not immunity persists. The owners of show dogs or therapy dogs may want yearly titers to satisfy themselves and others that their pet is immune. Titers are reliable and dependable.

or hire a dog sitter. There are folks out there who do dog sitting and house sitting for a living, including many who are bonded. My dogs prefer to stay at home when the family is away, anyway. If you have multiple animals, as I do, this can be a solution that will both reduce the risk of your pets contracting diseases and save you money in the bargain.

Doggy day care facilities should be handled the same way. Try to acquaint them with the latest thinking of the veterinary schools, or ask them to do some research on their own. Dog training schools may likewise need to be enlightened. Therapy dog facilities do generally accept titers, although they usually require an entire set of tests.

The point is, don't be reluctant to let the people most involved with your dog know what you want and how you arrived at that determination. In addition to making things a lot easier for you, it just may help increase the speed at which the times are a-changin'.

Chapter 10

Cancer Prevention and Treatment

Whether its called cancer, the big C, a malignancy, the silent killer, a tumor, or a growth, it's just plain frightening. For loving dog owners, cancer is the most feared disease. Unless the mass is bulging out noticeably from the skin, cancer grows invisibly inside the body, which is why it's called the silent killer. Many of the symptoms and signs that tell the owner and the veterinarian that something is very wrong are discovered only after cancer is well established. The later the cancer is found, the more time the cancer cells have had to spread. Unfortunately, there is no "marker cell testing" for dogs (as there is for humans) for early detection of certain types of cancer.

Malignant tumors are made up of cancerous cells. As they break away from a malignant tumor, these cancer cells can invade nearby tissues and organs. Cancer destroys life by invading an essential organ, where the disease grows out of control. Different types of cancer have different behaviors. Some cancers grow only locally, while others, such as lymphatic cancers, in which cancerous cells enter the bloodstream, spread rapidly to multiple areas in the body.

The spread of a malignant cancer is called metastasis. In contrast to a cancerous tumor, a benign mass does not spread, and degenerative changes are not present.

Most cancers are named for the type of cell or the organ in which they begin. There are numerous types of cancers, and there are many ways to treat them. Some treatments are done by trial and error; others are based on detailed research on the causes of cancer. Often several mechanisms used in combination prove more effective than just one. The best choice to make about conventional or holistic treatment (or both) depends on the kind of cancer and how far the disease has progressed—as well as what medical treatment the patient has already received.

Cancer takes a terrifying toll on both young and old dogs. The statistics on the number of dogs who get cancer only increase over time.

Cancer is now the number one cause of death in canines. Most types of cancer, once found, are difficult to stop. Cancer is an illness for which the proverbial ounce of prevention is definitely worth that pound of cure.

Ounces of Prevention

There is solid evidence that improved nutrition strengthens the immune system and helps prevent cancer. Believe it or not, we'll all get cancer multiple times in our lifetimes. But before those tiny cancer cells get a firm hold, our immune system takes charge of the situation and cleans it all up, unbeknown to us. While you're reading this, the antioxidants in your dog's body are countering the destructive forces of free radicals, discussed in chapter 7.

His immune system is locating and destroying abnormal cells. His genes (DNA and RNA) are making proteins to repair damage done by carcinogens. These natural processes are helping your dog fight cancer, but they need a helping hand themselves. You can do that by feeding your dog a healthy, cancer-fighting diet.

Vast numbers of studies show that excessive fat intake and a deficiency of important vitamins and minerals are related to higher rates of certain cancers. Figures from the National Cancer Institute show that 35 percent of all cancers can be attributed to dietary imbalances. The increased consumption of meat, poultry, fish, dairy, fats, and processed foods has steadily risen over the past decades, in step with the rising cancer rates.

Diet plays an important role in both cancer prevention and in cancer formation. Carcinogens in the environment and in dog food work to alter genetic information and make cells into potential cancer cells. Just as seeds planted must be watered for them to grow, cells with damaged DNA need a certain diet to make them turn into true cancer cells. Although the

Aflatoxins

Avoid commercial dog foods that have peanut by-products or peanut husks or hulls in them. Peanuts are often contaminated with a fungus that produces carcinogenic toxins called aflatoxins. Dr. Colin Campbell, author of *The China Study*, received grants from the National Institute of Health to research the presence of these aflatoxins, among *the most potent carcinogens* on the planet, in food. All 29 jars of peanut butter tested, purchased at local groceries, were found to be contaminated with aflatoxins—as much as 300 times the amount judged to be acceptable in food in the United States. The food industry uses the moldiest peanuts to make peanut butter. Corn is also high in aflatoxins.

genetic makeup of a dog factors into susceptibility to cancer, I believe that not only poor diet but also overvaccination combined with environmental toxins have a definite role in causing cancer. The National Cancer Institute states emphatically that many cancers can be prevented by making appropriate lifestyle changes. The following sections discuss the kinds of changes I believe need to be made.

Protect Your Dog with Diet

The majority of commercial dog foods are preserved with ethoxyquin, along with other carcinogens. Not only is the dog who is fed this diet being pumped with carcinogens, but the high protein content, rancid fat, heavy metals, and poor-quality food also add to the factors that help create cancer.

An estimated 80 to 90 percent of all cancers in people are prevented by lifestyle choices. This can, of course, also be true for dogs. Dr. Colin Campbell's *The China Study*, published in 2006, proved that a diet with over 20 percent animal protein had a significant effect on whether cells with altered DNA did, in fact, turn into cancer cells. Cancer cells will not grow and multiply unless the right conditions are met. While our dogs cannot live in a bubble to prevent themselves from being exposed to the carcinogens in the environment, they can eat a diet that will help prevent cells from becoming cancer cells.

Adding vegetables to a diet affords your dog the benefit of the phytonutrients present in these foods. Studies with humans have demonstrated a reduction in cancer risk in those who ate the most fruits and vegetables. Plants contain generous amounts of cancer-fighting antioxidants and phytonutrients. Cruciferous vegetables such as cabbage, kale, bok choy, turnips, rutabagas, mustard greens, and brussels sprouts contain substances that demonstrate a genuine ability to protect your dog from cancer.

Carotenoids are what make plants colorful. Leafy greens and orange and yellow vegetables such as squash and sweet potatoes contain beta-carotene and other phytonutrients that help protect cells from cancer. Broccoli contains compounds that inhibit the effect of carcinogens and boost production of cancer-blocking enzymes.

Vegetables can be fed raw or lightly steamed or grated, mixed into your dog's food. Organically grown vegetables give the best benefit because they are far richer in minerals and enzymes.

Saturated animal fats have been shown to increase risk factors for cancer. When these animal fats are heated and cooked, the risk factor becomes even higher. Cancer-preventing diets for humans are low in animal fats. Remember, most people buy meat that is much leaner than the meat by-products that is found in dog food.

Although cooked animal fat is undesirable, not all fats are bad. Studies show that omega-3 fatty acids act to suppress tumor growth. The best sources of omega-3 fatty acids are cold water fish and flax seeds. Give your dog a minimum daily serving of 1 to 2 tablespoons of flax oil or ¼ cup freshly ground flax seeds. Flax seeds, flaxseed oil, and all other oils should be stored in the refrigerator. I recommend olive oil as the only oil to use for cooking because it does not decompose into toxic compounds as other cooking oils do.

Keep the level of animal protein, including dairy, to below 20 percent of your dog's diet. If you feed a commercial dog food, don't add more animal proteins or dairy to a food that already has over 20 percent protein. If you cook for your dog, follow the recipes in The Canine Café section, and keep the animal protein low. If you want to feed a raw diet, feed lots of vegetables and add well-cooked grains to provide a healthier, cancer-fighting balance.

Cancer-Fighting Foods

Garlic
Parsley
Tomatoes
Garbanzo beans
Yogurt with no sugar
Fish
Olive oil
Butter
All herbs
Apples

Whole grains
Wheat bran
Lentils
Brown rice
Organic chicken and turkey
All vegetables, especially carrots,
　broccoli, cauliflower, red and
　yellow peppers, and leeks
Seeds and nuts, especially sesame
　seeds and almonds

Foods That Cancer Patients Should Avoid

Beef
Pork
All organ meats—liver, heart, brain
Sugar
White flour
Unsaturated fatty acids (corn oil,
　sunflower oil)
Margarine
Sausages, bacon, cold cuts

Tuna (a 6-ounce can of tuna
　fish contains an average of 17
　micrograms of mercury)
Beef jerky
Bone meal (contains toxic heavy
　metals including cadmium, which
　depletes selenium)
Dog treats
Processed typical commercial dog
　foods

Give Your Dog Cancer-Fighting Supplements

You know now that a healthy diet is the first step toward cancer prevention, but it's impossible to get enough nutrients through diet alone.

VITAMINS AND MINERALS

A good-quality multivitamin–mineral pill is a necessity. Begin with a multi-vitamin-mineral supplement with high doses of the antioxidant vitamins A, C, and E as well as beta-carotene and the mineral selenium. These nutrients have been shown to protect the cells' DNA from free-radical damage. Such damage is a major step toward the initiation of cancer. Studies have shown that supplemental selenium reduces cancer death rates by as much as 50 percent. Taking selenium at 200 micrograms a day repairs the damage in the DNA molecule to ensure normal cellular function and puts out the "spark" that ignites tumor growth.

Cancer begins when the DNA of a single cell is damaged or mutated, often by a free radical. The cell's normal repair mechanisms must break down for these abnormal cells to replicate into full-blown cancer. Vitamin C works on two fronts to fight cancer. First, it protects cellular DNA from free-radical damage. Second, it enhances the immune response. Although, unlike primates, dogs produce their own vitamin C, supplementation is needed in today's toxic environment. Your dog's diet may contain from 500 to 3000 extra milligrams of vitamin C daily.

Vitamin E is an important antioxidant in your dog's fatty tissues. We've mentioned that vitamin E and vitamin C complement each other when given together. Vitamin A is also highly recommended as part of a daily supplement, and vitamin A is actually used as a cancer treatment in conventional oncology.

GARLIC

One of the oldest and most popular botanical medicines is garlic. It is mentioned in ancient Egyptian medical texts. Several compounds in garlic have inhibitory effects on the growth of certain cancer cells. Garlic is one of the most versatile and widely used herbs in the world. It is best given chopped and in the raw form, because the compounds in garlic are easily destroyed by cooking and processing. You should chop the garlic fine and let it sit in the open air for ten minutes. This allows a special chemical reaction to occur. Allicin and other sulfur compounds in the garlic clove enhance the immune system, block carcinogens, and inhibit the formation of tumors.

TURMERIC

Turmeric is an ingredient that is effective against the progression of cancer. It also has the added benefit of helping your dog's joints and both alleviating and preventing arthritis. This is a very powerful anticancer herb, and it can be used to flavor food. Add ¼ to ½ teaspoon to your dog's meal.

> **CLEANING UP:** Damage to the DNA is always the first step toward cancer. Of course, there are numerous ways in which our DNA can be damaged, thereby later initiating fatal disease. Once the DNA is altered, the cell's genome changes and it has the potential, in the right environment, to become a cancer cell. The antioxidants mentioned act to clean up the free-radical debris in the cells and help them function as well as possible.

POLYSACCHARIDES

Polysaccharides are becoming very important molecules in preventing and fighting cancer. One polysaccharide peptide in particular has a very promising role in cancer prevention, for it creates an exceptionally healthy cellular environment in which the cell can repair damaged DNA. Damaged DNA is the single most important element that contributes to cancer cell formation. Polysaccharide peptide (PSP) is an alpha-glycan supplement, rather than a beta-glycan. The PSP supplement is a powder that can be added to your dog's food, and it works in the body at the cellular level, feeding the DNA, RNA, and mitochondria, thus supporting glucose energy metabolism. This special kind of nutrition is necessary to create and maintain healthy cells, healthy communication structures, and strong immune responses.

A proprietary processing technique produces unique functional characteristics of alpha-glycan PSP that are easily recognized by DNA, RNA, and genes. The extremely small molecular size of this product allows for 100 percent assimilation into the cell for maximum benefit. This is in contrast to the other known glycan supplements, known as beta-glycans, which consist of very large molecules and thus are limited in their ability to be assimilated into cells. Consequently, the alpha-glycan PSP is exponentially more effective than is the beta-glycan PSP.

The alpha-glycan provides the perfect fuel for the mitochondria in cells. Mitochondria act as a cell's power source, and the better the fuel, the healthier the cell can become. The healthier the cell, the better its ability to repair and correct itself. Alpha-glycan PSP acts within the cell as a perfect and natural nutritional source, and it causes toxins to be dumped out of the cell and an alkaline environment to be formed. In this incredible cellular environment, cellular repair is enhanced.

Administer Minimal Vaccinations

At the end of the last chapter, we discussed how overvaccination and vaccinations with cocktails of multiple viruses compromise and confuse your dog's immune system. The shame of it is that they are commonly unnecessary to start with. Research has shown that up to 15 percent of different types of cancer are caused by viruses. Vaccines are also easily contaminated with viruses and submicroscopic particles that can promote cancer. For example, a virus believed to contribute to a cancer called fibrosarcoma can be a contaminant of some rabies vaccines. Other cancer-associated viruses can potentially contaminate tissue culture media used to grow vaccines. If you must vaccinate your dog, make sure his immune system is performing optimally at the time of vaccination.

Minimize Environmental Toxins

According to a national report, there are more than 175 known carcinogens in human foods. Animal food is much less regulated, and many carcinogens that are banned for humans are used in animal food. Therefore, your dog's food may contain high doses of a number of serious carcinogens. We've mentioned ethoxyquin, which is not allowed in human food, as it is proved to be a very serious carcinogen. Yet the majority of the readily available supermarket dog foods may contain this preservative. Additionally, when the fats in dog food are heated, a very powerful carcinogen is produced—nitrosamines. The coloring agents, nitrites, and nitrates in dog food also contribute to cancer formation. If

Avoid Plastic

Store food in glass containers. If you must cook in a microwave, use only glass containers. When you heat food in the microwave in plastic containers or cover food with plastic wrap, the heat in the microwave causes the poisonous substance dioxin, a carcinogen, to melt out of the plastic and into the food. Restaurants are moving away from plastic and foam containers to paper ones.

Dioxins can leach into water that is stored in a plastic bottle or container and left in the sun or in a hot car. Use a canteen or glass bottle for your dog's (and your own) water if you can. Do not freeze water in plastic either.

you cook for your dog, all fruits and vegetables should be washed with a soap designed to remove pesticides from food surfaces.

Lawns should be treated as naturally as possible. While we all imagine that a good rain will wash these toxic ingredients down into the earth, it actually forms a thick mist of the herbicides, fertilizers, and other chemicals used in lawn care that mists up a few feet off the ground. It's exactly the right height for dogs to easily inhale those toxins.

Do Yearly Blood Tests for Thyroid Function

The thyroid gland is located on either side of your dog's trachea. It's the taskmaster of the body. It regulates metabolism and how efficiently all of the organs work, and it also communicates with the other glands in the body, such as the adrenal and the pituitary, to regulate hormones.

When the thyroid gland is functioning as it should, your dog's body is working as a well-oiled machine. An underactive thyroid results in a sluggish immune system and suboptimal performance within the body's organs. Humans who have a hypothyroid condition are often overweight, but this is not always the case in dogs. Hypothyroid conditions have been shown to contribute to cancer in humans.

Broda Barnes MD, coauthor of *Hypothyroidism, the Unsuspected Illness*, observed in his clinical practice myriad patients with typical hypothyroid symptoms whose blood values for thyroid tested normal. So when getting your dog's thyroid function tested, it's important to have a good laboratory do the test and to have someone well versed in thyroid medicine interpret the results. Dr. Barnes presented evidence that suggests a relationship between low thyroid and cancer in humans. In my clinical experience, I have found the same to be true for dogs, and I make it a point to send my thyroid tests to the Hemopet/Hemolife laboratory of Dr. Jean Dodds in California.

As part of a study I conducted for a pharmaceutical company on a natural treatment for cancer, I tested the thyroid function of all dogs

Say "No" to Bone Meal

Don't use bone meal as a calcium source. First of all, the calcium in bone meal cannot be absorbed. And some bone meal contains toxic heavy metals such as lead and cadmium, which are absorbed. Cadmium appears to be the single largest contributor to autoimmune thyroid disease. This powerful toxic metal depletes the selenium in the body, as the selenium is used to remove the cadmium. The selenium combines with the cadmium, and both are excreted through the liver. The enzyme that creates active thyroid hormone needs selenium. Selenium is also very important in protecting the cells from cancer. When the heavy metals in bone meal deplete a mineral that helps protect against and treat cancer and lowers thyroid function, the effect is that of a double-edged sword. Vitamin E in the diet protects against cadmium toxicity.

accepted into the study. The majority of the dogs tested had a hypothyroid condition. While the stress of the cancer they were being treated for could have contributed to a low thyroid condition, many of the dogs were of breeds that were prone to hypothyroidism. So the question that remains to be answered is, what came first, the chicken or the egg?

Undetected hypothyroidism opens up the door for diseases, infections, and cancer. It's easy to administer supplemental thyroid medicine if necessary, and maintaining good thyroid function is good insurance for that.

Exercise

For so many of us with busy lives, the thought of taking time out to give our dog some extra exercise to help prevent cancer may seem a bit much. I'm going to ask you to look at it this way—when you walk your dog for thirty minutes to stir up his metabolism to help prevent cancer, you're doing the same thing for yourself.

Recognizing Cancer: The Symptoms

Visible lumps and bumps are the easiest symptoms to recognize. Yet often, the very visible lumps are benign fatty tumors and sebaceous cysts. Dangerous mast cell tumors within the skin are typically smaller and harder to find under the fur.

Many cancers begin deep inside your dog's body. These growths can go undetected until their sheer bulk causes discomfort and weight loss. Typical signs of cancer may include significant weight loss, increased water intake, and tiredness, but in many cases the patient may appear to be in good health until the cancer gets large enough to interfere with organ function.

Blood tests will not necessary tell you that something is wrong. You'd be amazed at how many dogs with cancer have perfectly normal blood tests. Ultrasounds are better tools for diagnosis; they are often able to reveal masses in dogs that cannot be detected by other tests, such as X-rays, which do not reveal nearly as much as ultrasounds do. Tumors can be hidden beside or behind organs and not reveal themselves in an X-ray. It is important that any ultrasounds be done by an experienced and competent practitioner if you are concerned about cancer.

During a physical exam, your dog's lymph nodes and abdomen should be palpated. Once a month, lightly run your fingers over his body in search of any unusual masses on, in, or below the skin. Many older dogs develop benign lipomas, which pose no threat. For concerned owners, I simply aspirate these with a small needle and syringe and stain them. It's relatively pain free, and when the owners and I view the streak of liquid fat I place on the slide—and see for sure that it is a lipoma— we're all happy! Suspicious lumps can be aspirated and examined right in the office. Mast cell tumors typically give good samples to be read by a pathologist. It's also good to know what kind of tumor is present before it is excised surgically.

Treating Cancer

A point that I cannot stress too strongly is that holistic supplements that *work to prevent cancer do not necessarily work to cure it.* Loving dog owners often come to my clinic after surfing the Internet and visiting the health food store, emptying shopping bags full of cancer-preventing products onto the exam table. Although all of these products are inherently valuable, many of them are not powerful enough to do the job that needs to be done, and all of them together may give a dog one bad case of diarrhea. It's important to choose the right products—the ones that hit the nail on the head, so to speak. Once cancer has taken hold, it has a life force of its own to be reckoned with. Holistic guerrilla warfare that is dead-on accurate is necessary to terminate cancer.

The malignancy has to be hit from different angles. Each type of cancer responds differently to the options available. Alternative therapies offer the advantage of bolstering self-healing capacities while avoiding the toxic side effects that accompany conventional medical treatment for cancer. And holistic therapies really can work, depending on the expertise with which they are used. Many of the cancer cases I have successfully treated with holistic medicine were those that were not amenable to chemotherapy, radiation, or surgery. Conventional options were not going to work, and the owners usually had nowhere else to turn.

Cancer in dogs is often recognized later than in humans; therefore, it has progressed further and become more entrenched before treatment of any kind begins. We humans can talk to our doctors about discomfort, so, for example, an uncomfortable feeling in the bladder will be explored early on with various diagnostic tests. Bladder cancer, if present, will be detected shortly through this testing. Bladder cancer in a dog, on the other hand, is often found after repeated "urinary tract infections" warrant an ultrasound. Prostate cancer follows a similar path. Unfortunately, our wonderful friends cannot tell us that they are uncomfortable, so we find out that there's a real problem only when the symptoms are visible to us. This is why I value diagnostic tests and recommend a yearly blood and urine analysis on older dogs.

Conventional Approach: Chemotherapy

The goal of chemotherapy is to purge the body of cancer. Because cancer cells divide more rapidly than normal cells do, chemotherapeutic agents target these rapidly dividing cells. Of course, there are many other cells in the body that also divide rapidly. Intestinal cells, bone marrow cells, and immune system cells are adversely affected by chemotherapy as well. The bone marrow incubates the immune system, so chemotherapy devastates the immune system at the very time the body is most in need of the protection.

Chemotherapy has a fairly dismal record. Very few dogs are actually cured by chemotherapy. In most cases, a few months' remission is all that can be offered. Often, it's only a month or two more than the amount of time the dog would have lived without the chemotherapy. That's depressing.

The quality of life that the dog has during the chemotherapy is another issue. Although some dogs go through it with flying colors, others simply cannot tolerate the treatments. Many different types of cancer do not respond at all to chemotherapy. The problem with dogs is that because their cancer is often found at a later stage than it is in humans, dogs' tumors are bigger, more established in the body, and less responsive to chemotherapy.

Chemotherapy can also be very expensive. Before deciding on the path you wish to take if your dog gets cancer, find out the facts. If chemotherapy is recommended, ask for the exact statistics, expected survival time, and projected costs.

For dogs that are undergoing chemotherapy, there are some natural methods of reducing the unpleasant side effects:

- High doses of antioxidants, especially CoQ10, vitamin E, beta carotene, and selenium.
- The homeopathic remedy Nux vomica 30c twice a day to help drain toxins from the body and repair the digestive system.

Holistic Approaches

Veterinarians who use holistic cancer therapies are often dealing with patients who have already been treated with chemotherapy, radiation, or both. By this time, the cancer has spread and the internal systems of the patient have been compromised. Yet, even with all of these barriers, holistic treatment can sometimes succeed. It depends on finding just the right ammunition.

CANCER SALVES

In the 1950s, the use of herbal cancer salves for tumor destruction had a 75 to 80 percent success rate. With the advent of radiation and chemotherapy, this method went underground, yet salves containing herbal preparations have been used to treat cancer for the past 2,500 years.

In my opinion, cancer salves do not cure deep cancer but are reasonable alternatives in many cases of skin cancer. These salves contain ingredients that penetrate and kill the cancer. They are the ideal when a cancer is not immediately dangerous and the dog owner is willing to participate in the treatment. I have used salves on mast cell tumors and squamous cell carcinomas on the skin with good success.

To use a salve, the area is first shaved of fur and a small amount of cancer salve is placed on the affected area. With some salves, it is recommended to wait ten to twenty minutes before wiping the salve off, while with others it is recommended to leave the salve on for a few hours. Within a few days, some swelling and redness develops in the area, which can be alarming to squeamish owners. After this, the tumor, or the part of the tumor the salve has reached, dries up and falls off. The site needs to be evaluated to see whether another application is needed. Many holistic veterinarians use cancer salves, and I recommend that you work with your veterinarian if you wish to try this technique.

ANTICANCER DIETS

It is accepted as a general fact that a high-fat, high-protein diet works against cancer that has already established itself in the body. It is true that cancer needs sugars and carbohydrates desperately for its metabolism, but it is not true that the high-fat, high-protein, low-carbohydrate diet is the best approach in every dog's situation to fight existing cancer. Quite simply, it is the result of taking one metabolic fact about cancer and not looking any further than that.

First of all, cancer cachexia (a wasting of the body that occurs in the course of a chronic disease) results from the high tumor burden that is using up carbohydrates to survive. The body is starved while the cancer uses the body's carbohydrates greedily. In this case, a diet low in carbohydrates will put the cancer at a disadvantage, especially if the cancer patient is thin as a rail with no fat stores available for the cancer to turn into carbohydrates. However, this is simply not the case with most dogs that have cancer. While some are emaciated, many are normal in weight and even plump. Giving such a dog a low-carb, high-protein diet will cause the cancer cells to turn the dog's body fat right into carbohydrates and will keep doing this until the dog is rail thin. Additionally, the high protein content encourages the cancer cells in a healthy-looking dog to multiply.

Additionally, dogs who have had their tumors removed will have little or no tumor burden to steal their bodies' carbohydrates. So, when placed on the high-fat, high-protein food, they are eating exactly what they shouldn't be eating; a diet high in heated, processed animal and saturated fat and animal protein, which causes an acidic pH and impairs any potential success from holistic cancer treatments.

Germany's premier biochemist in the second half of the twentieth century was Dr. Johanna Budwig. Educated in pharmaceutical science,

Dr. Budwig's Anticancer Diet

Dr. Johanna Budwig's directions *must* be followed precisely for the diet to work.

One cup organic low-fat cottage cheese (or yogurt, but must be good yogurt that is naturally made)
2–5 tablespoons flaxseed oil (must refrigerate)
1–3 tablespoons freshly ground flax seeds (a coffee grinder works in addition to a flaxseed grinder)
enough water to make the mixture soft
pinch cayenne
chopped raw garlic that has been allowed to sit for at least ten minutes

Examples of a canine anticancer meal following Dr. Budwig's plan:
✓ Break up three pieces of whole grain bread and mix with one cup of basic cottage cheese-flax mix.
✓ Boil a large potato with its skin on. Steam one cup of carrots, broccoli, or cauliflower. Add one cup of cottage cheese-flax mix.
✓ Chop or grate one apple and mix with with one cup of cottage cheese-flax mixture. Sprinkle with grated coconut.
✓ Mix two cups of well-cooked lentils with one cup of cottage cheese-flax mix.

In addition to the cottage cheese-flax mixture, there are other rules to follow with this diet, such as foods to avoid and foods that are recommended. Go to http://www.datadepo.com/cancercure/budwig.htm for more information on the Budwig diet.

biology, physics, and botany, she published a number of books on cancer, including *The Death of the Tumor and Cancer: A Fat Problem.* In 1951, she developed an anticancer diet based on flaxseed oil blended with low-fat cottage cheese. Dan Roehm, a medical oncologist, recently reviewed it and found it to be one of the most successful anticancer diets in the world.

Enormous amounts of research conducted on this particular diet proved that its benefits are undisputable. Dr. Budwig developed a perfect ratio within her diet, which has since been touted as a biochemical breakthrough. The flax and cottage cheese must be in the ratio she prescribes, and the two foods must be eaten together to be effective. Unrefined flaxseed oil inhibits tumor growth, but the oil-to-protein ratio is extremely important.

It may seem puzzling that there is now irrefutable research that shows that routine dietary dairy content above 20 percent promotes cancer, and yet here is an anticancer diet with cottage cheese as the main ingredient. How can this be? The answer is that this balanced blend of cottage cheese and flax has a precise biochemical effect on cancer cells. The two main ingredients of this diet work together to destroy abnormal cancer cells. The fact that routine dietary animal protein and dairy in excess of 20 percent has been shown to promote cancer in cells damaged by carcinogens does not contradict the fact that the balance of the cottage cheese and flax in Dr. Budwig's diet works on the malignant cells' metabolism to destroy the cancer cells.

I am not surprised at how many of my cancer patients quickly tire of cottage cheese. I can't say I blame them! But you can doctor it up with other ingredients recommended by Dr. Budwig (see the Web site given previously). While you must be relatively strict about the balance and the ingredients, chicken broth or flavoring is sometimes needed to make the mixture palatable to the dog.

An ideal diet for a dog with cancer is a low-protein, high-fiber, balanced diet containing 50 percent whole grains, 10 percent beans or apples (for fiber), 30 percent vegetables, and 10 percent fruit, such as berries. The grains are best cooked with kombu or a similar seaweed, available in health food stores. If you can, get organic nonirradiated foods.

- Almonds, ground (best nuts to fight cancer)
- Sprouts of wheatgrass and alfalfa

ELLAGIC ACID: Found in red raspberries, blueberries, and strawberries, this acid has been found to slow or stop tumor growth. Studies have shown that a cup of fresh raspberries per week can slow certain cancers. Adding some fresh berries to the cottage cheese diet or to some oatmeal or yogurt is not difficult, and most dogs will enjoy their berries "berry" much!

- Egg whites, cooked
- White fish, chicken, and turkey
- Whole grains like barley, buckwheat, oats, flax, wheat berries
- Brown rice
- Molasses
- Olive and walnut oils
- Apples
- Sweet potatoes
- Broccoli
- Cauliflower
- Garlic
- Herbs

ESSIAC TEA

In 1922, a Canadian nurse named Rene Caisse was told of an Ojibway Indian tea that could cure cancer. It consisted of burdock root, sheep's sorrell, slippery elm, and rhubarb root. Rene made this tea for her aunt, who had incurable cancer, which completely resolved.

Rene continued to use this tea to treat people with cancer. Because of this, she was persecuted for nearly forty years. When she was threatened with arrest, doctors and patients always came to her rescue. Rene Caisse never claimed that the tea was a cancer cure; rather, she said it does relieve pain and improves a person's odds of overcoming the disease.

In 1959 Rene Caisse introduced her Essiac formula to Dr. Charles Brusch, physician to president John F. Kennedy. She started a study, supervised by eighteen doctors, on both terminal cancer patients and laboratory mice with cancer. In both the mice and humans, the Essiac formula reduced the size of their masses. Human patients also reported a reduction in pain and discomfort. In 1990 Dr. Brusch commented that tumors were easier to remove surgically and there was less bleeding after patients had been on a course of Essiac. In fact, he had cured his own bowel cancer with Essiac.

The name Essiac is Caisse spelled backward. Most health food stores carry packets of the mixed herbs, which you brew on your own, or a prepared mix. It is convenient and inexpensive to use. Dosages for dogs are available along with preparation guidelines on the instructions that come with the tea. It should be used three times a day for twelve consecutive weeks.

FUCOIDAN

Extensive research has shown that fucoidan—a polymer found mainly in various species of brown seaweed such as kombu, wakame, mozuku, and hijiki—has the potential to dissipate cancer cells by activating the digestive enzymes contained in the cells themselves. This process is referred to as apoptosis. Fucoidan's ability to help control the proliferation of cancerous cells as well as its ability to boost the body's immune system has been widely researched in laboratories across the world. It also contains powerful antioxidant compounds and detoxifies the body of heavy metals. In fact, fucoidan is used as standard protocol in every single oncology clinic in Japan.

Extensive research on two very distinct forms of fucoidan, U-fucoidan and F-fucoidan, began in the 1970s and continues to this day. Fucoidan is isolated as a sulfated fucopolysaccharide. Over the years, fucoidan has been cited in approximately 700 studies. Articles on it have been published in many reputable medical journals, including *The British Journal of Pharmacology* and *The Journal of Molecular Immunology.* In 1993, French scientists found that fucoidan blocked a cancer cell's ability to replicate. In 1995 in Japan, researchers discovered that when fucoidan was introduced to cancer cells in a laboratory dish, they all died within seventy-two hours. In the same year, the Japanese found that fucoidan inhibited the spread of lung cancer.

The general consensus of these studies, the evidence of thousands of years of anecdotal uses in Japan, and the decreased cancer rates in populations using the brown seaweeds in their diets all support the anticancer effects of the product. Fucoidan fights cancer by inhibiting metastasis, decreasing tumor activity, and boosting the immune system. It's been clinically shown to increase natural killer cell activity as well as improve activation of T-cells and B-cells (white cells that have a role in the body's defenses). The Biomedical Research Laboratories of Takara Shuzo and the Research Institute for the Glycotechnology Advancement have confirmed that fucoidan causes certain types of rapidly growing cancer cells, such as human stomach cancer cells and colon cancer cells, to self-destruct. Normal cells were untouched.

A small dog would take at least 500 milligrams twice a day, while a large dog would take at least 1000 milligrams twice a day. Begin with 500 milligrams a day for 5 days and then increase it to the suggested dose.

Cooking Kills Garlic

Hippocrates was the first to comment on garlic's antitumor properties. This antitumor activity can be destroyed by just one minute of microwaving, as cooking kills garlic's antitumor properties. The best way to get the most out of garlic is to chop it up and let it sit for ten minutes, during which time the enzymes naturally present in the garlic will start a chemical reaction that produces the compounds that fight tumors.

Homeopathic Remedies

Homeopathic remedies can be helpful, often working to slow down the growth of the cancer. I have experienced cures in my canine patients who had some very severe cancers. Because good nutritional support is so essential in cancer patients, I commonly combine homeopathic treatment with the appropriate array of nutraceuticals.

IP6

IP6 is composed of the sugar inositol with six phosphate groups attached to it. This nutritional supplement stimulates and promotes the activity and effectiveness of killer cells, which are important immune-system cells in fighting cancer. IP6 is made from a natural rice bran extract. Readily available in health food stores, the dose is 2,000 milligrams two or three times a day. It has no toxic side effects and has been found to inhibit the growth of cancer cells.

Hoxsey Herbs

Harry Hoxsey was an herbal folk healer who developed an herbal therapy that he learned from his great-grandfather. In the 1840s the elder Hoxsey, a veterinarian, put a horse with leg cancer out to pasture to die. He watched as the horse grazed on certain plants, and the cancer diminished. He formulated a salve from these plants and used it to treat cancer in other horses.

Today, the Hoxsey therapy consists of herbal preparations for internal and external use. The formula is made up of red clover, buckthorn bark, burdock root, stillingia root, barberry bark, chaparral, licorice root, prickly ash bark, and Cascara amarga. The external formula also contains bloodroot, an old Native American herb used to treat cancer. Humans with lymphoma, melanoma, and skin cancer seem to respond most favorably to this treatment.

Magnets

In his book *Test and Grow Healthy,* Dr. Sanford Frumker details how to use magnets to reduce tumors. Cancer cells do not reproduce easily in an alkaline environment. That's why, in the diet section, I discussed how important pH is in maintaining health. An all-meat diet produces an acid pH—a situation ripe for the development of many serious diseases, including cancer. A magnetic field applied to an area changes the concentration of hydrogen ions, and the concentration of hydrogen ions determines pH. When the magnetic north pole is applied to any cell, it increases the alkalinity within the cell and brings in more oxygen. Cancer cells do not grow in a high-oxygen environment.

Dr. Frumker found that the homeopathic remedy Tuberculinum 100c is essential for his program to have the effect of eliminating cancer. He

Homeopathy for Cancer

The homeopathic remedies suggested for cancer will depend on the type of cancer. The potencies of the remedies and the dosage schedules are suggested ones. When I treat a cancer case, I decide on the remedy, potency, and dosage rate according to the unique presentation of each patient's illness. Consult with a professional who uses homeopathy for the duration of the treatment.

CANCER, GENERAL
✓ Carcinocin 30c—three times a day for two days only
✓ Thuja 200c—twice a day for thirty days
✓ Tuberculinum 100c—three times a day (also see section on magnets that follows)
✓ Viscum album 30c—twice a day

CANCER, ABDOMINAL
✓ Conium 200c—for hard tumors and abdominal masses; give once a day

CANCER, BLADDER
✓ Berberis vulg 6c—three times a day
✓ Taraxacum 6c—three times a day

CANCER, BONE
✓ Silicea 1m—once a day
✓ Phosphorus 30c—twice a day
✓ Symphytum 200c—twice a day
✓ Arsenicum album 200c—twice a day

CANCER, FIBROSARCOMA
✓ Calcarea fluorica 200c—once a day

CANCER, LIVER
✓ Hydrastis 3x—three times a day
✓ Chelidonium 3x—three times a day
✓ Cadmium sulph 30c—twice a day

CANCER, LUNG
✓ Arsenicum album 200c—once a day
✓ Conium 200c—once a day

CANCER, LYMPH
✓ Carbo animalis 30x—twice a day
✓ Aurum met 6c—three times a day
✓ Conium 200c—twice a day

CANCER, MAMMARY
✓ Asterias rubens 6x—twice a day
✓ Phytolacca 30c—twice a day

CANCER, MELANOMA
✓ Carduus mar 30c—three times a day
✓ Lachesis 200c—once a day
✓ Thuja 30c—three times a day
✓ Argentum nit 6c—three times a day

CANCER, PROSTATE
✓ Conium 200c—three times a day
✓ Sabal serrulata 6c—three times a day
✓ Crotalis horr 200c—once a day for three days

CANCER, TONSIL
✓ Nux muschata 10m—two to three times a week

recommends a dosage of three times a day during the period of treatment with magnets.

Many studies have been done on the effect of north- and south-pole magnets. In addition to producing a more alkaline tissue and being able to shrink tumors and arrest cancer, a north-pole magnet also provokes a sedative reaction, helps control pain, and slows down organ activity. In my clinical experience, I have never found magnets to be a cure for cancer; rather, they slow the cancer's growth and give time for other treatments to take hold. Dr. Frumker uses 12,500 gauss magnets to slow cancer growth. The resources section at the end of this book has more information on Dr. Frumker's book and where to buy north-pole magnets.

Neoplasene

Neoplasene is a holistic treatment that may be used as a salve or dosed internally to treat cancer. While one form of neoplasene comes as a salve, it does not work the same way as the cancer salves previously mentioned. Neoplasene compounds attack the tumor mass by triggering apoptosis in cancer cells while sparing healthy cells.

The cancer cell membrane has a different biochemical makeup than a normal cell has, and it transfers ions and metabolic products in a very different way. Because of this, the cancer cell is vulnerable. The mix of polysaccharides that form the communication channel on the cancer cell's surface is believed to expose them to preferential apoptotic attack by the compounds in the neoplasene. Squamous cell cancer, mast cell cancer, transitional cell cancer, melanoma, osteosarcoma, nerve sheath cancer, hemangiosarcoma, lymphoma, and other cancer types have been recorded as having resolved with neoplasene treatment. Neoplasene is only available through your veterinarian. (See *Theoretical Explanation of Neoplasene*, T. S. Fox et al., "The Treatment of Neoplasm, Proud Flesh, and Warts with Sanguinarine and Related Isoquinoline Alkaloids," accessed May 2008 at www.buckmountainbotanicals.net.)

Poly-MVA

Scientists are searching for better methods to cure cancer. Currently, chemotherapy and radiation therapy produce dangerous side effects because they lack specificity. A goal of medical researchers is to find treatments that act solely on cancer cells. The compound Poly-MVA combines the vitamin lipoic acid with the trace element palladium. Palladium is first dissolved in a suitable acid under high heat at an extremely specific concentration, and the vitamin lipoic acid is added.

Dr. Merrill Gamett discovered that all cancer cells have abnormal electron transfer systems. He found that the metal palladium is a nontoxic compound that affects the cancer cells' ability to grow and reproduce. Normal cell development requires normal energy flow. In laboratory experiments, Dr. Gamett found that, because of these particular pathways, Poly-MVA selectively destroys cancer cells. The Poly-MVA works because healthy cells have "oxygen radical pathways," while cancer cells do not.

Poly-MVA destroys cancer cells by interfering with their metabolism. It is administered orally and is very palatable. More information on how Poly-MVA works, suggested dosage, practitioners who recommend it, and more can be found at www.polymvasurvivors.com.

Selenium

The mineral selenium should be administered in cancer cases. Selenium is a trace mineral that is essential to good health but required only in small amounts. It is incorporated into proteins to make selenoproteins, which are important antioxidant enzymes. The antioxidant properties of seleno-proteins help prevent cellular damage from free radicals, which in turn helps prevent the development of chronic diseases such as cancer and heart disease. Other selenoproteins help regulate thyroid function and also play a role in the immune system.

This mineral is very important for thyroid health, heart health, and cancer prevention in your dog. The selenite form, called sodium selenite, is the only form that has been shown to directly stop tumor growth. The more common form, called selenomethionine, is stored in the liver, whereas sodium selenite goes directly to the tumors. Selenium works well when combined with vitamin E and can often be found in combination as a supplement.

Wobenzym N

Wobenzym N is a systemic enzyme supplement manufactured by a German company. The tablets are coated in order for them to be able to pass through the stomach acids without being dissolved. This special feature enables the enzymes, especially the key enzyme in the formula, chymotrypsin, to absorb into the bloodstream, where it is carried along to the cancer sites. The prime objective of chymotrypsin is to dissolve the protective outer protein coating of the cancer cells, enabling the immune system (or the products you are giving your dog) to enter and destroy the cancer cells.

Wobenzym N is best taken every four hours during the day without food until the cancer is resolved. If possible, this product should be included in every holistic cancer protocol, as it opens up the cancer cell to the immune system's attacks.

Choosing

When loving dog owners are confronted with cancer in their dogs, reason may fly out the window. A sense of urgency combined with shock and fear could impair the formation of a well-considered and educated decision.

My Ideal Scenario for Fighting Cancer

It's not easy to come up with the perfect regimen for each and every cancer patient. The following steps suggest products that are relatively easy to obtain and may be effective with many cancers, as some promote the healthy cells in the body while some destroy the cancer cells.

1. Either Dr. Budwig's Diet or an anticancer low-protein diet.
2. One to two cups of fresh berries added to the diet each week.
3. Raw garlic, chopped and allowed to sit for ten minutes before serving, added to a meal each day.
4. Fucoidan for cancer cell apoptosis—give on empty stomach. (See Resources for source.)
5. Polysaccharide-polypeptide for cellular DNA repair and normalization. Give at a separate time away from dairy and carbohydrates. (See Resources for source.)
6. Wobenzym N to open cell membranes to the effects of fucoidan.
7. A good multivitamin-multimineral supplement along with a sodium selenite supplement.
8. Other holistic modalities such as homeopathy, Hoxsley herbs, Essiac tea, and neoplasene.
9. Other additions to this regimen will depend on the type and location of the cancer.

Never be afraid to ask questions and ask for documentation. If chemotherapy is offered, request the statistics for that type of cancer treated with the proposed drug. Don't rush into therapy that doesn't work because you are too worried and frightened to do anything else. When choosing holistic alternatives to conventional cancer treatment, you may use the information about cancer prevention along with the information on products used to treat cancer. Don't forget that you don't have to choose just one therapy. You can create a program for your dog by combining conventional treatments with natural therapies or combining a few indicated natural and nontoxic programs. Remember that many of these treatments slow the growth of the cancer and do not kill the malignant cells outright. Protocols that boost the immune system and activate the killer cells can be combined with those that slow the growth of the cancer. Large tumors that can be easily removed should be taken out, as your dog's body will, as a result, have less of a cancer load it has to deal with.

Chapter 11

Dogs with Special Needs

Dogs with special needs include those suffering from diabetes, digestive problems, heart conditions, kidney failure, obesity, and separation anxiety. It's important to understand the underlying reasons for the problem, as this enables you to make smarter choices. Additionally, if you are concerned whether your dog's symptoms may suggest a problem, this section will help put things in perspective. Complementary holistic medicines can be very helpful. The Canine Café recipes also feature a section on special-needs diets that can help with the conditions discussed in this chapter. You can also visit my Web site, www.doctordeva.com, for information and updates.

Diabetes

When your dog eats food, he digests the complex food molecules into simple sugars, much of which is glucose. This glucose then enters the blood, where insulin from the pancreas manages the distribution and uptake of these simple sugars. Insulin opens the cellular "door" so glucose can then enter and be used for energy.

In cases of diabetes, the sugars needed by the cells cannot be absorbed. The sugar keeps circulating in the blood and is finally secreted by the kidneys into the urine. Glucose gives the cells the energy they need to survive. When the cells are starved of the sugar necessary to run their metabolism, a trigger in the brain for hunger goes on. Therefore, diabetic dogs exhibit both excessive thirst and hunger.

THE PANCREAS is a pinkish, semi-oblong-shaped organ that is a few inches in length. It helps digest food by producing digestive enzymes. The pancreas also produces insulin. Insulin allows sugar carried in the blood to transfer into the cells.

Signs and symptoms of diabetes include the following:

- Intake of noticeably more water
- More frequent urination
- Weight loss
- Increased appetite
- Unusual- or sweet-smelling breath and urine, or both
- Secondary bladder infection

Mabel's Story

Mabel was drinking lots of water and wanting more and more to eat. Yet, she was losing weight and her coat appeared lackluster and shabby. At first, her owner thought the summer heat was the reason for her thirst, but she was now drinking several bowls of water a day. After examining Mabel, I took a blood and urine sample from her. The urine was positive for glucose, and the glucose level in her blood was very high. Mabel began taking insulin that was appropriate for her weight. We started with a dose on the low side, and I instructed her owner on how to monitor Mabel's urine with test strips to check its glucose level. About every other day, Mabel's owner was to bring her in to the clinic a specific number of hours after giving the insulin shot so we could check Mabel's glucose level in her blood.

Within a few days, Mabel was feeling much better. Her sugar levels were moving toward normal, and her thirst was decreasing. We started her on 250 micrograms of chromium glucose tolerance factor (GTF) and 50 milligrams of vanadyl sulfate twice a day. Her owner began cooking for her and added parsley, garlic, and some green beans to her food every day. Her meals consisted of basic low glycemic-index grains and lean meat, poultry, or fish with some vegetables. Mabel got 2 tablespoons of olive oil mixed into her food each day and a multivitamin/multimineral supplement. Mabel was also given a combination homeopathic remedy formulated for diabetes and 300 milligrams of Gymnena sylvestre once a day.

It often takes a bit of work to find just the right insulin dose for a diabetic dog. It was no different for Mabel. A month after diagnosis, she was stable but needed a much lower dose of insulin than expected. This may have been due to the holistic supplements. Mabel will need to stay on her insulin and the holistic supplements for the rest of her life unless her pancreas regenerates and recovers fully from the diabetes. Her homeopathic remedies may be adjusted over time, but supplements such as the chromium GTF and vanadyl sulfate will continue to be given to keep her at optimal health. Diabetics require routine veterinary examinations and blood sugar evaluations. A well-thought-out diet with proper supplements helps to regulate and to control diabetes.

Designing a Diabetes Diet

Feeding several small meals a day, with a larger portion given before an insulin injection, works well for diabetic dogs. Vegetables can be grated and served either raw or lightly steamed. Vegetables such as green beans, squash, kale, dandelion greens, and parsley are recommended, and garlic should be used generously in these meals. Meats, which should be lean, can be cooked or raw. The grains should be well cooked; excellent grains to use are millet, brown rice, barley, and oatmeal. Olive oil is the best oil for you to use.

You may wonder why these diets call for lean meats but the addition of olive oil. The answer is that not all fats are alike. Animal fat, particularly cooked animal fat, is very unhealthy and has been shown to predispose one to diabetes. Olive oil, fish oils, and omega-3 oils, such as those contained in flax oil, are very healthy and help prevent and control diabetes.

In The Canine Café recipe section, you'll find several recipes for diabetic dogs. The recipes can be adjusted easily to incorporate the afore-mentioned suggested grains and vegetables. Recipes serve as a basic template that can change along with the best buys at the market.

Diabetes Diet: The Basics

The following is a basic guideline for a diet for a diabetic dog; more specific recipes can be found in The Canine Café.

⅓ lean protein: fish, chicken, turkey, or very lean beef (cooked or raw), or cooked egg whites

⅓ low-starch vegetables and some fruits: string beans, broccoli, cauliflower, blueberries, apples

⅓ slow-cooked oatmeal or slow-cooked barley

olive oil

cinnamon, garlic, parsley as healing herbs

Treatments for Diabetes

There are several types of treatments for dogs with diabetes, including vitamins and minerals, botanical medicines, and homeopathic remedies.

VITAMINS AND MINERALS

The following vitamins and minerals will help dogs suffering from diabetes.

Chromium—This mineral improves the action of insulin and helps move nutrients such as glucose into the cells. Research proved it to be so beneficial for improving the cells' uptake of insulin that the researchers named it Glucose Tolerance Factor. Give 100 to 300 micrograms twice a day.

Vanadium or Vanadyl sulfate—This unique trace mineral lowers blood sugar by mimicking insulin. It also helps improve the cell's sensitivity to insulin. This mineral plays a role in blood sugar balance and cardiovascular function and may help your dog's body with sugar metabolism. You can find vanadium in cabbage, mushrooms, parsley, and grains. The therapeutic level of vanadium is from 15 to 25 milligrams daily. To treat diabetes, 50 to 75 milligrams a day can be used. Vanadium is very safe; it appears to be nontoxic, and the consequences of deficiency are unknown. Vanadium is available in liquid, tablet, or capsule form and is sold in health food stores. It is often found in human multivitamins.

Vitamin E and fish oils—These oils are very important for diabetes along with being excellent antioxidants; they can be given twice a day. The dose of vitamin E can range from 100 to 400 IU a day, depending on the size of the dog. Fish oils would simply be added to the food.

A good multivitamin-multimineral supplement—this is important.

BOTANICAL MEDICINE

The following botanical substances can help a dog suffering from diabetes:

Gymnema sylvestre—From a plant native to India, this herb appears to have the ability to regenerate the insulin-producing beta cells in the pancreas. The recommended dose is 200 milligrams a day for a small dog, 300 milligrams a day for a medium dog, and 400 milligrams daily for a large dog.

Lagerstroemia speciosa, or banaba leaf—This plant from Asia contains a compound called colosolic acid, which activates glucose transport into the cells. The suggested dose is 5 to 15 milligrams a day, depending on the size of your dog.

Fenugreek seeds—These seeds, taken as a tea, can help lower blood sugar. Take 1 teaspoon of seeds and add 1 cup of boiling water. Give ½ to 1 teaspoon two or three times a day, or add a few teaspoons to the dog's food. Store in the refrigerator.

Polygonum multiflorum—This is a Chinese herb that is specific for controlling blood sugar levels. You may be able to find this in a Chinese pharmacy. It can be given as a powder, tea, or capsule twice a day. To figure out the correct dose, use ¼ of the suggested human dose (divided into two daily doses) for a small dog or ½ of the suggested human dose (divided into two daily doses) for a large dog.

Cinnamon—This spice comes from the inner bark of the shoots of a tree *(Cinnamomum zeylanicum)* that grows predominantly in India, China, and Ceylon. The inner rind, when dried and rolled into cylinders, forms the cinnamon of commerce. The fruit and coarser pieces of bark, when boiled, yield a fragrant oil. Cinnamon is aromatic and one of the best-tasting spices. Researchers have long speculated that foods, especially spices, could help treat diabetes. In lab studies, cinnamon, cloves, bay leaves, and turmeric have all shown promise in enhancing insulin's action. There has been a lot of talk these days about cinnamon because scientists have discovered that cinnamon extract has strong antioxidant activity and has the potential to help maintain healthy blood sugar.

HOMEOPATHY

There are many homeopathic remedies that can help control and treat diabetes. If the level of diabetes is low, with mildly elevated glucose levels in the blood, remedies, herbs, and diet may control or eliminate the diabetes. Pharmaceutical insulin will be needed in more severe diabetes.

- *Iris vers 6c*—This remedy has a specific beneficial effect on the pancreas. It can be given twice a day.
- *Syzigium 6c*—This remedy can be used when the animal has a very high level of thirst. Give this remedy two to three times a day.
- *Phosphoric acid 6c*—This remedy has been helpful in diabetes and can be given once a day.
- *Natrum muriaticum 6c*—This remedy has also been helpful with diabetes and can be given twice a day.

These remedies may help reduce symptoms and help stabilize diabetic patients on insulin by assisting in controlling insulin levels. With diabetes, the appropriate remedy often needs to be given to the dog for the long term.

If your animal is presently diabetic, you will need to watch the sugar in his urine and blood carefully as you begin these supplements and homeopathic remedies. Your veterinarian can show you how to monitor the blood sugar and check the urine. Your dog may need less insulin after taking these remedies for while, and you want to be on the alert so you know when it's time to lower the insulin dose.

Digestive Problems

Digestive problems in dogs include diarrhea, vomiting, and constipation. Some dogs may have the occasional digestive upset after getting into the garbage, while others may have such sensitive digestive tracts that *any* alteration of their diets results in days or weeks of discomfort. By knowing the basics facts about your dog's problem and learning some quick, easy, and workable solutions, you may be able to save yourself a lot of extra cleanup and trips out to the yard.

Diarrhea

Diarrhea is one of the most common medical problems that occur in dogs. If your dog goes to a remote area of your yard to make his deposits, the problem may elude you. Otherwise, it's pretty obvious, especially when there are accidents in the house. Dogs with diarrhea have soft, oftentimes watery, stool. The stool can have mucus and sometimes a little bit of blood in it. Your dog may have accidents in the house or ask to go out more often. Diarrhea can come on quickly and also go away quickly, but it can also persist and get worse and worse.

The common denominator in just about all cases of diarrhea is an imbalance in the flora and fauna of the intestine. The environment of the intestine is filled with good bacteria that help digest food and produce vitamins. Bacteria, protozoa, and other organisms exist in the intestinal tract in delicate balance. When that balance is tipped, diarrhea may result. Anything that upsets the digestive tract can cause diarrhea in your dog.

Imbalance in the intestine can come about because your dog ate something he shouldn't have, drank water that was foul, had a marrowbone or treat that was very rich, got into the garbage, or for any

---

Rice and Egg Drop Soup

This recipe is an excellent one for a dog with diarrhea. Yields 6 cups.

2 cups basmati rice
6 cups water
3 eggs, beaten

Cook 2 cups basmati rice in 6 cups water for 15 minutes. The mixture that results should be a little soupy; if not, add more water. Rapidly mix in the beaten eggs and allow to cool to room temperature. It should firm up as it cools. Serve when cool.

Kudzu (Kuzu) Root Recipe

In Japan and China, kudzu (kuzu) is the traditional medicine of choice for a host of digestive disorders. Kudzu's complex starch molecules enter the intestines and help restore health and stop diarrhea. Special antioxidants, flavonoids, in the kudzu inhibit the contraction of the smooth muscle tissue, stop cramping, and increase blood flow to the area. Kudzu is also a thickening agent, acting to thicken and regulate the intestinal contents and thus firming the stool. Kudzu is available in most health food stores.

1 heaping teaspoon kudzu
3 tablespoons cold water
1 cup cold water
2 cups cooked white rice, cooked with a chicken or beef bouillon cube
½ cup diced cooked chicken pieces

Dissolve by mixing the kudzu in the 3 tablespoons cold water. Put the rest of the water (1 cup) in a saucepan. Add the dissolved kudzu to the water in the saucepan, and further mix and dissolve the kudzu. Bring to a boil over medium heat, reducing to low until the liquid looks translucent, and stirring constantly to avoid lumping. Mix liquid with 2 cups of cooked white rice, and add cooked diced chicken to mix. Cool and serve.

reason ingested something that upset the balance of his GI tract. In these cases, rebalancing the intestinal tract with probiotics along with a bland diet can often correct the problem. The good bugs will begin to overgrow the bad bugs, correct balance will return, and the problem will be handled. Uncomplicated diarrhea is not hard to correct.

If it is not a simple case of the dog's having ingested the wrong thing, the cause of the problem must be isolated and corrected, as diarrhea can be caused by food allergies, irritable bowel disease, and parasitic infections such as worms or *Giardia*. Diarrhea accompanied by a fever may require an emergency trip to the veterinarian, as serious diseases such as parvovirus and distemper can cause diarrhea (that may or may not be bloody). Diarrhea along with repeated vomiting may also be due to a serious medical condition. Intestinal cancer can also cause diarrhea.

For recipes that can help dogs suffering from diarrhea, see the special needs section in The Canine Café. Many foods can be beneficial. For example, sweet potatoes and yams have a natural substance in them that decreases inflammation in the intestine and can work even better than the typically recommended chicken and rice dishes. There are also various types of treatment; the treatments discussed here are for uncomplicated diarrhea. If your dog's diarrhea persists, take him to a veterinarian.

PHARMACEUTICAL DRUGS FOR DIARRHEA

Kaopectate is an over-the-counter drug available in drugstores and super-markets. It contains a special mineral that absorbs the diarrhea-causing bacteria along with the toxins in the intestine. You can give your dog from 1 teaspoon to 1 tablespoon of Kaopectate every hour or two for several hours. It works best if given often on the first day or two.

Metronidazole (flagyl) must be dispensed or prescribed by your veterinarian. Often one pill in the very beginning of the problem will nip it in the bud. After the one tablet is given, add some extra probiotics to your dog's food for added benefit.

HOMEOPATHIC REMEDIES

Homeopathic remedies are ideal for problems such as diarrhea and vomiting. As they melt in the mucous membranes and do not have to be swallowed, they can be given easily, allowing you to rest the digestive tract and treat your dog with some very effective medicine at the same time. It's a win-win situation. The following homeopathic remedies are helpful for treating dogs with diarrhea.

You may find it helpful to assemble a first-aid homeopathic kit for common problems. Many homeopathic pharmacies sell a kit that contains fifty remedies and a list of their common uses.

Podophyllum 30c—This is a very good remedy for just about all diarrhea, especially light brown or yellow diarrhea, which is very common in young nursing puppies. Give this remedy four times a day. After the stool becomes firm, reduce the frequency of dosage to twice a day for two to three days after all is cleared up.

Aloe 30c—This remedy is good for diarrhea that has a jellylike mucus. With this type of diarrhea, rumbling may be heard in the dog's bowel, and

HOMEOPATHIC REMEDIES are easy to administer. Remedies come in the form of tiny white pellets that can be tucked into your dog's lower lip fold to melt. They also come in liquid form in which a few drops can be placed on your dog's gums. Additionally, a few pellets can be placed in a small amount of spring water and stirred, and this water can be given as a remedy.

Discontinue the remedy after the problem resolves. Homeopathic remedies work to assist the body to heal. When this is accomplished, the remedy is stopped.

> **RESTING THE DIGESTIVE TRACT:** It may also be a good idea to fast your dog for twelve to twenty-four hours in order to rest his digestive tract. After that, move on to one of the bland diets indicated for diarrhea listed in The Canine Café section. Of course, water should be offered.

he will have a great urgency to go out. This remedy may be given four times a day until the diarrhea clears up.

* Mixing Podophyllum 30c and Aloe 30c and giving the mixture four times a day will help quickly alleviate most cases of uncomplicated diarrhea.

Merc corr 30c—This remedy is for diarrhea in which there is much straining. Your dog may stay in the arched position and go several times, producing diarrhea with mucus and a slimy appearance. There also may be spots of blood in the stool. This remedy can be given three times a day. If these symptoms are present, take a stool sample to your vet to check for worms, take your dog's temperature, and get a veterinary exam if he does not begin to respond to this treatment in twenty-four hours.

Arsenicum album 30c—This remedy is especially useful for cases of diarrhea in which there is accompanying vomiting. The stool may have a very rank odor, and the dog may be restless. It is also good remedy for dehydration. It should be given every hour or two, and the dosing reduced in frequency as improvement occurs. Keep dosing at least twice a day until the condition is well under control. Again, go to the vet if your dog does not respond to treatment.

China 30c—This remedy is important to give when there has been a great loss of fluid, as it will help restore strength and maintain electrolyte balance. Give this remedy three times on the first day only.

Nux vomica 30x—This is a good remedy to alleviate the discomfort your dog may feel. Give once in the evening before bed.

PROBIOTICS

You can help restore the natural balance of the intestine by adding beneficial bacteria such as lactobacillus acidophilus to your dog's meals. Yogurt from the health food store often has a more desirable mix of bacteria than the big name-brand yogurts, made from mixed cultures that do not have the needed probiotics, from the supermarket. Several tablespoons, or even a whole container, of yogurt from the health food store can be added to your dog's food as part of a meal. Probiotic bacteria in powder form, liquid preparations, tablets, and capsules are widely available over the counter at your health food store. Good intestinal bacteria should be part of your dog's routine diet, so I recommend that you continue giving probiotics even after the diarrhea clears up.

CHINESE HERBS

Po chai is a common Chinese herb that you can find in the Chinatown section of most large cities. It usually sold in sets of twelve small vials filled with tiny pellets. This herb works wonderfully in dogs with diarrhea. The dosage for a large dog is usually one vial three times a day. A small dog can get one half of a vial three times a day. Administer this herb until the diarrhea has fully cleared up. Do not continue use beyond that point.

BOTANICAL MEDICINE

Two substances that can be used for diarrhea are slippery elm and carob powder. Slippery elm can be mixed with water. A small amount of powdered slippery elm bark in water forms a jellylike substance that can be administered to your dog to help slow the diarrhea. Typical dosage is 1 to 2 teaspoons three times a day, depending on the size of your dog.

Carob powder can also be mixed with water and given to your dog. The recommended dosage is ½ to 1 teaspoon three times a day, depending on the size of the dog. You also can mix 1 teaspoon of slippery elm with teaspoon of carob powder and administer the two remedies together.

Vomiting

Many dogs occasionally eat grass and vomit. Dogs can also regurgitate their food once in a while, particularly if they have eaten quickly. This type of intermittent vomiting is not serious, but repeated episodes of vomiting, in which a dog cannot keep his food down, is a serious situation and requires a full veterinary examination. If the vomiting is spasmodic and continual, it is considered an emergency.

TREATING SIMPLE VOMITING

The first step in treating acute vomiting (that which comes on suddenly) is to stop feeding your dog and fast him for twelve to twenty-four hours to rest his digestive tract. Start by removing both food and water. If your dog doesn't vomit over the next few hours, reinstate the water—but only in small amounts. Don't put down a large bowl of water and let him drink most of it, as the result will probably be more vomiting. Instead, offer water to your dog in small amounts, about ½ cup at a time for a medium-sized dog and less for a small dog, every half hour or so.

After all is well for twelve to twenty-four hours, you can feed him a light homemade meal of cooked yams, scrambled eggs or chicken, and rice. If the vomiting continues, you must call your veterinarian. Additionally, if your dog has a temperature above 102.5 degrees F, bring him in to see a veterinarian. Severe problems such as pancreatitis can cause vomiting.

HOMEOPATHIC REMEDIES FOR SIMPLE VOMITING

Here are some simple homeopathic remedies to help a dog with vomiting.

Arsenicum album 30c—This is a good remedy for vomiting. It is very useful in a case where the dog has both vomiting and diarrhea. It is to be given every few hours until the condition improves; reduce the frequency of dosing as the problem starts to clear up. For example, it can be given every hour for three doses, then every two hours for two doses, and then three times on the next day. Once the problem is resolved, stop the dosing altogether. It should begin to work within three hours after the initial once-an-hour dosing starts. Of course, your dog should be resting his digestive tract as previously mentioned.

Nux vomica 30c—This has a beneficial effect on the entire intestinal tract. It is best used for the dog who routinely has the occasional vomiting with grass and has regurgitated his food. In cases in which this remedy is indicated, the dog is ready to eat again almost immediately after he throws up. It can be given three times a day for three days.

Ipecac 30c—This homeopathic remedy can relieve the symptoms of vomiting. If ipecac is given as the straight compound, it induces vomiting, but as a homeopathic remedy, it treats and relieves vomiting. Ipecac is an excellent example of "like treats like." This remedy would be used in the dog who has no interest in food after vomiting. This remedy can be given three times over a period of a day.

HOMEOPATHIC REMEDIES are easy to administer. Remedies come in the form of tiny white pellets that can be tucked into your dog's lower lip fold to melt. They also come in liquid form in which a few drops can be placed on your dog's gums. Additionally, a few pellets can be placed in a small amount of spring water and stirred, and this water can be given as a remedy.

Discontinue the remedy after the problem resolves. Homeopathic remedies work to assist the body to heal. When this is accomplished, the remedy is stopped.

Constipation

If your dog is in good health, he will have one or two (or more) bowel movements every day. But if a day or more goes by without bowel activity, he's constipated. Other symptoms of constipation are the dog's straining to move his bowels, producing small or very hard feces, or producing a very small amount of feces.

It's not difficult to prevent or relieve simple constipation. In fact, many of the same things that work for people will also help your dog keep regular. If, however, the situation doesn't respond to early treatment and becomes chronic, it can be a signal of a larger problem.

CAUSES OF CONSTIPATION

One of the two basic causes of constipation in dogs is problems with food. Most commercial foods, even those of the poorest quality, are designed to produce normal, firm, and easy-to-pick-up stools in most dogs. Manufacturers have long known that people look at their dog's excrement as a reflection of food quality.

Lack of roughage in the diet is the most common cause of simple constipation. This is particularly true of a diet very high in fat and meat and very low in roughage. Scan dog food labels for things such as blueberries, apples, beets, and herbs—all elements of good roughage—and purchase foods that have roughage. You won't find these ingredients in most of the low-end dog foods available at supermarkets. Dog foods available in health food stores do tend to have more fresh ingredients and higher levels of roughage.

The other basic cause of a dog's constipation is metabolic or organic problems. The dog's colon is the part of the intestinal system that absorbs water. When the colon absorbs an abnormally high amount of water, stools become hard, dry, and difficult for your dog to pass. A few of the conditions affecting the colon, generating constipation through high absorption of water, are kidney failure, heart failure, and diabetes.

Constipation is far less common in dogs than is diarrhea, and it is more likely to occur in older and less active dogs. Homeopathic remedies and herbs can be used in mild cases of constipation that are of short duration. If your dog seems uncomfortable, go right to your veterinarian and get your dog an examination. If constipation occurs for a period of time or even for short durations with severity and straining, you also should see your veterinarian.

HOMEOPATHIC REMEDIES

Here are two homeopathic remedies to help dogs who are suffering with constipation.

Nux vomica 6x or 30x—This remedy is good for acute constipation. It tones and detoxifies the digestive organs. It is the first remedy to consider for constipation or sluggish bowels. Give this remedy three or four times a day for a few days and then reduce the dose to twice a day for a week.

Lycopodium 6c—This remedy is good to give to a dog with chronic digestive problems. He may have a poor appetite and may be the kind of dog who could be described as a worrier. Give this remedy twice a day for ten days to benefit the digestive tract.

PREVENTION AND CARE

Canned pumpkin is an excellent addition to a dog's diet to help with constipation. You can add from ¼ to 1 cup of this into the dog's food every day. It is an excellent source of fiber, and it works extremely well to prevent, correct, and counteract constipation.

Additionally, be sure to:

- Keep the water bowl full.
- Take your dog for walks; the activity of a longer walk helps encourage the bowels to move.
- Make sure that food has enough fiber and roughage. Dietary fiber absorbs water in the intestines, making the stools larger, softer, and easier to pass. A sprinkle of bran cereal on the food will add a healthy dose of dietary fiber. Psyllium husks and flax seeds are also very high in fiber and good for the bowels. Make sure your dog is drinking plenty of water when you add fiber.
- Add cooked vegetables and fresh fruit to your dog's diet.
- Try some home cooking as suggested in the recipes in The Canine Café section.
- Add probiotics (acidophilus and other beneficial bacteria) to your dog's food. About ½ a teaspoon in each meal is an adequate amount. Probiotics that contain acidophilus and other beneficial bacteria help build the stool and create the normal passage of stool.
- Add digestive enzymes to your dog's food. This is especially important for the older dog, whose system does not make as many digestive enzymes as it once did. This will help him digest and utilize his food better and will promote better stools. Digestive enzymes are available in a powdered form at pet supply stores.
- Do not use laxatives made for humans unless your veterinarian recommends it, as these products may give your dog diarrhea and upset the bowel further.
- *Raw garlic* is also good for constipation.
- *Olive oil* can be added to the dog's food. The suggested amount ranges from 1 teaspoon to 2 tablespoons, depending on the size of the dog.

Heart Conditions

Dogs can develop a variety of heart problems. Just like people's, a dog's heart can become weak and enlarged, but dogs do not get hardening and thickening of the arteries as people do. Dogs also do not get the same kind of heart attacks as people do.

Your dog's heart is made up of four chambers, separated by heart valves. The valves open in rapid sequence, allowing each chamber to fill and close, sealing the chamber so that a rhythmic muscular contraction will drive the blood on to the following chamber.

The most common heart condition in dogs is a heart murmur. This murmur is detected when your veterinarian listens to your dog's heart with a stethoscope. When a valve is "leaky," the sound that the leaky valve makes is called a heart murmur. When your veterinarian hears your dog's heart murmur, he assigns the murmur a grade. The grade of a heart murmur tells us the degree of seriousness, or how badly the valve is leaking. A valve typically becomes leaky due to scarring. A chronic low-grade infection, such as that which occurs with chronically infected teeth, can become systemic. The immune system quickly clears up the infection, but sometimes the bacteria settle on the delicate, paper-thin valve. The infection is resolved, but the valve scars and so contracts. The scarred valve does not shut tightly, as it used to. Blood back flows when the heart contracts, and this is heard as a murmur.

The heart has to work harder to get the blood out to the body, and the heart muscles begin to tire and stretch as time passes. When the heart is so stretched that it cannot do its job, the kidneys sense that the blood pressure is getting low and try to help by retaining fluid. Finally, as the kidneys desperately hold fluid in the body in an attempt to compensate, this fluid begins to pool in the lungs, and the result is congestive heart failure.

Hold the Salt

With most heart conditions in dogs, it is important that your dog go on a strict no-salt diet with no break from this routine. Even just an occasional salty snack, like a piece of bacon on Sunday morning, will have a dramatic effect on the system, and fluid can rapidly build up in the lungs.

First, your dog won't miss salt in his diet because dogs don't particularly like it that much. Second, the dog's kidneys will have no salt to assist them in drawing in and retaining water. This will keep water from being retained in the body and will help stabilize the heart condition somewhat.

Zippy's Story

Zippy is a ten-year-old female Chihuahua. When her folks brought her in for her first visit, I couldn't find her. Her healthy sister had come along for the visit, and I began to examine her. "Wrong dog," I was told. I found Zippy under her owner's shirt. When she peeked out, I could see that she was not well at all. It was easy to see that she was very thin, and her whole body had a blue tinge. Her tongue and gums were almost purple. She was terrified. Upon examining her, I found that she had a very loud heart murmur. She had already been to a veterinary cardiologist, and X-rays had revealed that her heart was huge. It was so big that it pushed her trachea out of its normal position in the chest. The echocardiogram and EKG showed that she had a severely damaged mitral valve, an irregular heartbeat, and a collapsing trachea. Of course, she was in congestive heart failure.

She was on three different conventional heart drugs. She had been on them for some time and was just getting worse. She was so weak that she was not allowed to walk very far or climb stairs without supervision. Her owners were told that she did not have long to live, and it sure looked that way when I first saw her. They really didn't think that she was going to be around much longer and were uncertain whether I could help, but they loved her so much that they decided to make one more try.

Zippy's people were willing to cook for her and make her a healthy no-salt diet, and we also started her on a good multivitamin-mineral supplement. I prescribed 30 milligrams of CoQ10 twice a day to give her heart the fuel it needed to run. She also began taking a few drops of a tincture made from hawthorne berries three to four times a day. I made a homeopathic combination remedy with ingredients such as Cratageous, Cactus grandiflorus, and Convallaria in the 3c, 6c, and 30c potencies—all mixed together—and gave her this three times a day. She received a product made by Standard Process (a company that makes natural veterinary formulations) for heart problems in dogs, taking one tablet twice a day. I also gave her an asparagus-parsley tablet to act as a natural diuretic to help keep the fluid from pooling in her lungs. She received acupuncture for her heart, and a special light laser was used to encourage her heart tissues to regain their strength.

After five or six weekly visits, Zippy's external appearance was that of a perfectly healthy dog. She had gained weight and, instead of looking like an emaciated blue-tinted dog, was plump and pink. Her eyes were bright, she was interested in life, and she no longer hid in her dad's shirt. Rather, she looked at me cheerily, without fear in anticipation of her treatment.

I am told that Zippy runs and gallops about the house with her sister, is playful, and eats well. Her heart is not totally well and will remain damaged. She has stopped some of her conventional drugs, but we still depend on certain medications to keep her heart working well. But now her owners can look forward to more time with her, and she will enjoy a quality life.

A mild heart murmur can and should be treated holistically. Very advanced murmurs benefit from holistic treatments, but often some conventional medicines may be necessary to maintain homeostasis in the body. It is important to incorporate holistic medicine in the beginning as well as in more advanced states, for holistic medicine works very well in supporting the heart's ability to function. Even if you need to use conventional medications, it is also necessary to support the heart with nutrition, remedies, and herbs.

The symptoms for congestive heart failure include:
- Heart murmur, audible through a stethoscope
- Exercise intolerance
- Coughing, especially in the morning or after sleeping and resting
- Increased thirst

If you understand why a heart fails, it's not surprising that the best time to treat your dog for a heart condition is at the onset, before the heart stretches and becomes enlarged. Regular examinations allow your veterinarian to listen for a murmur; this is another reason why annual veterinary examinations are important.

Nowadays, we are fortunate enough to have specialists in veterinary cardiology. Because of this, your dog's heart can be evaluated in detail and its condition ascertained. The echocardiogram that a cardiologist performs is an ultrasound of the heart, and it can reveal the condition of the heart's valves and walls.

Remember, the grade of a heart murmur indicates how severe it is; the higher grades indicate louder murmurs. The time to begin treating a heart problem is when a heart murmur is found. Congestive heart failure, in which the lungs are congested with fluid that the heart cannot eliminate from the body, occurs in later stages. Nutritional supplements, herbs, and homeopathy effectively strengthen the heart tissue and assist in maintaining health. And again, make sure that you put your dog on a no-salt diet. There are recipes for dogs with heart conditions in the special needs section of The Canine Café.

Treatments for Heart Conditions

In my practice, I have found holistic products to be immeasurably helpful in prolonging the life of the heart. Zippy was one of many dogs who enjoyed an extended and fuller life because healthy natural supplements and homeopathic remedies were added to her heart regimen.

TREATMENTS FOR MURMURS AND CONGESTIVE HEART FAILURE

Here are some treatments to help dogs with heart murmurs and congestive heart failure.

No-salt diet

Coenzyme Q10—This wonderful antioxidant helps produce the energy molecule of the body, called adenosine triphosphate (ATP). The heart works all the time and needs energy molecules to run efficiently. CoQ10 helps keep the heart healthier and improves the function of its muscle tissue. A small dog would take 30 milligrams once a day; a large dog would take 30 to 100 milligrams once a day. The dose should be doubled in cases of very advanced heart failure.

Omega-3 fatty acids—Omega-3 fatty acids, fish oils, and flaxseed oil are readily available in health food stores. Omega-3 fats act as tissue stabilizers.

Hawthorne berries (Cratageous)—This very important herb improves myocardial function and is beneficial to the heart muscle. Give 500 milligrams twice a day orally to a medium-size dog. This herb has incredible benefits to dogs with heart conditions.

Multivitamin-multimineral supplement—Combination supplements from a good source contain the minerals and vitamins needed for heart function.

Vitamin E— Give your dog 400 IU once a day.

HOMEOPATHIC REMEDIES FOR THE HEART

These remedies do not interfere with the use of or effect of conventional drugs. Whichever remedies are indicated for your dog's condition can be given in pellet form or can be combined in a little liquid, stirred, and administered a few drops at a time. Whether given in individual pellets or combined in liquid, the frequency of dosage is twice a day unless otherwise specified.

Crataegus 3c—This is the homeopathic form of the hawthorne berry. It is a remedy that should be given for all heart conditions.

Convallaria 3c—This remedy is good when there is an arrhythmia, or uneven heartbeat.

Digitalis 6c—This is a wonderful remedy for the heart without the side effects of the conventional drug of the same name.

HOMEOPATHIC REMEDIES are easy to administer. Remedies come in the form of tiny white pellets that can be tucked into your dog's lower lip fold to melt. They also come in liquid form in which a few drops can be placed on your dog's gums. Additionally, a few pellets can be placed in a small amount of spring water and stirred, and this water can be given as a remedy.

Discontinue the remedy after the problem resolves. Homeopathic remedies work to assist the body to heal. When this is accomplished, the remedy is stopped.

Cactus grandiflorus 6c—This is recommended if your dog seems uncomfortable and is not improving with the other remedies.

Calcarea fluorica 6c—This remedy helps strengthen the tissues of the heart and should be given once a day.

Pulmonary Congestion

When the heart has weakened to the point of congestive heart failure, fluid begins to pool in the lungs or extremities. If fluid is pooling in the lungs, your dog may cough during the night or in the early morning after he has been lying still for some time.

HOMEOPATHIC REMEDIES FOR PULMONARY CONGESTION

Here are two remedies that help reduce fluid in the lungs.

Apis mel 6x—This remedy helps drain the fluid out of the lungs and can be given three times a day. This remedy is specifically used for the fluid, not for a cough that is not caused by fluid.

Hydrastis 6x—This remedy helps drain the lymphatic system and can be given along with Apis mell to help the fluid move out of the body. It is given twice a day.

PLANTS AS DIURETICS

Plants can act as natural diuretics and help remove excess fluid from the body. Parsley and asparagus are both effective diuretics.

Parsley—Fresh parsley can be chopped up and put in your pet's food or made into a tea. To make a tea, put 1 teaspoon of chopped parsley in 1 cup of boiling water. Let this steep for half an hour. Add 1 to 3 tablespoons of this tea to your dog's food twice a day. Parsley has more vitamin C than oranges do, high levels of vitamin A, and a very high iron content. It also helps with liver detoxification. Parsley is also available in tablet form at health food stores.

Asparagus—I often dispense tablets containing asparagus and parsley in cases of pulmonary congestion. You can purchase asparagus at the supermarket and steam several stalks for your dog. A little salt-free butter or olive oil mixed with garlic will make the asparagus tastier.

Dandelion—It has been shown that a 4-percent dandelion extract is a more effective diuretic than the conventional drug commonly known as lasix. Lasix can cause serious potassium depletion and liver and kidney toxicity, but if your veterinarian feels that it is necessary to prevent or relieve fluid in the lungs, you should use it as directed. Natural diuretics such as dandelion can be used in conjunction with lasix, and with your veterinarian's approval, you may be able to reduce or stop the lasix. Dandelion detoxifies the kidney and liver and does not cause any depletion of minerals in the body, as it actually *supplies* potassium. Dandelion has no toxic side effects.

How the Whole Plant Heals

Dandelion is an excellent example of how the whole plant works to heal. It works as a diuretic, removing excess fluid from body cavities. Pharmaceutical diuretics remove potassium and stress the kidneys as they accomplish their task, but dandelion, being very high in potassium, restores the body's potassium and tones the kidneys.

The fresh juice of the plant is the most powerful way to use this herb. Capsules containing dandelion are often available from health food stores, as are herbal tinctures or extracts. You can also make an infusion by placing several dandelion plants or 2 full tablespoons of dandelion powder into 2 cups of boiling water. Steep this infusion for about twenty minutes.

Capsules containing 200 to 500 milligrams of the powder can be taken three times a day. A small dog would take 200 milligrams two times a day. Dandelion can have a powerful effect on the digestive system, particularly the gall bladder, and this may cause your dog to have diarrhea. Therefore, start with a quarter of the recommended dose and increase the dose slowly. If the bowels are affected, lower the dose. The appropriate dose would be one that prevents your dog from coughing and retaining fluid without causing diarrhea. If one tablet a day does the job, you do not need to give a higher dose. It is important that you work together with your veterinarian because a dog in advanced congestive heart failure is compromised.

Kidney Failure

The kidneys are very important organs, for they are responsible for concentrating and removing waste from your dog's body and excreting it in the urine. They are very efficient organs and are excellent at their job. People can lose a kidney in an accident or donate a kidney to a relative and maintain excellent kidney function with only one remaining kidney. With one kidney, or 50 percent kidney function, the body is cleaned and maintained perfectly. The kidneys have to be at least 75 percent destroyed to just begin to show elevations of wastes (called the blood urea nitrogen and creatinine) in blood tests. The elevations reflect the inability of the kidney to concentrate and therefore dispose of the body's wastes. By the time a blood test registers any damage to the kidneys, they have already become severely damaged.

Your dog will drink more water in an effort to compensate for the reduced kidney function. If the kidneys can concentrate wastes at only 50

WHAT GOES IN MUST COME OUT: Owners often think that their dog's kidneys must be just fine because the dog is urinating well. In fact, the dog in kidney failure is urinating more because he is drinking more water.

percent of what they used to, your dog will want to drink twice the water he normally does in order to correct the situation. Your dog may start drinking more water to compensate even before the blood tests show any sign of kidney failure.

Signs of kidney disease include:
- increased water intake
- bad breath
- increased urination
- picky eating or poor appetite due to the increased waste level in his system, making him feel ill
- vomiting and diarrhea (in the last stages)

Annual blood and urine tests are important for dogs over six years of age so that kidney failure can be detected as early as possible.

Designing a Kidney Diet

The protein content and the type of protein are important when designing a kidney diet. Typically, pet foods that are low in protein are recommended for animals in kidney failure. However, many of the commonly used commercial pet foods have very poor-quality protein. This protein cannot be digested well or easily utilized in the body, and it therefore becomes a burden to the kidneys. The protein content of a diet for a dog in kidney failure should be low, and the proteins chosen should be those that burden the kidney the least.

A high-quality, digestible protein will be utilized well and will cause less stress on the kidneys. Proteins from dairy and legumes have a different structure and cause much less stress on the kidneys than do meat proteins.

The kidneys are responsible for a lot more than just filtering out waste products. They also are linked to the heart and circulatory systems, where they maintain a mineral and pH balance in the body. An alkaline pH is important for the health of the whole body, particularly the kidneys. In the case of impaired kidneys, an alkaline pH helps them function at their optimal level. In an acidic environment, the kidneys are much less efficient. The kidney diet should help keep the kidneys in their healthiest state.

Proteins in the diet are acid forming. Parsley is an alkaline-forming food and is therefore healthy for the kidneys. Other common foods that help maintain the alkaline balance of the body are sweet potatoes, yams, daikon radishes, miso, pineapples, watermelons, broccoli, and lentils. Foods such as garlic, asparagus, parsnips, and molasses also help promote an alkaline balance. For specific kidney-friendly recipes, see the special needs section in The Canine Café.

Treatment for the Kidneys

Treatments for dogs suffering from kidney problems include acupuncture, botanical medicines, homeopathy, and intravenous fluids.

ACUPUNCTURE

Acupuncture can be very helpful to promote blood flow and *Qi* to the kidneys.

I have found acupuncture and Chinese herbs very helpful. Nowadays, there are many certified veterinary acupuncturists, who administer acupuncture to balance and strengthen the kidneys.

BOTANICAL MEDICINE

Dandelion is an excellent herb for kidney health. Make dandelion tea by placing 2 tablespoons of dandelion powder or several dandelion plants into 2 cups of boiling water and steep for 15 to 20 minutes. Serve and refrigerate the remaining portion. You can give 2 tablespoons of the tea to your dog each day. Other beneficial teas can be made in the same way, substituting the dandelion with parsley or dried corn silk.

HOMEOPATHIC REMEDIES

Homeopathic remedies for kidney problems can be difficult to choose because the symptoms are not very differentiated. There are homeopathic remedies, however, that specialize in draining and treating a particular organ such as the kidneys.

Kidneys for Kidney Problems

Raw or cooked kidneys can be found at ethnic grocery stores and specialty shops. Your dog may enjoy them, and the organ contains many of the enzymes needed by failing kidneys.

Kidneys are very perishable. If your dog does like them, you'll need to cut and divide them into portions and freeze them until you are ready to use them. The kidneys can be fed raw or can be cooked. You can bake, broil, or sauté the kidneys or serve them with a sauce to increase their palatability.

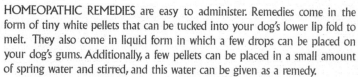

HOMEOPATHIC REMEDIES are easy to administer. Remedies come in the form of tiny white pellets that can be tucked into your dog's lower lip fold to melt. They also come in liquid form in which a few drops can be placed on your dog's gums. Additionally, a few pellets can be placed in a small amount of spring water and stirred, and this water can be given as a remedy.

Discontinue the remedy after the problem resolves. Homeopathic remedies work to assist the body to heal. When this is accomplished, the remedy is stopped.

Berberis vulgaris 6x, 6c, 30x, or 30c—This is a remedy that drains and cleans the kidneys. It also detoxifies the liver. Because the liver becomes more taxed when the kidneys cannot do their job, this is an excellent remedy. It can be given three or four times a day.

Helonias 6x or 6c—6x is very good for kidney failure in which there is protein in the urine, and it is also good for the anemia that can occur with chronic kidney failure.

Lycopodium 6c—This remedy works to drain and tone the kidneys. It also helps with digestion and with liver function. Give this remedy two times a day.

Solidago 6c—This can be a useful remedy for draining the kidneys and promoting the excretion of toxins. Give this remedy once a day.

Arsenicum album 6c—This remedy is indicated for the patient who craves warmth and drinks small amounts of water frequently. The dog's coat may be dry with some white flakes. This remedy can be given twice a day.

INTRAVENOUS FLUIDS

Intravenous fluids at the veterinary hospital or subcutaneous fluids at home are necessary in severe cases of kidney failure. These fluids flush the toxins out of the body, which is necessary to allow treatments such as acupuncture and homeopathy to gain a hold. In my practice, I put vitamin C into the fluids to help the pH balance of the body and promote detoxification. Acupuncture is given daily to hospitalized patients. While the intravenous fluids flush the toxins out, the acupuncture increases the blood flow to the kidneys.

Obesity

If far too many people tend to be overweight these days, so, too, do their pets. Dogs who have been eating commercial dog food all their lives, however, probably have a better excuse for putting on those extra pounds. Although the stuff isn't all that nutritious, its heavy fat content and combined ingredients are likely to contribute considerable girth to your

Thyroid Check

Make sure to have your dog's thyroid function checked. The thyroid gland controls the speed and strength at which the body functions. An underactive thyroid gland will slow down the body's metabolism, which will slow down the perfusion of blood to the kidneys. Correcting an imbalanced thyroid gland will allow your dog's kidneys to have the blood flow and metabolic support that they need.

canine companion. In addition, most dogs today don't get nearly as much exercise as they should, given their owners' busy schedules. All told, it's an unhealthy situation that can lead to a variety of medical problems, just as with humans.

If you're worried about your dog's weight, especially if he eats relatively little and is also relatively chubby, the first thing I'd suggest is having his thyroid tested. Hypothyroidism, an underactive thyroid gland, can contribute to obesity in dogs.

Barring any thyroid problems, my next recommendation is that you start your dog on a weight-reduction diet. The recipe for chubby dogs in the special needs section of The Canine Café is a healthy regimen I've prescribed for many overweight dogs. It's one I've rarely known to fail, as it consists of foods that dogs love and helps them lose weight naturally.

On this diet, your dog may have as many steamed or grated vegetables as he wants. You can cook the veggies in meat broth or flavor them with garlic and a little olive oil or a small amount of butter if vegetables are not his favorite. Frozen mixed vegetables are a great time-saving alternative to fresh.

The amount of food recommended depends on the size of the dog; a smaller dog would get less, and a larger dog would get more. Provide plenty of fresh, clean water for your dog at all times. Don't forget that a superior multivitamin-multimineral supplement is also very important.

Watch your dog. In addition to losing weight, he should have more energy and his skin and coat should continue to improve on this diet. If he seems listless, go to your veterinarian for an exam and appropriate testing.

Separation Anxiety and Other Emotional Problems

The feelings experienced by our dogs are pretty much the same kinds of feelings that we have. We have all been able to observe the wide range of emotions that every dog can have. Because I spend so much of my time in the world of dogs, it is a fairly easy task for me to gauge how a dog is feeling. For example, a Golden Retriever can jump onto my chest, emanating love and trust. His mood is obvious. The wonderful thing about dogs is that their emotions weigh in on the positive scale—with lots of love and playfulness. Perhaps that's why they are such a tonic to us. Dogs offer so much love and devotion and so often exhibit a wonderful sense of fun.

Dogs can also feel afraid and insecure, just as we can. Dogs who have had bad experiences can display mistrust, with probable good reason. Dogs can get upset and concerned, just as we can. Sometimes a dog can become anxious or worried when left alone. It can be difficult for even the most loving dog owner to understand why his dog is experiencing unwanted or unpleasant emotions. It can also be frustrating because we cannot simply sit down and have an open chat with our dogs as we could with a human friend who is afraid or worried.

When pets are left alone for the majority of the day, they may get bored, lonely, or anxious. It is important to understand that they need love and quality time. All of us, including myself, can get so wrapped up in our work and projects that we forget that our furry friends who give us so much love also need love to be sent their way, along with some attention and playtime.

The following information suggests some remedies for separation anxiety and some other common fear problems in dogs. Additionally, a calming diet is given in the special needs recipes section of The Canine Café.

Separation Anxiety

Many families who own pets are out of the house for the majority of the day. This leaves their animals at home for extended periods of time. Dogs can become anxious and sometimes destructive when left at home alone.

SOLUTIONS

Here are some suggested solutions for helping a dog who is suffering from separation anxiety.

- Have more than one pet. Get two dogs who are compatible with each other, as they will provide each other with company. A compatible cat can also provide your dog with company.

MELATONIN TO THE RESCUE! Based on a study of published cases from Nicholas Dodman and Linda Aronoson at Tufts Veterinary School, melatonin has been found to help with separation anxiety, destructive chewing, and the fear of thunderstorms and loud noises. A typical fifty-pound dog would take 3 mg twice a day during thunderstorm season. The same dose can be used for dogs suffering from separation anxiety and destructive chewing.

- Tell your dog that you are leaving and when you will be back. Picture in your mind your return and send that picture to your dog with your words.
- Leave soothing music, such as Mozart, playing softly in the background.
- Leave your dog with safe toys to chew on and play with.
- Hire a professional dog walker or a trustworthy neighbor to take your dog for an afternoon walk and break up his day.
- Stuff almond butter or treats into a "Kong" or similar toy to keep your dog challenged and busy during the day.
- Take your dog for a run or long walk in the morning before you leave to burn up some of his excess energy.
- Set up a tape recorder or other device to record during the day. Listen to the recording to discover if any particular event, such as the mailman's arrival, triggers unwanted behavior.
- Set aside a specific time every day to spend quality time interacting with your dog.

HOMEOPATHIC REMEDIES AND BOTANICAL MEDICINE

There are several homeopathic and botanical remedies that can be used for dogs suffering from separation anxiety.

Ignatia 30x—This is one of the best remedies to use for separation anxiety. If the lower potencies do not produce the desired effect, move up to the higher potencies. Give this remedy three times a day for two to four weeks.

Pulsatilla 30c—This remedy would be suitable to give to sweet, gentle, loving, and clingy dogs. These dogs typically have soft loving eyes and devotedly follow their owners all over the house. It is a remedy predominantly used with females. Give this remedy twice a day for two to four weeks.

Lycopodium 6c or 30c—The dog who needs this remedy does not like solitude. He will not cling, but will stay in the same area that you do. He will move from room to room with you. He may also be the type who worries. Give this remedy once a day for one month.

Phosphorus 6c or 30c—This remedy is good for the dog who loves people and company. He will push for attention and often be the star of the moment. A sense of fun will predominate in this dog's personality. The dog who needs this remedy may be fearful of loud noises such as gunshots and thunder. Give this remedy once a day for one month.

St. John's Wort—This herb is used to treat anxiety, and it is easily available at health food stores. This herb works to calm the emotions and can be given along with any of the aforementioned indicated homeopathic remedies. Give one or two tablets, depending on the dog's size, twice a day.

HOMEOPATHIC REMEDIES are easy to administer. Remedies come in the form of tiny white pellets that can be tucked into your dog's lower lip fold to melt. They also come in liquid form in which a few drops can be placed on your dog's gums. Additionally, a few pellets can be placed in a small amount of spring water and stirred, and this water can be given as a remedy.

Discontinue the remedy after the problem resolves. Homeopathic remedies work to assist the body to heal. When this is accomplished, the remedy is stopped.

Fear of Thunderstorms

Fear of thunderstorms has become more and more common in recent years, and a number of homeopathic remedies have proven helpful. One of the problems with treating this condition is that it is often difficult to know when a thunderstorm is coming. Therefore, the indicated remedies may be given during storm season. Beginning the remedy at least one week before thunderstorm season or before a storm is predicted would be advantageous. After the remedies start to work, the dosing can be reduced and then stopped. In many cases, dogs have been cured of their fear with the appropriate remedy.

Borax 6x—This refers to a homeopathic remedy, not the cleaning product! This remedy is specific for fear of thunderstorms and can be given twice a day for one or two months.

Phosphorus 30x—This remedy is good for animals that are afraid of thunder and the sound of gunshots. Give this remedy once every other day for twenty days. Increase the frequency to twice a day if you think it is helping but not doing the whole trick.

Natrum muriaticum 6c—This is a good remedy for the quiet dog who tends not to look directly in the eye. Give this remedy twice a day for one month.

Aconite 30c—This is a specific remedy for fear and can be given every

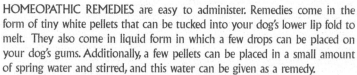

Flower Remedies

Flower remedies, also called flower essences, are commonly available in health food stores. These flower remedies are prescribed specifically to correct emotional and mental problems. The first flower remedies were those developed by Dr. Edward Bach, a homeopathic physician. There are thirty-eight Bach flower remedies. Many other flower remedies from a variety of companies have also become available. Rescue remedy, which is also sold as calming essence, is a combination of flower remedies to use in times of stress.

Fear Remedy

Aconite 30c stands at the forefront of remedies that are used for fear. It is usually given right before the situation that causes the fear and can be given every fifteen minutes or every half hour for several doses. It can also be used immediately after a fearful situation to help alleviate the fear.

fifteen minutes for one hour during a thunderstorm.

Rescue remedy—This is a Bach flower remedy that soothes troubled nerves. Give this remedy every fifteen minutes until noticeable calming occurs.

Nervousness

Here are some remedies for dogs who are nervous:

Gelsemium 6c or 30c—This is an excellent remedy for nervousness. It is particularly good when given before a particular event that causes nervousness. For example, it may benefit animals who are nervous in the show ring. Give this remedy every half an hour for a few doses before the event.

Argentum nitricum 30c—This remedy is also excellent for nervousness. Sometimes, the dog who needs this remedy will get diarrhea as a result of his anxiety and nervousness.

Arsenicum album 6c or 30c—Dogs who need this remedy can appear to be fidgety and meticulous. Some of the dogs who need this remedy may enjoy going over to the water bowl often for a drink. Give this remedy once or twice a day for two weeks.

Phosphorus 6c—This remedy can be used for the nervous dog who is needy for affection and is afraid of sudden loud noises. Give this remedy twice a day for a few weeks.

Chapter 12

When It Comes Time to Say Good~bye

"It's only a dog," some will say to console you
when your loyal companion is gone
It's hard not to let this memory control you
That's all that is left from now on.

Yes, it's only a dog—giving love and affection
when all daily tasks are complete
Always alert for his master's protection
and closely curled at his feet

When death's at his doorstep he'll look up toward you
while licking your trembling hand
A final gesture of love to reward you
and tell you, "I understand."

Yes, it's only a dog, devoted and caring
on whom you can always depend
Lucky are those who choose to be sharing
the love of a four-legged friend.

—Ben Shulman

There are no feelings quite so "pure," so selfless and devoted, as those of dogs for their owners. The extent to which a dog's focus revolves completely around the members of his human family is so strong as to transcend either peril or pain. An older dog will readily disregard the stiffness and aching joints of arthritis to enjoy the pleasure of walking with his beloved master or mistress or to check out any unusual noise in the house. From my years of experience, I can assure you that dogs' concerns about the safety of their human companions far outweigh any concerns they might have for their own well-being. And when they feel themselves slipping away, I'm firmly convinced that their greatest anxiety is about how their owners will manage without the presence of their physical and emotional support.

Many years ago, I was asked to examine a German Shepherd named Gretchen whose owners lived in Maryland, some distance away from my practice. Gretchen had been seen by several specialists, and none of the medications they prescribed could put a stop to her continual seizures, the frequency of which had increased to about one every twenty minutes. Her owners did not have an air-conditioned car, and it was a hot summer's day. I evaluated the situation and concluded that there was nothing I could do to help her condition—something I explained to the owners as Gretchen listened. They were very worried about taking her home in the hot car, as her temperature was already quite elevated due to the seizures.

As Gretchen looked at me, we seemed to make a telepathic connection as the images of three young children suddenly flashed across my mind. I asked the owners if they had any children at home. "Yes," they replied, "we have three small children, and she behaves like a nanny to them." Tears came to my eyes as I conveyed to them what it was that Gretchen seemed to be saying—that she wanted to see the children just one more time. I explained to Gretchen that she might not make it through the hot ride home. She seemed to understand and accept that her time had come, her only concern being how the children might react and whether her loved ones would be all right without her watchful eye and constant devotion.

The Gift of a Golden Twilight

As with all veterinarians, there have been times when people have brought their pets to me, convinced that it is time to end their suffering. Often, the whole family will show up, emotionally distraught. I know that they have gone through hours, perhaps days or even weeks, of heart-wrenching decision making and have finally prepared themselves to face this difficult and dispiriting decision. But sometimes, when I have looked at the dog whose fate seemed to have been decided, I will notice a certain brightness still residing in his eyes, reflecting the tenacity to hang on to life despite the distress and pain of the affliction.

While I know it would be much easier for the family at that point to simply end the ordeal, as a healer of animals I feel obligated to convey to them what I sense to be the dog's viewpoint. In such instances, I will quietly tell them, "It is not yet his time. He is not ready to go now." Their eyes will brighten up as well, and they will look at the dog as if to say, "OK then, you continue to hang in there with us, buddy, and you tell us when your time has come." The special kind of love that they have had between them for years becomes even more powerful as they respect their pet's desire to have perhaps just a few more cherished days with them.

Many people, upon learning that their pets have only a short time left to live, have found a new perspective on life and love. So many of the things that they had long taken for granted suddenly began to take on a precious and beautiful glow. Whether it be a sunrise or a special gift received from a loved one years ago, each experience was now savored and remembered with a heartfelt reverence. Arguments and disagreements suddenly seemed petty, and sharing love became all important.

Just as that love proves to be the eternal aspect of our lives, so it is with the lives of our pets. If anything, their depth of feeling for the families with whom they live is even purer (and more forbearing and forgiving) than that of most people. And because their time on earth is so much shorter than that of other loved ones, every day they spend with us is that much more meaningful. That's why, even when a dog has been discovered to have a terminal illness, it shouldn't necessarily be viewed as a cause to cut short his remaining days simply to "put him out of his misery." For what may seem like a painful existence to us is likely to be mitigated for the dog by the chance to spend additional precious times with the people to whom he is so devoted—a kind of golden twilight you can give your companion as a parting gift.

Such was the case with KC, a wonderful black Cocker Spaniel I had treated for many years. I had pulled KC through a number of serious health crises. Finally, it came time for her owners to make a painful decision. She was suffering from severe heart failure, her abdomen was filled like a tight drum with fluid, and she was breathing with difficulty. I looked into her eyes, and she looked back at me. "Not now," she seemed to be saying.

"It's not yet her time," I told her owners. But they were clearly worried, since they would be leaving shortly for their son's wedding, which was to be held high atop a mountain in New Hampshire. How could they take her in such a condition? Who could they possibly leave her with? "We'll do whatever it takes," I said. I proceeded to manually drain a good deal of the fluid from her abdomen, making her breathing somewhat easier, and altered the schedule of her herbs and medications. KC not only attended the wedding on that mountain, she became the "guest of honor," traveling in high style in a baby carriage. She knew how excited her family was over this event, and she got to be an important part of it. The quality of her life, in fact, remained good for several more months. And when the time finally came that nothing more could be done to make her comfortable, and she was obviously failing fast, I explained it to her and sensed that she agreed.

But euthanasia is not something that should simply be dictated by convenience or by the understandable desire to prevent a dog's quality of life from diminishing as an illness progresses. Far too often, people are influenced by people who tell them that the dog should be put to sleep

Mother Nature's Balms for Grief

Rescue remedy is a Bach flower remedy that can be administered to both humans and pets to counteract the distraught feelings that can accompany the death of a companion animal. A few drops in water, sipped over a period of a few minutes, can help ease the shock, unsteadiness, and surreal feelings that often occur after such a loss.

Ignatia (30x or 200x) is also an excellent homeopathic remedy for grief that can be given to people and pets three to four times daily over a period of one or two weeks.

---

simply because he does not walk as well as he used to, or that it's better to simply get a new dog rather than to prolong the health problems of their current dog. Offensive though it may seem to some people's sensibilities, I feel compelled to share with you a hypothetical example I often give to clients who are torn over what to do with a dog who has been given only a short time to live. Imagine that a close relative—say, an aunt who has always been a kind, gentle, and loving person, asking little for herself—has just been diagnosed with liver cancer. Can you imagine the rest of the family coming to the hospital to tell her they have decided that she should be "put to sleep" because she has only six months to a year remaining and it would be just too painful for everyone to see her through the ordeal?

The Afterlife of a Dog, as Reflected in Eternal Love

While Western theology has perpetrated the belief that only human beings are blessed with a divine spark and a spiritual existence beyond death (based on the idea that man is created in God's image), anyone who has shared a relationship with a dog is likely to find that hard to accept. Dog owners know that the unconditional love exhibited toward us by our canine companions can be one of the most precious things in the universe—a sublime and powerful flow of energy that is about as close to divine love as any experienced on earth. And they know that a dog has a soul as pure as that of the most noble of humans. That's why I strongly believe a dog's affection for his master to be a form of spiritual energy that transcends earthly existence—an energy that we can call upon any time we need it, even long after our four-legged best friends have departed this life.

There is another spiritual aspect of a dog's passing that should be a source of great comfort to those left behind. Some of my own experiences have firmly convinced me that dogs and their masters can be reunited

> "If there are no dogs in Heaven,
> then when I die I want to go where they went."
> —*Will Rogers*

after death; this is a theme that has been reflected in both song and story throughout the ages. Many years ago, I treated an English Setter named Morgan who was suffering from a terminal illness. His owners preferred that he go naturally rather than be put to sleep. His condition was not particularly painful, so I concurred. They needed to work during the day, so they left him at my practice so he could be with us. When they called to see how he was doing, I told them that they needed to communicate with him mentally and tell him it was OK for him to go.

A while later, I returned to the kennel area where Morgan was lying on a soft comforter. In between the stainless steel cages, I saw an elderly man with white hair and a closely cropped beard holding Morgan's head gently in his lap and stroking him. When I got to his cage, however, the stranger was gone. Then Morgan let out a small sigh and peacefully passed away. I called the owners to tell them that Morgan had passed, and I described the apparent apparition I had seen. They said little in response to my story.

Two weeks later, the owners came to the clinic to pick up Morgan's ashes. They took me aside and produced a picture of an elderly gentleman, asking, "Was this the man you saw?" Taken aback, I told them that it was indeed. "He was my father," one of the owners said. "Morgan and he were the best of friends until my father passed away three months ago."

My experience with families grieving over the loss of beloved pets has also convinced me that there are times when animals attempt to communicate with us from the other side, to reassure us in their own way that they are happy and at peace. One such case involved Torro, a German Shepherd who came to be my good friend. He came to my clinic once a week for acupuncture to alleviate the effects of a spinal disease that made his back legs weak, and he seemed to especially enjoy the visits. After Torro died, his owner related to me a strange tale told to her by a friend. The friend said he had seen Torro in a dream, jumping and playing and running so as to convey to him that he was happy and just fine. She added that if anyone else had told her that, she would have thought it was just an attempt to make her feel better—but this was an extremely down-to-earth sort of individual, and it would be completely unlike him to say anything like that unless it had actually happened.

A Final Display of Affection and Admiration

Just as it is for a person, the most desirable way for a dog to leave this life is in the comfort of familiar surroundings and in the company of loved ones. Many dogs are able to pass away in such a beautiful manner, sometimes in the arms of a beloved master or mistress. Whenever they seem to be reasonably comfortable and able to cope with their condition, it is usually best to allow them to choose their own time. When the time that a pet needs help to pass on does come, and I can't emphasize this enough, animals need to be treated with the greatest of love and respect. It helps them to be surrounded by the family members they love so much, who will let them know that they will be eased out of their pain. This is the time for them to be shown admiration and appreciation for the protection, comfort, healing, and love they have provided and to be properly honored with a ritual of recognition. Such a ceremony is equally important for any other animals in the house, who should be given the message about what's become of their friend. Often, pets will wander the house for days or weeks in search of companions who have left and never returned.

Animals do not fear death, having never been exposed to ideas that would predispose them to worry about what awaits them. I believe they know when their bodies are no longer serving them and in their own way are aware that their spirits will continue to exist in another realm. When they have reached this stage, what concerns them most, I am convinced, is leaving behind their loved ones. That's why it is so important to euthanize a pet only when the animal is ready.

There must be a preparation period in which loving communication transpires between the dog and the rest of the family. The owners should sense that the dog has given his consent to the procedure. In my practice, I talk to the dog, reassuring him that we will be gentle and loving, and I often administer a sedative. As it takes effect, the owners and family members are asked to surround their pet with loving thoughts and to recall the special times they had together. I suggest that they focus on the emotional bond they have shared with their companion all these years so that it fills the space around their pet. I ask that they concentrate on their admiration and appreciation for all that this animal has taught them and for all the love and loyalty he has brought into their lives. And if they cannot hold back the tears, I explain to the dog that this is only because he is so special to them and will so be missed. The better this is communicated and the more harmonious the environment, the easier it is for the pet.

When a pet departs this life surrounded by love and respect, it can be a beautiful and peaceful experience for those to whom the pet was closest. If the weather permits and the animal and the family seem to like the idea, we often perform the procedure outside, on the serene and picturesque grounds that surround my clinic. As the dog ascends into the spirit world, his last impression of the earth is at its most ideal, with the sound of chirping birds and the scents of flowers and pine trees.

Giving a dog such a farewell ceremony is no more silly or frivolous than a funeral for a person. In fact, if there are any clients in the waiting room at the time, we often find them in an emotional state and extending their condolences, although typically they knew neither the dog nor the people involved.

Several years ago, a most unusual-looking dog named Nicholas started coming to my clinic for treatment of severe arthritis in his hips and multiple disk problems in his back. At first, he was frightened and in a great deal of pain, but as the treatments gradually relieved some of his discomfort, he began to genuinely enjoy his visits. As I reflected on his distinctive appearance, it occurred to me that he looked like a sort of cross between a herding dog and a wildebeest, and I laughed as I told his owner that Nicholas must have been a rare "great wildebeest herding dog." From then on, it became our personal joke, and the owner began to describe him as such to anyone who wanted to know his breed. She also began putting a different bow tie on him each time he came to visit the clinic.

My heart warmed whenever Nicholas entered the door, at which point I would exclaim, "Look who's here!" He, in turn, seemed to revel in the attention.

Nicholas grew to be very old, and when he had reached the point at which it was no longer possible to alleviate his suffering, he waited outside, lying on a blanket on a warm sunny day. He looked at me with trust and love and seemed to understand that it was his time. Afterward, I received a letter of gratitude from Nicholas's owner, who after recalling how her dog had showed his happiness at visiting my office by becoming its "self-appointed social director, greeting all two- and four-legged creatures as they came to the door," went on to tell me the following:

> Nicholas' spirit was released where he wanted to be. He was surrounded by love and filled with joy and trust. To ease him along that final step was your loving gift to him. I know as he gazed at you at that final moment, he was at peace and felt all the love you had for him. I too am finding peace in remembering that last day.

It's fitting that I began this chapter with a poem by my cherished departed friend Ben Shulman. Ben, my son's piano teacher's father, was my friend for many years. My two boys began their piano lessons when they were three years old, so I had many years of piano recitals to attend. Ben and I spent years together, standing in the back of these piano recitals, joking around and generally exhibiting behavior unbecoming of a

The Rites of Passage
for Dog Owners

Talk to your dog. Let him know that you understand that he is suffering and that you will help him heal in any way you can. The effectiveness of this holistic approach cannot be underestimated.

If it is clearly obvious that the dog's condition is terminal and nothing can be done to save him, let him know that you are there to support whatever decision he makes about how much longer he wants to hang on.

If his eyes and attitude indicate that he still cherishes life, try to keep him as comfortable as possible and provide him as often as you can with those things that he finds most enjoyable.

If he gives you signals that he's ready to go, as pets often do, allow him to say good-bye to any other animal companions, and let them all know what is happening. If you need to have the veterinarian put him to sleep, allow all those who knew and loved him to pay their final respects before he goes.

Stay with him during the procedure, and surround him with loving and caring thoughts. Focus on things like wonderful walks or games of catch, along with the protection he gave you and your family and how special he was and always will be to you.

Have a mild sedative given to him and, if you can, hold his head and stroke it comfortingly.

After the final injection has been administered, say a special silent prayer for him and envision the love between you as a unique and special gift that you will never misplace. If you are among those who believe in such things, tell him that he would be welcome to rejoin your family in a new body, if he desires. Take whatever time you need to feel that your personal farewell is complete.

If you choose to bury your dog at home or in a pet cemetery, make sure that it is done with a proper ritual in his honor, much like a funeral for a person. If you have him cremated, do the same when his ashes are returned.

Upon your return home, tell the other animals in your house what happened both by talking to them and mentally conveying the image of the passing to them.

Mourning for a pet requires a period of time. But following the above steps can help mitigate the grief with a sense of serenity, comfort, and spiritual elevation that stems from a recognition of the eternal bond of love between you and your special companion.

mother and an elderly gentleman. We laughed at each other's terrible jokes (retold in all their glory twice a year at the recitals), huddled together and chortling at the back of the room. On some occasions, we even broke into the food that all of the parents had brought for the end of the recital.

As the years went by, Ben began to tell me of his aches and pains. He was a wise and happy man who had always enjoyed living. He came to be in chronic pain, with a heart condition and all sorts of aches. One day, he was rushed to the emergency room and placed in intensive care. Without the injections and monitoring that he could only receive in intensive care, he would not live more than a few days. Ben took a good look at what his life had become and made his decision. He was ready to go. He wanted to leave with all of his friends and family around him.

I rushed to his house to be with him. His daughter and I fell into each other's arms crying, thinking of how much we would both miss his loving wisdom. Oddly, the atmosphere in the house was ethereal and beautiful. Ben had made his decision and was at peace. He laughed at my same old tired jokes and listened to stories and music. Within a few days, as predicted, he serenely passed on. His poems were read at his funeral and his music was played. Just as he wanted.

That's the way it should be and that is what, among many other things, Ben taught me. Being surrounded by your loved ones, listening to stories that elucidate how much you were loved, and hearing about the favorite moments of a wonderful life work to heal and comfort both the dying and the ones who loved them most.

The "great wildebeest herding dog" Nicholas.

Part 3

THE CANINE CAFÉ

L ook into his loving brown eyes around 6 p.m., and you know what's on his mind: "What's for dinner?" This section will help you give your dog an answer to that question. Many of the dishes described herein can be prepared and frozen for up to six weeks, so you can cook on more leisurely days to have meals ready for a busy work week. The section on quick meals will enable you to throw together a nutritious meal in minutes. If you're like most people, you won't always be able to prepare a homemade meal for your best friend, no matter how much tail-wagging goes on. But that's OK. You'll still be a good person and your dog will always love you.

The point of this book is to enhance both your dog's health and your relationship with your best friend—not to make you feel guilty if you are short on time. I have only one request: that you enjoy the time you spend on and with your dog. Have the wisdom to know when you can relax and when you want to be cookin' for the canine. And just as with kids, if you have a picky eater, every meal may not be a hit, but you will surely find several recipes in this section to be real winners. Knowing that there is a special family member who enjoys his "mom's" or "dad's" good cooking adds another something special to the dog-owner relationship.

There are many wonderful meal options available in The Canine Café. Be forewarned, as most of these recipes will have you smacking your lips along with your dog. They just smell so good as they cook. My husband tells me the egg shells we add to the hearty man stews are the only things that keep him at bay!

For more recipes, you can also check out my Web site, www.doctordeva.com, for the recipe of the month. Readers are invited to share special recipes—we can even name them after your dog, if you wish.

Toppers add diversity and healthy fresh ingredients to routine fare and store easily in the refrigerator or freezer. Unknowingly, I invented my first topper as a young veterinary student. I lived in a big old seven-bedroom Philadelphia house with six other students. Every week I baked a nutritional oatmeal dish that, when cooked, had the look of bread. I would store it in the refrigerator and treat my dog to some of it every day. It smelled good and looked good, so I had to start leaving notes in the refrigerator saying, "Please don't eat my dog's food!" My fellow tenants ate it nearly as fast as I could bake it!

Vet School Oatmeal Bread

The popular bread that I invented during veterinary school can be used as a meal, a topper, or even a reward.

5 cups uncooked oatmeal
½ cup olive oil
¼ cup powdered milk
1 teaspoon kelp powder
1 teaspoon garlic powder
½ teaspoon ground rosemary
½ cup nutritional yeast

Preheat oven to 375 degrees. Mix all dry ingredients in a bowl, add the oil, and then add enough water to cover. Blend until the consistency of thick mush is achieved. Spread in a single layer in an oiled rectangular cake pan.

Bake for one hour. Remove from oven and let cool. Break into bite-size chunks to feed.

VEGGIE TOPPERS

The healthy yummy additions presented in this section are sure to please many a canine when added to healthful kibbled dog food.

RALEIGH'S FAVORITE HEALTHY AND FRESH TOPPER

Yields 8 to 12 servings

2 cups diced carrots
2 tablespoons chopped parsley
2 cups chopped broccoli stems (each broccoli stem makes about one cup)
3 eggs (with shells)
3 cups chicken or beef broth or water
4 cups whole wheat bread squares
4 diced garlic cloves
½ cup olive oil

Heat the garlic in olive oil in a large skillet. Add the diced carrots, broccoli stems, and parsley and sauté for about 5 minutes. Add the chicken or beef broth or water and simmer for 15 minutes. Blend the eggs and shells in the blender. Add the bread squares to the vegetables in the skillet and stir.

Lower the heat, add the beaten eggs to the pan, and stir again for about three minutes. Cool, store, and serve as needed.

SQUASH PORRIDGE TOPPER

3 butternut or acorn squash (to yield 6 cups cooked and mashed)
⅔ cup olive oil
½ cup chicken broth
6 eggs, beaten
1 teaspoon garlic powder

Cut the squash in half and bake in oven at 350 degrees until soft (about 40 minutes). Let them cool, then scoop out the insides. The squash seeds are very healthy, and you can place the inner seeds in the blender and chop them up, adding them to the mix.

Blend the eggs (shells optional), chicken broth, and garlic powder in blender. Mix blended liquid with mashed squash (and seeds, if desired). Pour into oiled casserole dish.

Bake at 350 degrees for 45–50 minutes or until a knife inserted in the center comes out clean. Cool and serve as a topper.

CAULIFLOWER AND CHEESE TOPPER

3 cups diced cauliflower
¼ cup ground walnuts (optional)
3 tablespoons nutritional yeast (optional)
½ cup toasted wheat germ (optional)
½ cup grated Parmesan cheese
3 tablespoons butter

Steam the cauliflower until tender but not soft. Strain and coat in butter. Add the rest of the ingredients and toss. Cool, then serve or store.

CRUNCHY TOPPERS

Sometimes, we all feel the need for something crunchy and toasty, like popcorn or granola. These crunchy toppers freeze and store very well.

OATMEAL AND GARLIC CRUNCH

8 cups rolled oats
4 cloves garlic
1 cup olive oil

Dice garlic cloves. Warm oil in a large frying pan. Add garlic and cook lightly, stirring for 1 or 2 minutes. Stir oatmeal into hot oil and immediately remove from heat.

Spread mixture onto two greased cookie sheets. Bake at 250 degrees for 20–30 minutes, stirring occasionally. Cool completely. Store in airtight container.

COAT-NOURISHING TOPPER

6 cups rolled oats
2 cups shredded coconut
1 cup wheat germ
2 teaspoons rosemary
1¼ cup olive oil

Heat the olive oil with the rosemary in it. Stir in rolled oats, coconut, and wheat germ and remove from heat immediately.

Spread mixture onto two greased cookie sheets. Bake at 250 degrees for 20–30 minutes, stirring occasionally. Cool completely. Store in airtight container.

WHOLE WHEAT CRUNCHY BREAD TOPPER

2 loaves whole grain or whole wheat bread (day-old bread is fine for this recipe)
1 tablespoon garlic powder
½ teaspoon dried rosemary
1 tablespoon dried parsley
½ to 1 cup Parmesan cheese
1 large plastic bag

Preheat oven to 300 degrees. Place bread slices on oven rack for 30 minutes. Place toasted slices in the plastic bag, and roll it with a rolling pin to make crumbs. When crumbs are made, add the garlic powder, parsley, rosemary, and Parmesan cheese to the bag and shake.

Store in an airtight container. Some of the mix can be stored in the freezer, as it defrosts quickly when needed.

PANCAKE TOPPER

1 bag whole wheat or buckwheat pancake mix (available at health food stores)
2 tablespoons fresh chopped parsley or 2 teaspoons dry parsley
butter (enough to coat a large frying pan)

Prepare the pancake mix according to directions, and stir batter until smooth. Add the parsley. Heat butter in a large frying pan. Pour in the pancake batter, and let it heat for just a few minutes; then begin to stir the mixture just as you would scrambled eggs until the batter is completely cooked. Cool and serve.

CHEWY TOPPERS

Fresh and filling, the following chewy toppers are full of nutrients that help in maintaining good health. The best part of all is how good good health can taste!

Protein Source

One cup of lentils has 7.8 grams of protein.

LENTIL SURPRISE TOPPER
Yields about 8 servings

1 cup lentils
3 cups water or chicken stock (or water with 1 salt-free chicken
  bouillon cube)
1 cup carrot, finely chopped
2 tablespoons parsley
3 cups chopped bread squares
3 eggs (with shells), blended
4 tablespoons olive oil
2 cloves garlic

Add lentils to water and bring to a boil in water, chicken stock, or water
with bouillon cube. Lower heat and simmer for about 20 minutes or until
soft. (Different types of lentils cook at different rates.) Add the carrot and
parsley, and cook for 15 more minutes.

Lightly heat the olive oil and garlic in a large frying pan. Add the lentil
mixture and stir, then mix in the bread squares. Pour in the beaten eggs
and mix well over medium heat.

Cool and serve or store.

MILLET MIX TOPPER
Yields 8 to 12 servings

1 cup millet
4½ cups water
1 no-salt beef bouillon cube
½ cup blended sunflower or pumpkin seeds
1 tablespoon olive oil
½ teaspoon sage
½ teaspoon rosemary
½ teaspoon thyme
1 teaspoon garlic powder
1 to 2 cups leftover cooked vegetable bits (such as broccoli stems,
green beans, carrots, parsnips, kale)

Add millet, stirring while adding, to boiling water and bouillon cube. Cover
and simmer on low heat for about 40 minutes until all water is absorbed.
Add 1 tablespoon of olive oil, blended seeds, spices, and garlic powder
and stir. Add cooked vegetables and mix everything together.

Remove from heat, cool, and serve or store.

PUMPKIN NUT LOAF TOPPER

Yields 8 to 10 toppers

2 cups whole wheat flour
2½ teaspoons baking powder
½ teaspoon baking soda
1½ teaspoons cinnamon
2 cups pumpkin pulp (can be canned or fresh)
½ cup molasses
½ cup milk
3 eggs
¼ cup olive oil
1 cup pumpkin seeds, finely chopped (easy to do in food processor)

Mix or sift together flour, baking powder, baking soda, and cinnamon. Combine pumpkin, molasses, milk, olive oil, and eggs in a mixing bowl or blend in a blender. Add dry ingredients and stir in the chopped pumpkin seeds.

Spread in a well-greased standard loaf pan, and bake at 350 degrees for 45–55 minutes or until a toothpick comes out clean. Cool and crumble on kibble.

Note: If you use fresh pumpkin, you can bake it in the oven and put the seeds and pumpkin in the blender. Use these seeds rather than dried pumpkin seeds.

 ## MEALS IN A MUFFIN

This is a wonderful way to prepare and store meals, particularly for a small-breed dog, or you may choose to use mini-muffin tins and use these recipes for mini-muffin snacks. Note: The baking times given in the following recipes are for regular-size muffins. If you are going to make mini-muffins, the baking time will be a little more than half of what's indicated in the recipe. Using this as a general guideline, bake until done.

Dogs are pack animals and like to eat when their humans eat, so some of these recipes are wonderful for breakfast and some for dinner. Make a few dozen and freeze and store, defrosting on schedule for the next meal. I give my dogs a large breakfast, and they each get one or two mini-muffins for a snack at dinner. They just love them! The meals in a muffin can also be crumbled and used as toppers.

OAT AND CHICKEN MUFFINS
Yields 12 medium-size muffins

2½ cups whole wheat flour
2 cups oats
1½ teaspoons baking soda
½ cup olive oil
3 beaten eggs (shells optional; can put whole eggs with shells in blender)
2½ cups yogurt or buttermilk
1 cup grated chicken

Mix together the oats, flour, and baking soda. Blend the olive oil, yogurt or buttermilk, and eggs. Add the wet ingredients to the dry ingredients. Stir in the grated chicken. Pour into oiled muffin tins, and bake at 300 degrees for 30 minutes or until toothpick comes out dry.

Extra muffins can be frozen for six weeks.

APPLE, BANANA, AND TURKEY BREAST MUFFINS
Yields 18 medium-size muffins

1 cup yogurt
1 cup chopped-up turkey breast lunch meat
3 medium-size very ripe bananas
2 teaspoons baking powder
4 cups unbleached flour
⅔ cup olive oil
2 teaspoons cinnamon
½ teaspoon powdered sage (optional)
1 cup chicken broth
4 eggs with shells, beaten
3 medium-size apples, peeled and grated

Place the yogurt, bananas, chicken broth, olive oil, and whole eggs in a blender and blend until smooth. Combine the unbleached flour, baking powder, sage, and cinnamon. Mix the liquid mixture with the flour mixture. Add in the turkey breast and grated apples.

Bake at 350 degrees for 30 minutes or until the top is brown and a toothpick inserted into the center comes out clean.

MUFFIN MEAT LOAF
1 pound ground round or chuck
½ cup milk
2 eggs
¾ cup whole wheat bread crumbs
1 cup frozen carrots and peas
1 tablespoon Italian spices

Beat eggs and milk together; then mix in seasonings and bread crumbs. Fold in this mixture with the meat and frozen vegetables. Bake at 350 degrees for 20–25 minutes.

Muffins and Loaves

Muffins can be made into loaves, or loaves can be made into muffins. The recipes are interchangeable.

HEALTHY BRAN MUFFINS

1 cup whole wheat flour
1 cup all-bran cereal
2½ teaspoons baking powder
½ teaspoon baking soda
½ cup honey
¾ cup yogurt or buttermilk
1 egg, slightly beaten
¼ cup butter or olive oil

Combine flour, baking powder, and soda in large bowl. Mix in the bran cereal. Beat the egg and add in the yogurt (or buttermilk) and butter (or olive oil) along with the honey. Mix wet and dry ingredients together. Grease muffin tins and pour mixture into muffin molds. Bake at 375 degrees for about 20 minutes.

THANKSGIVING MUFFINS

2 cups whole wheat flour
2½ teaspoons baking powder
½ teaspoon ground cinnamon
4 teaspoons ground nutmeg
⅓ cup olive oil
2 large eggs
1¼ cups canned pumpkin puree
½ cup milk
1 cup coarsely chopped turkey breast
1½ cups coarsely chopped cranberries, fresh or frozen

Preheat oven to 400 degrees. Oil a twelve-muffin pan well. Mix the flour, baking powder, cinnamon, and nutmeg. Mix together the oil, eggs, pumpkin, and milk. Combine wet and dry ingredients. Fold in the turkey and the cranberries. Fill the muffin tins. Bake for 20–25 minutes. Cool and serve.

Creamy Topping

A bit of creativity can make cooking even more fun. For special occasions, muffins can be topped with cream cheese icing (page 270) and become party cupcakes!

WHITEFISH, OAT, AND BLUEBERRY MUFFINS

1½ cups whole wheat flour
6 tablespoons honey
1 tablespoon baking powder
1½ cups rolled oats
1 cup milk
1 large egg
4 tablespoons olive oil
1 cup blueberries, fresh or frozen (frozen or fresh veggies can be substituted for blueberries)
1 cup tilapia or bland whitefish, baked and coarsely chopped or flaked

Preheat oven to 425 degrees. Mix the flour and baking powder together, and then mix in the oats. Mix the milk and egg, lightly beating the egg, and add in the honey and olive oil. Combine the dry and wet ingredients. Fold in the tilapia or whitefish and blueberries. Bake for 12–15 minutes. Cool and serve.

CARROT LIVER MUFFINS

2 cups whole wheat pastry flour
¼ cup wheat germ
1 tablespoon baking powder
½ teaspoon powdered nutmeg
½ teaspoon grated fresh ginger
½ teaspoon cinnamon
½ cup milk
½ cup olive oil
½ cup honey
3 eggs
1½ cups grated carrots
½ cup cold liver bits, diced, sauteed, and cooled

Preheat oven to 400 degrees. Set aside the carrots and liver. Combine the dry ingredients, and then combine the wet ingredients. Mix wet and dry ingredients together; then add carrots and liver. Spoon batter into oiled muffin tins. Bake for 15 minutes (or 8 minutes for mini-muffins).

ALLERGY-FREE MUFFINS

1 cup rice flour
1 teaspoon baking soda
½ cup oat bran
1 cup millet flour
1 cup goat's milk
½ cup water

In a large bowl, mix dry ingredients. Mix wet ingredients separately. Mix wet and dry ingredients together. Spoon mixture into oiled muffin tins. Bake for 40 minutes at 375 degrees.

HIGH-PROTEIN VEGETARIAN MUFFINS #1
Yields 12 muffins

1½ cups whole wheat flour
1½ cups powdered whey
1 cup wheat germ
4 teaspoons baking powder
3 eggs
¼ cup olive or walnut oil
1 cup yogurt
2 cups chopped pumpkin seeds

Preheat oven to 350 degrees. Mix together the whole wheat flour, whey, wheat germ, and baking powder. Combine the eggs, yogurt, and oil. Mix the flour mixture and the egg mixture together, and then stir in the pumpkin seeds. Pour into muffin tins. Bake 30 minutes until lightly browned.

HIGH-PROTEIN VEGETARIAN MUFFINS #2

1 cup whole wheat flour
1 tablespoon molasses
¼ cup sunflower seeds, ground in a blender
2 tablespoons dry milk powder
1 cup milk
2 tablespoons olive oil

Preheat oven to 350 degrees. Combine all ingredients, and pour into an oiled and floured muffin tin. Bake 30 minutes until lightly browned.

 CASSEROLES AND LOAVES

These recipes smell so good in the oven and keep smelling good after they are taken out to cool. My dogs know when we are cooking for them, and the look on their faces seem to say to me, "I know I am loved soooo much." I think I might have the same look when I bite into some really good chocolate.

CARROT, PEA, AND TURKEY LOAF
4 cups frozen mixed carrots and peas
4 cups cooked brown rice
2 cups chopped raw turkey (chicken or ground beef can substitute)
1 cup whole wheat bread crumbs
4 eggs
3 tablespoons minced parsley

Combine all ingredients and place in a loaf pan that has been greased with olive oil. Bake at 350 degrees for 45–50 minutes.

BROCCOLI AND BEEF CASSEROLE

2 cups ground beef
1 cup buttermilk or yogurt
2 cups bread crumbs
1 cup instant oatmeal
1½ cups broccoli stems, chopped and very lightly steamed
3 eggs, beaten
3 tablespoons olive oil

Combine all ingredients and pour into a loaf pan or casserole dish that has been greased with olive oil. Bake at 350 degrees for 45 minutes.

THREE Ps AND CARROT LOAF

2 cups diced potatoes
1 cup diced parsnips
1 cup diced carrots
3 tablespoons fresh chopped parsley
6 beaten eggs
1 cup yogurt
3 tablespoons flour
½ cup olive oil

Steam potatoes, parsnips, parsley, and carrots for 20 minutes. Blend eggs, yogurt, olive oil, and flour in blender. Mix cooled vegetables and blended liquid together. Pour into a well-oiled loaf pan. Bake at 350 degrees for 45 minutes. Cool and serve in portions.

MACARONI CUSTARD

1 cup whole wheat macaroni
1 cup whole grain bread crumbs
1½ cups milk
3 eggs, beaten
1 cup grated cheddar cheese
pinch of cayenne
2 tablespoons mixed fresh herbs or 1 tablespoon dried Italian herbs

Cook the noodles according to package directions. Soak the bread crumbs in milk, and stir in the eggs and seasonings. Place the noodles in an oiled casserole dish, and crumble the cheese on top of the noodles. Pour the bread crumb, milk, egg, and seasoning mixture on top of the noodles without stirring in. Set the casserole in a pan of hot water, and bake at 325 degrees for 1 hour.

POTATOES AU CANINE
Yields 4 cups

3 cups sliced potatoes
¼ cup grated cheese
½ cup cottage cheese
2 tablespoons grated vegetables
1 tablespoon nutritional yeast
¼ cup whole milk

Boil 3 cups of sliced potatoes for 45 minutes. Place a layer of potatoes at the bottom of an appropriate-size buttered casserole dish. Spread a layer of cream cheese over the bottom layer of potatoes, add another layer of potatoes, and then spread cream cheese over this layer of potatoes as well. Pour the milk over the layered mixture, and top with grated cheese and grated vegetables. Bake until the cheese on top is melted and slightly brown; this usually takes about 15–20 minutes in a 350-degree oven. Serve when cool. Can be refrigerated covered for up to five days.

LIVER LOVER'S LOAF
2 cups chopped broccoli, including stems
2 cups chopped string beans
1½ to 2 pounds beef liver
1 cup olive oil
4 cloves chopped garlic
3 fresh sage leaves, minced, or ½ teaspoon powdered sage
2 fresh sprigs thyme or ½ teaspoon powdered thyme
12 cups (about 1 large loaf) whole grain bread, torn into smaller pieces
6 eggs, beaten (shells optional)

Chop up the vegetables, and add the herbs and garlic to the vegetable mix. Chop the liver into smaller pieces. Put the 12 cups of bread pieces into a large bowl. Mix in the olive oil and cubed beef liver, then mix in the vegetables. Add the beaten eggs to the mixture. Add enough water (1 to 2 cups) to moisten the bread. Bake for 1 hour at 350 degrees in 2 loaf pans or a square cake pan.

SALMON LOAF

2½ cups whole wheat flour
2 cups rolled oats
1½ teaspoons baking soda
3 cups yogurt, kefir, or buttermilk
1 teaspoon dried rosemary
2 tablespoons chopped fresh parsley
2 garlic cloves, chopped
16-ounce can salmon

Mix the flour and baking soda together, and add in the oats. Add the yogurt, kefir, or buttermilk. Mix in the herbs and garlic, and then mix in the canned salmon. Pour into an oiled loaf pan, and bake at 300 degrees for 45 minutes.

HERB AND CHICKEN LOAF

2 cups cubed whole grain bread
1 tablespoon parsley
2 cloves chopped garlic
1 teaspoon dried tarragon
2 cups chopped cooked chicken
½ cup yogurt
3 eggs, beaten
⅓ cup olive oil

Mix the bread, chicken, and herbs together in a large bowl. Beat the eggs and add the yogurt and olive oil to the eggs. Pour over the bread and chicken mixture and mix together. Pour into a greased loaf pan. Bake at 350 degrees for 35–40 minutes.

OLD-FASHIONED MEAT LOAF
2 cups broccoli stems, finely chopped
2 pounds ground chuck
½ cup minced Italian parsley
1 teaspoon garlic powder
3 large eggs
½ cup milk
2 cups rolled oats

Preheat the oven to 350 degrees. Mix together the meat, broccoli stems, garlic powder, and Italian parsley in a bowl. Beat the eggs and milk together; add to the meat mixture and mix. Add the rolled oats and continue mixing. Put mixture in a 10 x 13-inch baking dish, and bake at 350 degrees for about 50 minutes. Cool and slice into portions.

SWEET POTATOES AND EGGS
Yields 5 cups

4 cups sweet potatoes (or yams)
½ cup cream
4 eggs, beaten
1 cup whole milk

Bake sweet potatoes until thoroughly cooked (usually about 60–90 minutes at 400 degrees). Then dice sweet potatoes and place in a blender while adding the remaining ingredients. Puree all ingredients in blender; you want a consistency similar to that of pancake batter, so add enough cream and milk to achieve this consistency. Pour pureed mixture into a 13 x 9-inch pan, and bake at 350 degrees for 40 minutes. Cool and serve. Can be refrigerated covered for up to five days.

POTATO CHEESE PUDDING
5 medium potatoes with skins on, cooked and mashed
2 eggs
1 cup cottage cheese
¾ cup milk

Mix eggs and milk together in a blender. Add the cottage cheese to the blended mixture, and mix again until smooth. Stir the blended mix in with the mashed potatoes. Pour mixture into an oiled 2-quart casserole. Bake at 350 degrees for 1 hour or until the top is brown and a toothpick comes out clean.

PASTA, LENTIL, AND VEGGIE LOAF

1⅓ cups brown lentils
2 cups whole wheat pasta in small shapes
½ cup olive oil
3 chopped garlic cloves
1 large chopped carrot
1 stalk chopped celery
1 egg, beaten
2 tablespoons chopped fresh parsley

Bring water to a boil in saucepan, and stir in lentils. Simmer uncovered for about 40 minutes or until lentils are soft. Preheat oven to 375 degrees. In another large saucepan, cook pasta shapes until tender. Heat olive oil in another saucepan, and add garlic, celery, and carrot and lightly sauté until soft. Add the cooked lentils and pasta to the vegetables, along with the parsley and beaten egg. Bake in oven for 40 minutes. Cool and serve.

 YUMMY STEWS AND SOUPS

There is no need to heat up the oven for these recipes, for they are all done on the stovetop. Even better, these yummy stews are one-pot preparations. Cleanup consists of a knife and a cutting board. Remember to not have the flame on too high and to stir and watch the mix during the cooking process. I often let these stews cool and store them in the stainless steel pots in the refrigerator.

Everyday Stews and Soups

Once you get the hang of it, these recipes are easy to prepare. Leftover vegetables from the dinner table can be saved in the refrigerator and "liberated" into a stew or soup. In the Middle Ages, a large cooking pot over the fire was continually filled with leftovers and cooked and recooked. We're not going quite that far, but stews and soups are wide open for all kinds of leftovers. Dogs do not think that you ruined the recipe when you add more yummy things to it.

Be Patient!

Large pots of stew take a few hours to cool. If your dog just can't wait for the stew to cool, you can take a portion out of the pot and spread it on a cookie sheet to speed cooling.

NUIT'S FAVORITE STEW

2 pounds ground beef, turkey, or chicken
1½ cups brown basmati rice
½ cup barley
garlic (fresh or granulated)
1 cup chopped parsley
1 16-ounce package frozen chopped veggies, thawed

FOR MEAT BROTH (MADE FROM MEAT/BONES):
bones, such as chicken wings, soup bones, chicken thighs
2 quarts water

Cook bones in 2 quarts of water to make broth. Remove bones, pull any meat from the bones, and put the meat back into the broth. Add ground meat, basmati rice, barley, garlic, and parsley, and simmer until everything is cooked and tender. Add water if needed; it should be moist but not runny when it's done. Add the thawed veggies and stir into the mixture. Do not cook the veggies, as the heat from the mixture will be enough to blend them into the dog food. Serve in portions based on your dog's size and needs.

CHICKEN AND ROOT VEGETABLE STEW
Yields 12 cups

3 cups chicken parts (boneless)
2 tablespoons olive oil
4 large boiling potatoes
4 large carrots
¼ cup chopped fresh marjoram
3 large parsnips
6 cups canned low-salt chicken broth
3 medium turnips
¾ cup heavy whipping cream

Place chicken in a large pot. Wash potatoes well and cut into pieces. Wash carrots well and slice. Peel parsnips and slice into pieces. Peel and dice turnips. Add these ingredients into the pot with the chicken.

Add olive oil, chopped garlic, marjoram, chicken broth, and whipping cream to the pot. Simmer for 1 hour. You can add more chicken broth until desired consistency is achieved. Can be refrigerated covered for up to five days or frozen for up to one month.

BEEF, BARLEY, AND VEGETABLE STEW
Yields about 15 cups

2 cups pearl barley
4 cloves chopped garlic
5 cups water
1 teaspoon lemon juice
4 cups beef broth
2 tablespoons olive oil
1 pound beef stew meat
1½ cups frozen peas
3 stalks celery, chopped
2 small bay leaves
3 carrots, chopped

Place the pearl barley in a large pot with 4 cups of the water and 2 cups of the beef broth, and simmer for 1 hour. Add the remaining ingredients, and simmer for an additional 30 minutes. Add more water to achieve desired consistency. Serve when cool. Can refrigerate covered for up to five days or freeze for up to one month.

RICE AND BEANS
Yields 3 cups

1 cup cooked beans (kidney, navy, or pinto)
2 cloves chopped garlic
2 cups cooked rice (basmati or brown)
4 tablespoons olive oil

You can use canned precooked beans or you can soak and cook them yourself. The rice can be cooked with a meat-based stock or bouillon cube for extra flavor. Sauté the garlic in the olive oil for 1 minute. Add in the beans and stir, rewarming the beans. Add the rice and mix well to warm the entire meal. Serve when cool. Refrigerate covered for up to five days.

CHICKEN AND RICE
Yields 12 cups

2 cloves diced garlic
2 cups chicken pieces without bones
4 tablespoons olive oil
1 cup diced carrot
2 cups brown rice
½ cup diced celery
6 cups water or chicken stock
¼ cup chopped parsley

In a large pot, lightly sauté the garlic in the olive oil. Add the uncooked rice and stir thoroughly. Add the water or chicken stock, and simmer for 1 hour. Next, add in the boneless chicken pieces and vegetables (carrots, celery, and parsley). At this point, you may want to add more water or chicken stock to achieve the desired consistency. Cook the mixture for an additional 20 minutes. Serve when cool. Refrigerate covered for up to five days.

Be Creative!

Don't be afraid to be innovative with these recipes. You can add a twist to the same recipe each time you make it by checking your refrigerator for fresh leftovers that will add a new perspective to each batch.

RICE AND EGG DROP SOUP
Yields 6 cups

2 cups basmati rice
6 cups water
3 beaten eggs

This is the same recipe as given in chapter 11, suggested for dogs with diarrhea. Cook 2 cups basmati rice in 6 cups water for 15 minutes. The mixture that results should be a little soupy; if not, add more water. Rapidly mix in the beaten eggs, and allow to cool to room temperature. It should firm up as it cools. Serve when cool.

HUNGARIAN GOULASH
2 pounds diced chuck or round
½ cup olive oil
16-ounce bag of frozen carrots and peas
2 cups yogurt
dash of paprika
8 cups cooked whole wheat macaroni or pasta

Put oil in a skillet and add diced meat. Sauté meat in oil until the outside is browned. Add the frozen peas and carrots, and mix in until cooked with meat. Stir in the yogurt and paprika. Remove from heat and cool. Mix in the pasta. Cool and serve.

Hearty Dog Stews
These economic and ecologically prepared stews allow you to make enough to feed several dogs or a large dog for several days. We save all of our healthy leftovers, such as broccoli stems, egg shells, cauliflower leaves, carrot tops, potato peels, and the like. These "hearty man" stews are really fun to make, as there is always some innovation in every dish. Once you get the hang of it, you'll find yourself inventing new and even better ways to make a big pot of delicious stew, and your dog will love you all the more for it. For example, one of my clients bought a slow-cooker and loves the way it works. He has several chestnut trees and often adds fresh chestnuts to the recipes.

HEARTY MAN PORK STEW

3 pounds pork with bones or 1 pound cubed or diced pork
3 quarts water
5 cloves garlic
shells from several eggs (optional)
leftover vegetables
2 cups parsnips or carrots (leave the peels on, but wash well)
rosemary, either 1 tablespoon dried or 3 tablespoons fresh
½ cup olive oil
3½ cups brown rice

Put the pork and 3 quarts water into a 5-quart stock pot, and bring to a boil. If using pork with bones, cook for 1½ hours until meat is very tender; then cool and pull pork off the bones. If using minced or cubed pork, you do not need to cook it first; simply cook everything together. Only the pork with bones needs to be cooked first so that the bones can be removed. Add garlic, rosemary, olive oil, vegetables, eggshells, and brown rice to the meat, whether pulled from the bone or minced/cubed. Bring to a simmer and cook for 1 hour and 15 minutes. Cool and serve. Divide the rest into portions for subsequent meals, and refrigerate or freeze in ziplock bags.

STICK YOUR NECK OUT HEARTY MAN STEW

2 pounds chicken necks
6 medium potatoes
shells from 4 to 6 eggs, crumbled
leftover vegetables, any kind
4 large carrots
3 cups quinoa
1 teaspoon sage
3 tablespoons parsley
3 no-salt chicken bouillon cubes
3 quarts water

Place all ingredients into a large pot and bring to a boil. Reduce to simmer; simmer for 40 minutes. Remove from heat and let cool. Divide into meal-size portions, and store in plastic containers or ziplock bags. Refrigerate or freeze portions.

Note

Always give these recipes an occasional stir, and add more water if in doubt.

TARRAGON CHICKEN HEARTY MAN STEW

1 large chicken or 12 chicken legs or 7 chicken breasts (frozen or fresh)
large pot water
¼ cup olive oil
3 cups sliced carrots
3 cups cubed potatoes
4 sliced parsnips
2 cups broccoli stems, sliced
6 cloves garlic, sliced
leftover shells from 3 to 6 eggs
1 teaspoon tarragon

Place chicken in large pot with 2 quarts of water, bring to boil, and then reduce to simmer and cook until meat is tender. If using chicken with bones, cool, remove meat from bone, and return meat to the pot. Add olive oil, carrots, potatoes, parsnips, garlic, eggshells, tarragon, and broccoli stems. Return to a boil, and simmer for 30 minutes or until done. Remove from heat and let cool. Store in ziplock bags and refrigerate or freeze.

SWEET AND WOOLLY HEARTY MAN STEW

2 pounds minced lamb
8 cups diced sweet potatoes or yams
2 tablespoons molasses
2 diced apples
2 teaspoons ground cinnamon
leftover shells from 3 to 6 eggs
10 cups water

In a large stockpot, combine all ingredients. Bring to a boil, and then simmer for 35–40 minutes or until potatoes or yams are tender. Cool, serve, and store.

Organic Skins

In any of the recipes that call for potatoes or carrots, leave the skins on if the vegetables are organic. These skins contain many minerals and nutrients. If the veggies are not organic, they should be peeled.

BEEF AND BARLEY HEARTY MAN STEW

1½ pounds cubed beef
3 cups barley
2 cups cubed potatoes
1 cup sliced carrots
½ cup sliced celery
2 cups canned corn
5 cloves garlic, sliced
½ cup olive oil
leftover shells from 3 to 6 eggs
leftover vegetables

Fill large stockpot with 3 quarts of water, and add all ingredients. Bring to a boil, and then reduce to simmer for 70 minutes. Cool and serve. Divide the rest into meal-size portions, and refrigerate or freeze for future meals.

FRUITS OF THE SEA HEARTY MAN STEW

2 pounds cubed tilapia
1 flat sheet kombu seaweed
6 (or more) crumbled eggshells
3 tablespoons parsley
5 cloves garlic, sliced
2 cups sliced carrots
4 cups basmati or jasmine white rice
3 quarts water

Place all ingredients in large stock pot. Bring to boil, and then simmer for 30 minutes and cool. Remove sheet of kombu. Serve and store.

LIVER AND BROWN RICE HEARTY MAN STEW

2 pounds liver
4 cups brown rice
2 cubed beets and beet greens
3 tablespoons or more fresh parsley
1 teaspoon rosemary
⅔ cup olive oil
3 quarts water

Lightly sauté liver in olive oil in a large stock pot. Add rest of ingredients and water. Bring to boil, and then simmer for 75 minutes. Cool, serve, and store.

 ## TOSS AND SERVE

Your dog is in the mood for some canine cooking, and you want to make something special. Toss and serve meals can be prepared with a minimum of fuss. If you are in a rush, you can substitute pasta for potatoes.

FISH AND CHIPS
1 pound frozen breaded fish sticks
8 medium potatoes (white, sweet, or yams)
½ cup olive oil
2 tablespoons chopped parsley

Slice potatoes into smallish wedges. Place wedges on oiled tray, and sprinkle with olive oil and parsley. Place in 350-degree oven, and bake for 45 minutes. Consult the instructions on the fish-stick package, and add them into the oven so that they bake along with the potato wedges and finish at about the same time. Cool, mix together, and serve.

YAMS AND GINGER
Yields 3–4 cups

2 yams
ginger, either ½ teaspoon grated fine or ¼ teaspoon powdered ginger
1 tablespoon butter

Bake yams until thoroughly cooked. Mash yams with ginger, and add butter to the warm mixture. Serve when cool. Refrigerate covered for up to five days.

MACKEREL AND OATMEAL

1 cup steel-cut oats
1 12- to 16-ounce can mackerel
2 tablespoons fresh chopped parsley (or 2 teaspoons dried)

Put 1 cup of steel-cut oats in 3½ cups of water. Bring to a quick boil, and then simmer on very low heat for 30–40 minutes, checking during the cooking process to see if more water is needed. Put cooked oatmeal in a large bowl, fluff it up, and allow it to cool a bit (should yield about 3 cups). Mix canned mackerel and parsley into oatmeal. Finish cooling and serve.

TILAPIA AND POTATOES

1 pound fresh tilapia or other whitefish
4 cups chopped white potatoes (with skin on)
1 teaspoon dried rosemary
⅓ cup olive oil
water

Place potatoes in pot with rosemary, olive oil, and enough unsalted water to just cover potatoes. Bring to boil and cook until potatoes are tender. Slice fish into strips and add to potatoes and water. Mix in well and bring to boil again for another 10–15 minutes until the fish flakes or is cooked through. Remove from heat and cool.

QUINOA, CAULIFLOWER, AND TASTY TURKEY

1 cup quinoa
turkey parts—thighs and/or wings
1 cup cauliflower, chopped
2 tablespoons fresh parsley, chopped
⅓ cup olive oil

Rinse quinoa with tap water to remove any bitter taste from outer husks, and set aside. Place 4 cups of water in a saucepan, and add the turkey pieces. Bring to a boil and then simmer, covered, until the turkey is cooked. Cool, remove the turkey bones, and place the turkey meat back into the water. Add the quinoa, cauliflower, and olive oil. Bring back to a boil and immediately reduce to simmer, covered, for 30 minutes. Remove from heat and mix in parsley. Let cool and serve.

Quinoa

Quinoa is a grain with high protein content. It is also a complete protein. This grain was historically grown in the Andes of South America. Most health food stores carry this product.

YAMS AND CHICKEN
Yields about 8 cups

4 skinned yams
3 cups boneless chicken
1 cup grated vegetables, any kind

Bake skinned yams until thoroughly cooked. Cut chicken into pieces. Cook boneless chicken however you like (please do not fry). Mash cooked yams and mix in cooked chicken pieces and grated vegetables. Serve when cool. Refrigerate covered for up to three days.

POTATOES AND CHEESE
2 cups potatoes, diced
1 stalk broccoli stems, chopped
½ cup ricotta cheese
1 tablespoon parsley, chopped
½ cup half and half

Boil diced potatoes for 45 minutes. Strain potatoes through a colander. Add the remaining ingredients and mix well. Serve when cool. Refrigerate covered for up to five days.

SALMON AND POTATOES
Yields about 3½ cups

3 medium potatoes
1 can low-salt salmon
½ cup grated carrot

Cook potatoes however you desire; then add in the salmon and carrots and mix well. Serve when cool. Refrigerate covered for up to three days.

VENISON AND POTATOES

3 cups diced potatoes with skins on
1 cup cubed venison
1 cup frozen peas and carrots
⅓ cup olive oil
½ teaspoon powdered rosemary
water

Place diced potatoes in unsalted water, using just enough water to cover potatoes. Bring to boil and then simmer until potatoes are soft. Add the cubed venison, rosemary, and olive oil. Simmer for another 10 minutes. Add the cup of frozen peas and carrots, and simmer for another 10 minutes. Cool and serve.

POTATO SALAD

Yields 3 cups

2 cups potatoes, sliced
3 eggs
½ cup mayonnaise

Boil potato slices for 45 minutes. While waiting, boil three eggs for about 20 minutes. In a casserole dish, mix the potatoes, eggs, and mayonnaise together well. You can leave the eggshells on if you choose. Serve when cool. Refrigerate covered for up to five days.

LIVER TOSS

2 cups cubed liver
½ cup olive oil
3 diced garlic cloves
3 cups whole wheat pasta
1 tablespoon Italian herb mix

Cook pasta according to package directions and drain. Add liver to warm olive oil in frying pan. Add diced garlic. Sprinkle on Italian herbs. Cook liver for about 10 minutes, stirring, until light pink inside. Combine liver mixture with the whole wheat pasta and toss.

RICE AND SALMON
Yields 3½ cups

1½ cups basmati rice
water for cooking rice
1 can low-salt salmon

Cook the basmati rice in 3½ cups boiling water for 3 minutes (will yield about 3 cups cooked). Let sit covered on stove for 20 minutes. Add salmon and mix. Serve when cool. Refrigerate covered for up to three days.

 ## EGGS AND OMELETS

Since dogs do not get hardening and thickening of the arteries as people do, be assured that you cannot overdose your dog on eggs. They are simple to make, and dogs love them.

EASY EGGS AND TOAST
3 eggs
3 pieces whole grain bread
1 tablespoon fresh parsley, chopped

Soft-boil eggs in a pan of water. Toast the bread lightly in the toaster, and then crumble the bread in the bottom of a bowl. Mash the eggs (leaving the shells on) with a fork. Place mashed eggs and shells on top of toast. Sprinkle with parsley. Serve when cool.

SCRAMBLED EGGS AND COTTAGE CHEESE

1 tablespoon olive oil
1 tablespoon butter
½ cup cottage cheese
2 tablespoons parsley, chopped
8 eggs

Place butter and oil in large frying pan. When butter has melted, stir in cottage cheese, and cook until creamy. Pour beaten eggs mixed with chopped parsley into pan and lower heat. As soon as eggs begin to set, stir until moist. Cool and serve.

SCRAMBLED EGGS WITH MEAT AND SPINACH

2 tablespoons olive oil
½ cup meat, either chicken, steak, turkey, bacon, or ham
8 eggs
1 cup fresh spinach, chopped

Place oil in large frying pan. Add meat to oil and sauté until done. (If you are using deli-type precooked lunch meat, wait and add it with the spinach.) Beat the eggs and add them to the pan, stirring lightly in with the meat. Immediately add the spinach and stir into eggs quickly. Stir in pan until done. Cool and serve.

SCRAMBLED EGGS AND ROSEMARY RICE

4 tablespoons olive oil
4 eggs, beaten
2 cups cooked brown rice
½ teaspoon rosemary

Heat oil in 12-inch frying pan. Combine beaten eggs, rice, and rosemary, and pour the mixture into the hot pan. Cook over medium heat until eggs are set. Cool and serve.

Eggshells

Using a blender to beat the eggs and placing the whole egg (with the shells) in the blender will add extra healthy calcium to the meal.

POTATO, FETA, AND HERB OMELET

2 tablespoons olive oil
1 cup of cooked (steamed or baked and cooled) diced potato with the
  skins on
½ cup crumbled feta cheese (or any kind of cheese)
5 eggs, beaten
¼ teaspoon sage
¼ teaspoon thyme

Place the oil in a 10- or 12-inch frying pan. When pan is warm, add potatoes, sage, and thyme. Stir lightly in pan. Immediately pour beaten eggs on top of potato mixture and lower heat. Sprinkle cheese onto mixture, and put cover on frying pan. Reduce heat and cook over very low heat for 4–6 minutes or until done. The cover eliminates the need for flipping the omelet, but if you wish to live dangerously, flip it. Cool, cut into slices or pieces, and serve.

EAT YOUR VEGETABLES OMELET

2 tablespoons olive oil
1 cup broccoli, finely chopped
½ cup kale, finely chopped
1 clove garlic, diced or crushed
1 tablespoon parsley
4 eggs, beaten

Warm the oil in a 10- or 12-inch frying pan. Add the garlic and lightly sauté for a few seconds. Add the broccoli, kale, and parsley, and sauté lightly for 1 minute. Pour the beaten eggs over the vegetables. Cover and cook over low heat for 4–6 minutes or until done. Cool and serve.

 RAW DIETS

If you wish to feed a raw-food diet, you will want to have plenty of variety to afford your dog a good balance of vitamins, minerals, and other essential nutrients. While variety is the key to all diets, I like to pay particular attention to the mineral balance in raw diets.

Studies have shown that some raw diets tend to be deficient in calcium, linoleic acid, and iodine. Calcium is a very important mineral that must be added to raw-food diets. Linoleic acid, or omega-6 fatty acid, is found in grains and seeds. The word *linoleic* comes from the Greek word *linon*, which means "flax." Coconut oil, walnut oil, olive oil, and, of course, flax seeds and flaxseed oil contain linoleic acid.

Quick Mix and Match Meals

Pick one from Column A and one from Column B and just mix them together. You can make these meals al fresco or prepare ahead of time and store.

COLUMN A

2 cups whole-grain no-sugar breakfast cereal

2 cups soaked or cooked whole oats

2 cups cooked white potatoes

2 cups cooked sweet potatoes or yams

2 cups cooked whole wheat pasta

2 cups rice

2 cups crumbled whole grain bread

COLUMN B

1 cup buttermilk

1 cup plain yogurt

1 cup kefir

3 large scrambled eggs

3 large hard-boiled eggs, mashed with shells left on

1 cup cottage cheese

1 cup farmer's cheese

1 cup beef

1 cup chicken

1 cup salmon

1 cup whitefish

1 cup canned kidney beans

1 cup frozen fish sticks, baked and cooled

Seaweed and seaweed products are chock full of iodine. I do like to use cooked grains along with raw meat, and these grains can be cooked with a piece of kombu seaweed in the water to add iodine to the diet. Nori seaweed comes in flat dry sheets, and my dogs love to have nori as a snack. Powdered seaweed products are also available in health food stores.

Meat preparation will be different with a raw diet. The fat does not need to be trimmed from raw meat. Cooked animal fat has a negative health value, but raw animal fat is healthy for your dog. However, you may want to freeze raw meat for fourteen days before you defrost and serve it, as this effectively eliminates most parasites that the meat may be harboring.

We've mentioned how essential added calcium is to a raw-food diet, and it is important that the calcium be bioavailable calcium. Meat is high in phosphorus and low in calcium. Calcium must be added to the food to ensure the correct balance of these minerals for bone growth and bone

Flax Seeds

Ground flax seeds are an excellent addition to any diet, especially a raw diet. These seeds need a special grinder to grind them; this type of grinder can be found in most health food stores. Ground flax seeds need to be refrigerated.

density. Dry, desiccated, ground bone meal is not bioavailable. Following are some ways of preparing healthy bioavailable calcium at home. Furthermore, the resources section lists sources from which you can purchase bioavailable calcium supplements.

EASY EGGSHELL RECIPE #1
eggshells
lemon juice or vinegar

Save your eggshells. Wash them with water, break into small pieces, and cover with lemon juice or vinegar. Let sit for a few days. The shells will dissolve completely, resulting in an excellent source of calcium that will be easily assimilated.

EASY EGGSHELL RECIPE #2
organic eggs
organic lemon juice

Place whole, washed, uncooked, uncracked, organic eggs in a clean glass or ceramic bowl. Cover the eggs with freshly squeezed organic lemon juice (concentrated lemon juice is pasteurized and should never be used as a substitute). Cover the bowl loosely, and place it in the refrigerator. A few times during the day, gently—very gently—agitate the liquid in the bowl. As the calcium from the shells is leached by the lemon juice, bubbles will appear around the eggs. Approximately 48 hours later, when the bubbling has stopped, carefully remove the eggs and try not to break the egg membranes. Put the remaining liquid in a glass jar, close the lid tightly, and shake the mixture. You now have "Lemon Egg." (Courtesy of Ian Shillington)

CHICKEN AND BARLEY RAW DIET
1 cup raw chicken
2 cups well-cooked barley that has been cooked with kombu seaweed in the water
1 cup broccoli stems, finely chopped
1 tablespoon coconut oil, or 3 tablespoons of olive or walnut oil
1 teaspoon ground flax seeds
2 cloves raw garlic, diced
1 teaspoon eggshell calcium or suggested dose of water-soluble calcium

Mix all ingredients together and serve.

Raw~Food Diet Facts

Here are some facts to keep in mind about raw-food diets:

✓ The protein and grain sources can vary in raw-food diets.

✓ Grains, except for oatmeal, must be cooked (see chapter 5 for amounts and cooking) or sprouted.

✓ All meals should include olive oil, walnut oil, or coconut oil.

✓ Cooking with seaweed or adding nori seaweed increases the nutritional value of the meal.

✓ Spices, such as rosemary and garlic, along with Italian spices, are healthy to add to the mix.

✓ All raw diets should be supplemented with calcium.

BEEF AND OATMEAL RAW DIET

1 cup cubed raw beef
2 cups oatmeal, soaked overnight in water
1 cup carrots, squash, or yams
3 tablespoons olive oil
1 tablespoon molasses
1 teaspoon ground flax seeds
2 pieces nori seaweed, torn into small pieces
1 teaspoon of eggshell calcium or suggested dose of water-soluble calcium

Mix all ingredients together and serve.

 INDUSTRIOUS STOCKS

In the grain section in chapter 5, recipes for cooking grains and stews were covered. Plain water can always be used to cook grains and food in general. Grains can also be cooked in stocks to make them more flavorful and to increase the protein content of the meal. A stock can be prepared from scratch when you have the time. You can also use canned beef or chicken stock. Bouillon cubes can be used for flavor also. Vegetarians can find meatless soups to use that impart a nice flavor. Stocks that include vegetables are mineral rich.

MEAT STOCK
Yields 14 cups

3 pounds beef or lamb bone
8 long parsley sprigs
2 pounds stew beef or lamb
½ teaspoon dried thyme
4 carrots
½ cup vinegar
3 ribs celery
4 quarts water
5 garlic cloves

Place bones in a large pot. Cut stew beef or lamb meat into cubes and place in pot. Cut carrots and celery into one-inch pieces and add to pot. Peel the garlic cloves and place in pot. Chop the parsley sprigs and add to the pot along with thyme, vinegar, and water.

Bring stock to a boil, then reduce to a simmer, and cook uncovered for one hour. Remove all bones from stock; the vegetables can be left in or strained through a colander. Refrigerate for up to one week, or freeze for up to one month.

CHICKEN STOCK
Yields 12 cups

2½ pounds chicken wings or chicken thighs
¼ teaspoon dried thyme
2 carrots
1 tablespoon vinegar
3 ribs of celery
4 garlic cloves
6 sprigs parsley
10 cups water

Place chicken in a large pot. Add 2 carrots, 3 ribs of celery, and 6 sprigs of parsley, all coarsely chopped. Add the rest of the ingredients into the pot. Bring stock to a boil; then reduce to a simmer and cook uncovered for 1 hour. Strain through a colander, carefully remove any chicken bones, and put veggies and meat back into the stock if you desire. Refrigerate for up to one week or freeze for up to one month.

FISH STOCK
Yields 8 cups

1 pound bones/trimmings of any type whitefish
12 long parsley sprigs, chopped
2 tablespoons fresh lemon juice
8 cups cold water

Combine all ingredients in a large pot. Bring to a boil, and then reduce to a simmer for 30 minutes. Strain through a colander, and remove any fish bones. Use the stock only. Refrigerate for up to three days or keep frozen for up to one month.

 # FRUITS

Fruits are full of live nutrition and definitely have their place in a dog's diet. My dogs love slices of apple, and sometimes I spice them up with some nut butter (I do not use peanut butter, but I do use almond butter and cashew butter, available in most health food stores). You'd be surprised at how many dogs enjoy a slice of watermelon on a hot summer day. Besides being refreshing, it provides them with healthy electrolytes.

BEAUTY AND COLE'S FAVORITE FROZEN TREAT

assorted fruits
yogurt or kefir
hollowed marrow bones, ice cube trays, or hollow toys

Mix fruit pieces with yogurt or kefir. Put the mixture in clean hollowed marrow bones, ice cube trays, or any hollow toys. Place in freezer until mixture is solid.

When treats are frozen, I call out, "Who wants a treat!?" Beauty and Cole come running. They have become connoisseurs of these favorite frozen treats.

APPLES, COUSCOUS, AND CINNAMON

3 apples, peeled, cored, and diced
2 cups dry couscous
5 cups water
½ teaspoon cinnamon
2 tablespoons butter

Place the water in large saucepan and add couscous, cinnamon, apple, and butter. Bring to a boil, and then simmer for 10 minutes. Cool and serve.

PEARS, HONEY, AND OATMEAL

3 pears, peeled, cored, and diced
4 cups cooked oatmeal
3 tablespoons honey

Mix pears with warm oatmeal. Cool and serve in dishes, with a dollop of honey on each serving.

BLUEBERRIES AND MUESLI

3 cups plain muesli
1 cup blueberries
1 cup cottage cheese

Mix all ingredients together and serve.

 # SNACKS, TREATS, AND BISCUITS

As far as our canine friends are concerned, we have finally gotten to the heart of the matter. A little nosh here and there is what makes a good day a great day! These treats store well in the fridge and are very welcome surprises.

BAKED YAM CHIPS

6 organic yams or sweet potatoes
1 tablespoon cinnamon
½ cup olive oil

Slice yams or sweet potatoes into thin slices. Place on oiled cookie trays, and drizzle with olive oil. Sprinkle cinnamon on top. Bake at 350 degrees for 35 minutes or until cooked and a little crunchy. Cool, store, and serve.

ALL DOGS LOVE 'EM LIVER TREATS

2 pounds calf liver
2 cups uncooked oatmeal
4 tablespoons whole wheat flour
4 cloves garlic
3 tablespoons parsley, chopped
4 eggs

Place all ingredients in blender, and mix until smooth. Place a good amount of olive oil on a 10 x 15-inch cookie tray. Spread mixture onto tray until it is about a ½ inch or so thick. Bake at 350 degrees for 30–35 minutes or until mixture is firm. Cool and cut into treat-size squares. Freeze extras and defrost as needed.

FLAXSEED TWISTS

2 cups all-purpose flour
¼ cup low-sodium beef or chicken bouillon powder
¼ cup flaxseed meal
1 egg
¾ cup warm water
1 cup cornmeal, for rolling out treats
½ cup flaxseed meal, for rolling out treats

Preheat oven to 325 degrees. Mix together the first five ingredients until well combined; then knead the mixture with your hands to form a soft ball (add more flour if needed). Put the cornmeal and flaxseed meal on a breadboard, and then drop the ball of dough on the breadboard and flatten. Flip the dough over to get the cornmeal on both sides. Roll out the dough to about ¼ inch thick. Use a sharp knife to cut the circle of dough into strips about ½ inch wide. Twist the strips to the desired length. Bake for 10–15 minutes or until golden brown on the bottom.

SALMON FUDGE
14-ounce can undrained salmon
1½ cups oat flour
1 tablespoon garlic powder or granulated garlic
2 eggs, lightly beaten
½ cup grated parmesan cheese

Mix together all ingredients in a bowl or food processor. Spread on oiled or nonstick cookie sheet to desired thickness. Bake at 350 degrees for 20 minutes. Slice with pizza cutter to desired size.

SAUSAGE BALLS
1 pound uncooked sausage
4 cups premade ready-to-cook biscuit mix
½ pound grated cheddar cheese
2 tablespoons parsley

Work all ingredients together and roll into balls. Place on lightly greased cookie sheet, and bake at 350 for 20 minutes. Freeze and defrost as needed.

EASY BRUSCHETTA TREAT
4 to 6 slices of whole wheat bread
2 tablespoons olive oil
1 tablespoon nutritional yeast*

Lightly brush the whole wheat bread slices with olive oil. Lightly sprinkle nutritional yeast on top of oiled bread. Cut the bread into one-inch strips, and place on a baking sheet. Heat the oven to 250 degrees, and cook for 1 hour. Serve as treats when cool. Can refrigerate for up to five days.
* *Note:* You can leave out the nutritional yeast, and when done cooking and cooling, spread some chopped liver or cream cheese on the bread as an additional treat.

FISH STICKS
a few pounds frozen fish sticks
olive oil
dried tarragon

Place fish sticks on oiled baking pan. Sprinkle with olive oil, and dust lightly with powdered tarragon. Bake according to directions on fish-stick package. Cool and serve.

SESAME BALL TREATS
Yields 6–8 treats

½ cup sesame butter
1¼ cups sesame seeds
2 tablespoons wheat germ

Mix together sesame butter, wheat germ, and ¾ cup of sesame seeds. Form into small round balls. Roll in the remaining sesame seeds. Refrigerate covered for up to five days, or freeze for up to six weeks.

HERB BISCOTTI
Yields 2½ dozen

2 cups whole wheat flour
¼ teaspoon dried rosemary
7 tablespoons butter, softened
1 teaspoon baking powder
1 teaspoon dried thyme
2 large eggs
1 teaspoon dried marjoram
1 tablespoon water

Preheat oven to 350 degrees. Combine all dry ingredients in a large mixing bowl and mix well. Add the softened butter, eggs, and water, using an electric mixer to combine all ingredients. The mixture will hold together in a soft dough.

Remove dough from mixing bowl, and place on a lightly floured surface. (Note: If the dough is sticky and hard to work with, it is too soft. To achieve the desired consistency, flatten the dough into a disk, cover with plastic wrap, and place in refrigerator for at least 1 hour.) Divide the dough into three equal pieces. Work each piece into a 1½-inch-diameter rope of a length that will fit on your baking sheet, taking into consideration that they spread as they bake.

Place two of the biscotti ropes on a parchment-covered baking sheet, and bake until golden brown, approximately 30 minutes. Remove from oven and cool slightly on baking sheet. Using a serrated knife, slice the biscotti diagonally into ½-inch-long cookies while they are still warm.

Reduce the oven temperature to 300 degrees, and put the slices back in the oven for another 10–15 minutes. Repeat the process for the third rope, or use two baking sheets to bake all three at one time.

Serve when cool. Store in airtight containers at room temperature for two weeks or freeze for up to two months.

FLAXSEED AND CHICKEN BISCOTTI
Yields 2½ dozen

2 cups whole wheat flour
7 tablespoons cold unsalted butter
2 tablespoons flax seeds
2 large eggs
1 teaspoon baking powder
1 tablespoon water
1 unsalted chicken bouillon cube, mashed

Preheat oven to 350 degrees. Combine all dry ingredients in a large mixing bowl and mix well. Add the butter, eggs, and water, using an electric mixer to combine all of the ingredients. The mixture will hold together in a soft dough.

Remove dough from mixing bowl, and place on a lightly floured surface. (Note: If the dough is sticky and hard to work with, it is too soft. To achieve the desired consistency, flatten the dough into a disk, cover with plastic wrap, and place in refrigerator for at least 1 hour.) Divide the dough into three equal pieces. Work each piece into a 1½-inch diameter rope of a length that will fit on your baking sheet, taking into consideration that they spread as they bake.

Place two of the biscotti ropes on a parchment-covered baking sheet, and bake until golden brown, approximately 30 minutes. Remove from oven and cool slightly on baking sheet. Using a serrated knife, slice the biscotti diagonally into ½-inch-long cookies while they are still warm.

Reduce the oven temperature to 300 degrees, and put the slices back in the oven for another 10–15 minutes. Repeat the process for the third rope, or use two baking sheets to bake all three at one time.

Serve when cool. Store in airtight containers at room temperature for two weeks or freeze for up to two months.

EASY CHICKEN NECKS
a few pounds chicken necks
olive oil
garlic powder

Preheat oven to 350 degrees. Cut chicken necks into bite-size pieces, appropriately sized for your dog. Put them on oiled cookie trays; drizzle with olive oil and sprinkle with garlic powder. Bake for 25 minutes. Cool, then serve or store.

ALMOND BUTTER COOKIES
Yields 3 dozen

½ cup butter
1 cup almond butter
⅔ cup firmly packed brown sugar
½ teaspoon baking soda
1 egg
1½ cups unbleached white flour

Preheat the oven to 375 degrees. Beat the butter and almond butter together until it is soft. Add the sugar and beat until light and fluffy. Add the egg and beat until all of the ingredients are mixed together.

Add the remaining ingredients, starting with one cup of flour and the baking soda. Mix until just combined. Add more flour, but just enough to form a nonsticky dough. Roll the dough into small balls. Place on a buttered cookie sheet and flatten with a fork. Bake at 375 degrees for 10–12 minutes.

Serve when cool. Store in airtight containers at room temperature for up to two weeks.

OATMEAL COOKIES
Yields 3½ dozen

8 ounces unsalted butter
1 teaspoon cinnamon
½ cup firmly packed brown sugar
pinch of nutmeg
3 tablespoons honey
4 cups rolled oats
2 eggs
1½ cups pecans
1½ cups whole wheat flour

Preheat the oven to 375 degrees. Cream the butter and brown sugar in a large mixing bowl. Beat in the honey and eggs until smooth. Sift the flour, cinnamon, and nutmeg together, and stir into the butter mixture. Add the oats and pecans and stir well.

Shape the dough into 1-inch balls. Place on a buttered cookie sheet and flatten with a fork. Bake until light brown, approximately 15 minutes.

Serve when cool. Store in an airtight container at room temperature for up to two weeks.

POULTRY DELIGHTS
Yields about 2½ dozen

2 cups whole wheat flour
2 tablespoons olive oil
⅔ cup cornmeal
½ cup chicken broth
½ cup mixed seeds (flax, sunflower, or sesame)
2 eggs
¼ cup low-fat yogurt

FOR EGG GLAZE:
1 beaten egg
1 tablespoon milk

Preheat oven to 350 degrees. In a large mixing bowl, mix together all the dry ingredients. Combine the 2 eggs with the ¼ cup low-fat yogurt. Next, mix the wet ingredients (egg/yogurt mixture, oil, and broth) with the dry ingredients. The result should be a firm dough.

Allow the dough to rest for 20 minutes. Roll out the dough on a lightly floured surface to a thickness of ¼ inch. Cut out shapes using your favorite cookie cutter. Brush shapes with egg glaze, and bake for 30 minutes or until golden brown.

Serve when cool. Store in an airtight container at room temperature for up to two weeks.

MEAT-LOVER BISCUIT
Yields 6 dozen

1 pound lean ground beef
1½ cups rolled oats
2 eggs, beaten
1½ cups water
3 cups whole wheat flour

Preheat oven to 325 degrees. Mix together the beef and eggs in a bowl, using your hands if necessary to mix completely. In a separate bowl, mix the flour with the oats; then gradually mix in the beef/egg mixture, again using your hands, until mixed thoroughly. Add the water to form a sticky dough.

Knead dough on a lightly floured surface for 3 minutes. Roll dough to ¼-inch thickness, and cut into desired shapes with a cookie cutter. Use a greased cookie sheet, and bake for 80 minutes. Allow to cool in oven for several hours, and then store at room temperature for up to four weeks.

HOT DOG DELIGHTS

a few pounds hot dogs, either turkey, chicken, or beef
olive oil
mixed Italian herbs

Preheat oven to 350 degrees. Slice hot dogs into bite-size pieces, and place on oiled cookie sheet. Drizzle with olive oil and sprinkle with Italian herbs. Bake for 15 minutes. Cool and serve.

BAKED LIVER LICKS

2 pounds liver
½ cup olive oil
garlic powder
powdered parsley

Preheat oven to 350 degrees. Dice liver into treat-size portions. Place on well-oiled cookie trays, and dust with garlic powder and dried parsley. Bake for 25 minutes. Cool, serve, or store.

TARTAR FIGHTERS

Yields 5 dozen

¾ cup skim milk
1 cup all-purpose flour
½ cup stone-ground cornmeal
1½ cups low-salt chicken broth
¼ cup bulgur wheat
1 cup rolled oats
1½ cups whole wheat flour
1 egg, beaten

Preheat oven to 350 degrees. In a large bowl, mix together the dry ingredients. Heat the chicken broth until warm. Add the rolled oats to the chicken broth, and allow to stand for 5 minutes. Next, mix in the beaten egg. Slowly add the egg mixture to the dry ingredients while mixing thoroughly.

Knead dough on a lightly floured surface for about 5 minutes. The dough should stick together and be easy to work with. Roll dough to ¼-inch thickness, and cut into desired shapes with cookie cutter. Use a cookie sheet lined with foil and bake for 45 minutes. Allow to cool in oven for several hours, and then store at room temperature for up to four weeks.

VEGETARIAN TREATS
Yields 8 dozen

1¼ cups rolled oats
1 egg, beaten
½ cup olive oil
1 cup cornmeal
1¾ cups hot water
1½ cups wheat germ
3 cloves garlic, crushed
2 cups all-purpose flour
½ cup whole wheat flour
½ cup ground sunflower seeds
½ cup powdered skim milk

Preheat oven to 325 degrees. In a large bowl, mix together rolled oats, olive oil, and hot water, and allow to stand for 5 minutes. In a skillet, sauté garlic in a small amount of olive oil. Add garlic, powdered skim milk, and beaten egg to the rolled oats mixture and blend well. In a separate bowl, mix together the flours, wheat germ, and sunflower seeds. Gradually add flour mixture until well blended.

Knead dough on a lightly floured surface for 3 minutes. Roll dough to ¼-inch thickness, and cut into desired shapes with cookie cutter. Use a cookie sheet lined with foil, and bake for 45 minutes. Allow to cool in oven for several hours, and then store at room temperature for up to four weeks.

CAROB CHEWS
Yields 2 dozen

½ cup carob powder
1 cup sunflower seeds
¾ cup honey
½ cup rolled oats
1 cup almond, sesame, or peanut butter
½ cup powdered milk

Combine carob powder, honey, and almond (or sesame or peanut) butter in a large bowl and mix well. Add in sunflower seeds and rolled oats and mix thoroughly. Form into small balls and roll in powdered milk. Cover and refrigerate for up to five days or freeze for up to six weeks.

SIMPLY BISCUITS
Yields 4 dozen

⅓ cup olive oil
2 teaspoons garlic powder
1¼ cups rye flour
¾ cup water
½ cup powdered skim milk
1 egg, beaten
2 cups whole wheat flour

Preheat oven to 350 degrees. In a large bowl, mix olive oil and flour together, and set aside. In a separate bowl, mix powdered skim milk and garlic powder in the water until dissolved. Next, mix in the beaten egg. Slowly stir egg mixture into the flour mixture until well blended.

Knead dough on a lightly floured surface for about 5 minutes. The dough should stick together and be easy to work with. Roll dough to ¼-inch thickness, and cut into desired shapes with cookie cutter. Use a greased cookie sheet, and bake for 45 minutes. Allow to cool in oven for several hours, and then store at room temperature for up to four weeks.

FLEA-BUSTER BISCUITS
Yields 8 dozen

2 cups low-salt beef broth
1 cup cornmeal
1 cup rolled oats
½ cup brewer's yeast
1½ cups all-purpose flour
3 tablespoons garlic powder
2½ cups whole wheat flour
¼ cup shredded carrot
½ cup olive oil
1 egg, beaten

Preheat oven to 325 degrees. In a large bowl, combine dry ingredients. Slowly mix the oil, egg, and beef broth with the dry ingredients until well blended. Knead dough on a lightly floured surface for 5 minutes.

Roll dough to ¼-inch thickness, and cut into desired shapes with cookie cutter. Use a cookie sheet lined with foil, and bake for 1 hour and 40 minutes. Allow to cool in oven for several hours, and then store at room temperature for up to four weeks.

SPECIAL HOLIDAYS AND BIRTHDAYS

I cannot imagine anything more special than celebrating your best friend's birthday with a cake. If you don't know when your dog was born, make up a date and stick to it. It will be just as much fun, and your dog will enjoy this special occasion. Invite friends to celebrate with you. I do, however, suggest that you make a "people" cake along with one of the recipes below. Dogs love these tried-and-true canine-friendly recipes but I prefer chocolate cake for myself!

BIRTHDAY CAKE #1:
CARROT CAKE WITH CREAM CHEESE ICING

CAKE:
1½ cups melted unsalted butter
3 teaspoons baking powder
1½ cups honey
1 teaspoon cinnamon
4 eggs
2½ cups finely shredded carrot
4 cups whole wheat flour
¾ cup sesame or flax seeds
½ teaspoon baking soda

ICING:
16 ounces cream cheese, softened
8-ounce stick of unsalted butter, softened

Preheat oven to 350 degrees. In one large bowl, mix together butter, honey, and eggs. In a separate bowl, sift together the dry ingredients including the flour, baking powder, baking soda, cinnamon, carrot, and seeds. Gently and slowly mix the dry ingredients into the butter mixture. Do not beat.

Generously butter one large pan or two loaf pans, and pour cake mixture into the pan(s). Bake for 45 minutes, and then remove from oven and allow to cool. Mix together the icing ingredients in a medium-size bowl. Ice the birthday cake with this softened mixture, and refrigerate when complete. Refrigerate cake for up to one week.

BIRTHDAY CAKE #2:
CAROB CAKE WITH PEANUT BUTTER FILLING

CAKE:
½ cup unsalted butter, softened
1 cup honey
2½ cups whole wheat flour
¼ cup water
2 teaspoons baking powder
⅔ cup milk mixed with 1 teaspoon vinegar
1 cup sugar-free peanut butter
1 cup carob powder mixed with ½ cup water
½ teaspoon vanilla
2 eggs

ICING:
1 cup carob powder
¼ cup honey
1 teaspoon vanilla
⅓ cup whole milk

Preheat oven to 350 degrees. In large mixing bowl, mix together butter, honey, eggs, water, milk-vinegar mixture, and vanilla. In a separate bowl, mix together carob powder–water mixture, flour, and baking powder. Slowly mix dry ingredients in with the wet ingredients, and mix well with a rotary beater. Pour into two well-buttered pans, and bake for 25 minutes. Allow time to cool.

Spread one cup of sugar-free peanut butter on top of one of the cakes, and then place the other cake on top of it, so that the peanut butter is the middle layer between the two cakes.

To make the carob icing, mix together the carob powder, honey, and vanilla. Slowly add the milk while gently mixing to achieve "icing" consistency. Cover with plastic wrap and refrigerate.

SPECIAL NEEDS DOG RECIPES

In chapter 11 we discussed complementary treatments for dogs with special needs. This section provides you with recipes designed specifically for dogs with particular medical and emotional problems.

RECOVERY BROTH
Yields 6 cups

This recipe is for very sick animals who are not eating. The sick dog may be drinking water but not showing interest in food. Drinking this broth will provide him with nourishment. The potato peels are filled with minerals, the carrots with vitamins, and the chicken legs or wings with fat and protein. Breaking the bones allows the marrow to be exposed, and this part of the bone has a very special nutrition.

5 organic potatoes
2 organic carrots
6 cups water
3 chicken legs or wings
2 cloves garlic, crushed

Peel the potatoes and keep just the peels for this recipe (you can use the potatoes for another meal). Place the potato peels in a large pot. Dice the carrots, leaving the skin on, and add them to the pot. Break the chicken bones, leaving the skin intact, and add the legs or wings to the pot along with the garlic and water. Simmer for 1 hour, and then strain through a colander. Be sure to discard all chicken bones. Serve broth when cool. Refrigerate broth for up to one week.

The Basic Formula

⅓ lean protein: cooked or raw fish, chicken, turkey, very lean beef, cooked egg whites
⅓ low-starch vegetables and some fruits: e.g., string beans, broccoli, cauliflower, blueberries, apples
⅓ slow-cooked oatmeal or slow-cooked barley
olive oil
cinnamon, garlic, and parsley as healing herbs

Recipes for Diabetic Dogs

DIABETIC DIET #1

2 cups cooked chicken
2 cups cooked barley
1 cup cauliflower, diced
1 cup apples, diced
chicken broth
1 teaspoon powdered cinnamon
½ cup olive oil

Dice or shred chicken when cool. Steam diced cauliflower and apples with cinnamon in 2 inches of chicken broth. Do not discard broth when done; use it to moisten chicken mixture to a consistency that your dog likes. Mix chicken, cauliflower, and apples in with cooked barley. Add olive oil over and mix in. Toss and let cool before serving.

DIABETIC DIET # 2

2 cups cooked lean beef
2 tablespoons fresh parsley, chopped
2 cups broccoli, lightly steamed
2 cups barley
½ teaspoon turmeric
½ cup olive oil

Sauté beef cubes in some of the olive oil until done. Just before meat is done, add parsley and stir in quickly. Remove from heat. Cook barley and turmeric. Remove from heat and let cool. Steam broccoli lightly and coat with olive oil. Mix beef, barley, and broccoli together and serve.

DIABETIC DIET # 3

2 cups tilapia
3 cloves garlic, chopped
2 cups slow-cooked oatmeal
1 teaspoon cinnamon
1 cup blueberries
1 cup cooked string beans, cut into 1-inch pieces
½ cup olive oil

Sauté tilapia in olive oil until done; add chopped garlic at very end. Cook oatmeal with cinnamon. Lightly steam string beans. Mix all of these ingredients together, then stir in uncooked blueberries.

Recipes to Correct Diarrhea

Note: These recipes appear in other sections but are also collected here, as they are effective in treating dogs with diarrhea.

KUDZU (KUZU) ROOT RECIPE

1 heaping teaspoon kudzu
3 tablespoons cold water
1 cup cold water
2 cups cooked white rice, cooked with a chicken or beef bouillon cube
¾ cup diced cooked chicken pieces

Dissolve by mixing the kudzu in the 3 tablespoons cold water. Put the rest of the water (1 cup) in a saucepan. Add the dissolved kudzu to the water in the saucepan, and further mix and dissolve the kudzu. Bring to a boil over medium heat, reducing to low until the liquid looks translucent, and stirring constantly to avoid lumping. Mix liquid with 2 cups of cooked white rice, and add cooked diced chicken to mix. Cool and serve.

SWEET POTATOES AND EGGS

Yields about 5 cups

4 cups sweet potatoes (or yams)
½ cup cream
4 eggs, beaten
1 cup whole milk

Bake sweet potatoes until thoroughly cooked (usually about 60-90 minutes at 400 degrees. Dice the baked sweet potatoes, and place them in a blender with the remaining ingredients. Puree all ingredients in blender; you want a consistency similar to pancake batter. Add enough cream and milk to achieve this consistency.

Pour pureed mixture into a 13 x 9-inch pan. Bake at 350 degrees for 40 minutes.

Cool and serve. Refrigerate covered for up to five days.

YAMS AND CHICKEN
Yields 8 cups

4 skinned yams
3 cups boneless chicken
1 cup grated vegetables, any kind

Bake skinned yams until thoroughly cooked. Cut chicken into pieces and cook however you like (other than frying). Mash cooked yams and mix into cooked chicken pieces and grated vegetables.

Serve when cool. Refrigerate covered for up to three days.

YAMS AND GINGER
Yields 3–4 cups

2 yams
½ teaspoon grated fine ginger or ¼ teaspoon powdered ginger
1 tablespoon butter

Bake yams until thoroughly cooked. Mash yams with ginger, and add the butter to the warm mixture.

Serve when cool. Refrigerate for up to five days.

RICE AND EGG DROP SOUP
Yields 6 cups

2 cups basmati rice
6 cups water
3 eggs, beaten

Cook 2 cups basmati rice in 6 cups water for 75 minutes. The mixture that results should be a little soupy; if not, add more water.

Rapidly mix in the beaten eggs, and allow to cool to room temperature. The mixture should firm up as it cools. Serve when cool.

POTATO SALAD
Yields 3 cups

2 cups sliced potatoes
3 eggs, hard-boiled (shells optional)
½ cup mayonnaise

Boil sliced potatoes for 45 minutes. While waiting, boil eggs for about 20 minutes.

Mix the potatoes, eggs, and mayonnaise together in a casserole dish. You can leave the eggshells on if you choose.

Serve when cool. Refrigerate covered for up to five days.

Cooking for the Heart

HEART DIET
3 cups either boiled and diced white potatoes, boiled and diced sweet potatoes, cooked brown rice, or cooked basmati rice
1 cup either beef, chicken, or fish
4 tablespoons fresh chopped parsley
1 can of asparagus pieces, or 1 cup of chopped cooked asparagus
1 tablespoon dandelion greens, chopped (optional)
⅓ cup olive oil
2 cloves garlic

Set the cooked potatoes or rice aside to cool. Finely chop the garlic, and let sit for 10 minutes in open air. Place the olive oil in the skillet, and add the beef, chicken, or fish. Add the parsley and dandelion greens (if using them), and sauté together until done. Cook the asparagus and set aside to cool. If using cannned asparagus, retain the juice. Mix all ingredients together and serve.

Finicky Eater

If your dog does not like a recipe, review the flavoring. Finicky dogs, for instance, will often refuse dandelion in their food, so try the recipe without the dandelion and then, if you want, add just a little the next time around.

Cooking for Healthier Kidneys

BISCOTTI FOR KIDNEY PROBLEMS

1 16-ounce bag dried red kidney beans
4 large eggs
1 cup parsley, stems included, chopped
1 head garlic, peeled
4 cups whole wheat flour
1 cup good chicken broth (salt free and reduced to concentrate the flavor)

Soak the dried kidney beans overnight; rinse well and drain. Preheat oven to 350 degrees. In a food processor, chop the garlic. Add the eggs and beat. Add the chicken broth and soaked kidney beans, and process until well blended but not thoroughly pureed. Mix in the chopped parsley. Put this mixture into a large bowl, and stir in flour, a little at a time, until it's completely mixed in and smooth.

Divide the mixture into two equal portions. Shape each into a loaf about 12 inches long by 3 inches wide, making the sides and top even and smooth. Place the loaves next to one another on a parchment-lined cookie sheet. Make sure they are several inches apart and several inches away from the sides of the pan. Bake until the loaves are golden and the tops spring back when poked gently. This usually takes 30–40 minutes.

Remove the loaves from the baking sheet, and reduce the oven temperature to 300 degrees. Cool the loaves until slightly warm but still soft enough to cut into ½-inch biscuits. You will need a sharp knife for this.

Lay the biscuits on their sides on parchment-lined cookie sheets (in order to allow enough space around the cookies as they bake, you will need two cookie sheets). Bake for 40 minutes, and then flip them over and continue baking for another 30 minutes or until they are crisp. Keep checking them to make sure they are baking slowly and drying out in the baking process.

Cool completely. Store in a covered container for up to two weeks.

BASIC KIDNEY RECIPE

2 cups high-fat cottage cheese
2 eggs, raw or cooked (my dog prefers them raw)
3 pieces whole wheat, whole grain, or sprouted grain bread, or 1 cup oatmeal soaked in chicken broth
2 cups mixed vegetables (can use frozen mixed veggies)
½ cup chopped raw kidney (e.g., veal kidney)

Mix all ingredients together and serve.

KIDNEY RECIPE #1

1 cup lentils, cooked
1 large yam or sweet potato, cooked
1 cup cooked broccoli (stems can be used as well as flowers)
2 cloves garlic, chopped
1 cup basmati rice, cooked (white rice is better than brown rice for kidney problems)
2 teaspoons olive oil

Mix all ingredients together and serve.

KIDNEY RECIPE #2

2 large cooked yams
½ cup pineapple, chopped
1 small banana
1 teaspoon molasses
2 eggs, hard-boiled and chopped
1 teaspoon flaxseed oil

Mix all ingredients together and serve.

KIDNEY RECIPE # 3

2 cups well-cooked kidney beans
2 cups basmati rice, cooked
2 cloves garlic, finely diced
½ cup asparagus, cooked
1 teaspoon parsley, chopped
1 tablespoon olive oil
1 teaspoon flaxseed oil

Mix all ingredients together and serve.

KIDNEY RECIPE #4

½ cup parsnips, diced
1 cup high-fat cottage cheese
2 teaspoons parsley, chopped
2 cups pasta, cooked

Mix all ingredients together and serve.

KIDNEY RECIPE #5

½ cup chicken, cooked
1 cup kidney beans or lentils, cooked
3 cloves garlic
3 tablespoons olive oil
2 cups basmati rice or pasta, cooked
½ cup broccoli, asparagus, or parsnips, diced

Sauté garlic in olive oil; when almost done, quickly mix in the parsley. Combine garlic-parsley mixture with the rest of the ingredients and serve.

Cooking for Full-Figured Dogs

CHUBBY DOG CHOW

The following recommended daily diet should be accompanied by a superior multivitamin-multimineral supplement. A range of amounts is given, as portions should be adjusted for the size of the dog.

Morning meal:
¼ to 1 cup of oatmeal
1 teaspoon coconut oil, uncooked
½ to 1½ cups of vegetables (or as much as you need to satisfy your dog)

Evening meal:
¼ to ½ cup of low-fat cottage cheese, ricotta cheese, or farmer's cheese;
   or ½ to 2 eggs; or ¼ to ¾ cup lean meat or poultry
¼ to 1½ cup of high-fiber bran breakfast cereal
vegetables, as many as your dog wants
1 teaspoon coconut oil, uncooked

Snacks can be:
• piece of apple
• piece of banana
• piece of sliced, toasted, whole wheat bread
• carrots, sliced, brushed with olive oil, and baked

Cooking to Calm and Soothe

CALMING DIET

Turkey is high in L-tryptophan, while barley soothes the nerves, as does the chamomile.

2 cups turkey, cooked
2 cups barley, cooked with 3 eggshells
2 teaspoons chamomile flowers, made into a tea with ½ cup water; or
   ½ cup of strong chamomile tea made with a tea bag
2 teaspoons parsley
2 cups carrots, cooked
⅓ cup olive oil

Mix all ingredients together and serve.

Acknowledgments

This book, from its original conception to its final form, was in the making for many years. It was given its present form after I moved to New Zealand, for I finally had time away from my busy practice and made it my first priority to finish the book. More important, this book was created as a gift to all of the wonderful people who brought their pets to me for so many years. Many people and many dogs and cats were so dear to me, and leaving all of them was one of the most difficult things I have ever done. I created this book for them. (No, I haven't forgotten the cats! That's next.) I also created an easy way for my clients to reach me in New Zealand, whether by e-mail or a U.S. toll-free number.

Most important, I thank my family for helping to make *Natural Dog* a reality. My husband, Monte, beamed love and support to me the entire time, and believe-you-me, one tends to wave people away repeatedly while writing so he deserves some real recognition. My two sons, Ethan and Damien, helped me with photography and proofreading. I would also like to acknowledge my deceased mother and father, who encouraged me to follow my dreams.

I am indebted as well to another family of mine: my associates and staff at the Animal Healing Center, a place that was a substantial part of my life for so many years. I would like to thank Dr. Sharon Marx, Tina, Toby, and so many others who supported my work and helped me to fine-tune these holistic modalities to perfection.

Yet more friends contributed mightily: Rosemary Rennicke, who gave me invaluable advice. Nina, Jerry, Dillian, Justie, and Spencer, who are a true extended family. One of my closest friends, a homeopathic MD, Dr. Lucy Nitskansky, meticulously reviewed sections with detailed feedback.

Of course, I am grateful to all those at Kennel Club Books and at BowTie Press who shepherded this project through the publishing process, including Andrew DePrisco, Jarelle Stein, and Amy Deputato—who was busy working on the editing and design almost right up to the moment she went into labor. A warm thanks to Kathy Hall, who introduced me to Andrew and BowTie Press.

Finally, I must thank my canine and feline patients and their people. People who requested, in cases in which there seemed to be no light at the end of the tunnel, that I try. With this came new successes and the development of better treatment modalities. Joyful successes that would benefit so many other pets destined to come my way. It was and still is exhilarating to create real health. I love being a veterinarian, and the heady bonus of seeing my patients thrive makes it that much better.

Associations and Organizations

Academy of Veterinary Homeopathy
PO Box 9280
Wilmington, DE 19809
(866) 652-1590
www.theavh.org

The American Botanical Council
PO Box 144345
Austin, TX 78714-4345
(800) 373-7105
www.herbalgram.com

American Holistic Veterinary Medical Association
2218 Old Emmorton Road
Bel Air, MD 21015
(410) 569-0795
www.ahvma.org

American Veterinary Chiropractic Association
442154 East 140 Road
Bluejacket, OK 74333
(918) 784-2231
www.animalchiropractic.org

Born Free USA united with Animal Protection Institute of America
PO Box 22505
Sacramento, CA 95822
(916) 447-3085
www.bornfreeusa.org

British Homeopathic Association
Hahnemann House
29 Park Street West, Luton, LU1 3BE
(+) 0870 444 3950
www.trusthomeopathy.org

The British Institute of Veterinary Homeopathy
580 Zion Road
Egg Harbor Township, NJ 08234
(609) 927-5660
www.bihusa.com

The Herb Research Foundation
4140 15th Street
Boulder, CO 80304
(303) 449-2265
www.herbs.org

International Veterinary Acupuncture Society
2625 Redwing Road
Suite 160
Fort Collins, CO 80526
(970) 266-0666
www.ivas.org

National Center for Homeopathy
801 North Fairfax Street
Suite 306
Alexandria, VA 22314
(703) 548-7790
http://nationalcenterforhomeopathy.org

Recommended Reading

CHAPTER 1

Boone, J. Allen. *Kinship with All Life: Simple, Challenging, Real-Life Experiences Showing How Animals Communicate with Each Other and with the People Who Understand Them.* San Francisco: HarperOne, 1976.

Clothier, Suzanne. *If Bones Would Rain from the Sky: Deepening Our Relationship with Dogs.* New York: Warner Books, 2002.

Curtis, Anita. *Animal Wisdom: Communications with Animals.* Animal Communications, 1996.

Fitzpatrick, Sonya, with Patricia Burkhart Smith. *What the Animals Tell Me: Developing Your Innate Telepathic Skills to Understand and Communicate with Animals.* New York: Hyperion, 1998.

Hartmann, Thom. *The Last Hours of Ancient Sunlight: Waking Up to Personal and Global Transformation.* Northfield, VT: Mythical Books, 1998.

McElroy, Susan Chernak. *Animals as Teachers and Healers.* New York: Ballantine Books, 1997.

Myers, Arthur. *Communicating with Animals: The Spiritual Connection between People and Animals.* Chicago: Contemporary Books, 1997.

Smith, Penelope. *Animal Talk: Interspecies Telepathic Communication.* Tulsa, OK: Council Oak Books, 2004.

Smith, Penelope. *Animals: Our Return to Wholeness.* Point Reyes Station, CA: Pegasus Publications, 1993.

CHAPTER 2

Animal Protection Institute of America. "Investigative Report on Pet Food," May 2007. (The Animal Protection Institute of America has since merged with Born Free USA. This paper can be found at www.bornfreeusa.org.)

Martin, Ann N. *Food Pets Die For.* Troutdale, OR: New Sage Press, 2008.

Subcommittee on Dog Nutrition. *Nutrient Requirements of Dogs.* Washington, DC: National Academies Press, 1985.

Rowe, John D. *Animal Nutrition.* Keene, KY: Setter Publications, 2007.

CHAPTER 3

Fahey, William J., and Peter R. Rothschild, MD, PhD. *Free Radicals, Stress and Antioxidant Enzymes: A Guide to Cellular Health.* Honolulu: University Labs Press, 1991.

CHAPTER 4

Anson, Suzan. *Bone Appetit! Gourmet Cooking for Your Dog.* Chicago: New Chapter Press, 1999.

Boyle, Carol. *Natural Food Recipes for Healthy Dogs.* New York: Howell Book House, 1997.

Cusick, William D. *Canine Nutrition: Choosing the Best Food for Your Breed.* Irvine, CA: Doral Publishing, 1997.

Dorosz, Edmund R. *Let's Cook for Our Dog.* Alberta: Our Pet's, Inc., 1993.

Laybourn, Carole. *The Original Gourmet Doggie Treat Cook Book.* Paws Publishing, 1995.

McKinnon, Helen L. *It's for the Animals! Natural Care & Resources.* Fairview, NC: Self-published, 1998.

Messonnier, Shawn. *Natural Supplements for Dogs: Alternative Ways to Promote Health In Your Pet.* Lincolnwood, IL: Keats Publishing, 1998.

Peden, James A. *Vegetarian Cats and Dogs.* Troy, MT: Harbingers of a New Age, 1995.

Schultze, Kymythy R. *Natural Nutrition for Dogs and Cats: The Ultimate Diet.* Carlsbad, CA: Hay House, 1998.

Weigle, Jaroslav. *A Little Recipe Book for Dogs: Sound Nutrition and Good Homecooking for Your Pet.* New York: Ballantine Books, 1997.

CHAPTER 5

Anderson, Nina, Howard Peiper, and Alicia McWatters, M.S. *Super-Nutrition for Animals! (Birds Too!) Healthy Advice for Dogs, Cats, Horses, and Birds.* Sheffield, MA: Safe Goods, 1996.

Billinghurst, Ian, V.V.Sc (Hons), .Sc.Agr., Dip.Ed. *Give Your Dog a Bone: The Practical Commonsense Way to Feed Dogs for A Healthy Life.* Bathurst, Australia: Self-published, 1993.

Billinghurst, Ian, V.V.Sc (Hons), B.Sc.Agr., Dip.Ed. *Grow Your Pups with Bones: The BARF Program for Breeding Healthy Dogs and Eliminating Skeletal Disease.* Bathurst, Australia: Self-published, 1993.

Goldstein, Martin, DVM. *The Nature of Animal Healing.* New York: Ballantine, 2000.

Kaufmann, Klaus, D.Sc., and Annelies Schneck. *Making Sauerkraut and Pickled Vegetables at Home: Creative Recipes for Lactic-Fermented Food to Improve Your Health.* Burnaby, BC: Alive Books, 2002.

Volhard, Wendy, and Kerry Brown. *Holistic Guide for a Healthy Dog.* New York: Howell Book House, 2000.

Weigle, Jaroslav. *A Little Recipe Book for Dogs: Sound Nutrition and Good Homecooking for Your Pet.* New York: Ballantine Books, 1997.

CHAPTER 6

Anderson, Nina, Howard Peiper, and Alicia McWatters, MS. *Super-Nutrition for Animals!(Birds Too!) Healthy Advice for Dogs, Cats, Horses, and Birds.* Sheffield, MA: Safe Goods, 1996.

Foster, Steven, and James A. Duke. *Peterson Field Guides: Eastern/Central Medicinal Plants.* Boston: Houghton Mifflin, 1990.

Gladstar, Rosemary. *Herbal Healing for Women.* New York: Fireside, 1993.

Keville, Kathi. *The Illustrated Herb Encyclopedia.* New York: Bdd Promotional Book Company, 1991.

Levy, Juliette de Baïracli. *The Complete Herbal Handbook for the Dog and Cat.* London: Faber and Faber, 1992.

Lust, John. *The Herb Book: The Complete and Authoritative Guide to More than 500 Herbs.* New York: Bantam Books, 1979.

Moore, Michael. *Medicinal Plants of the Pacific West.* Santa Fe, NM: Red Crane Books, 1993.

Mowrey, Daniel B., PhD. *Herbal Tonic Therapies.* New Canaan, CT: Keats Publishing, 1993.

Mowrey, Daniel B., PhD. *The Scientific Validation of Herbal Medicine.* Lincolnwood, IL: Keats Publishing, 1986.

Reader's Digest. *Magic and Medicine of Plants.* Pleasantville, NY: Reader's Digest, 1990.

Schwartz, Cheryl. *Four Paws, Five Directions: A Guide to Chinese Medicine for Cats and Dogs.* Berkeley, CA: Celestial Arts Publishing, 1996.

Theiss, Barbara, and Peter Theiss. *The Family Herbal.* Rochester, VT: Healing Arts Press, 1992.

Tierra, Michael. The *Way of Herbs.* New York: Pocket Books, 1998.

Treben, Maria. *Health through God's Pharmacy.* Champaign, IL: Balogh Scientific Books, 1994.

Weiss, Rudolph Fritz, and Volker Fintelmann. *Herbal Medicine.* New York: Thieme Publishers, 2000.

CHAPTER 8

Bach, Edward, MD, and F. J. Wheeler, MD. *Bach Flower Remedies.* New York: McGraw-Hill, 1998.

Biddis, K.J. *Homeopathy in Veterinary Practice.* London: Random House, 1987.

Cummings, Stephen, and Dana Ullman. *Everybody's Guide to Homeopathic Medicines.* New York: Jeremy P. Tarcher/Penguin, 2004.

Day, Christopher, MA, VetMB, VetFFHom, MRCVS. *The Homeopathic Treatment of Small Animals: Principles and Practice.* London: Random House, 2005.

Dooley, Timothy R. *Homeopathy: beyond Flat Earth Medicine.* San Diego: Timing Publications, 2002.

Fox, Michael, MRCVS. *The Healing Touch: The Proven Massage Program for Dogs and Cats.* New York: Newmarket Press, 1990.

Goldstein, Martin, DVM. *The Nature of Animal Healing.* New York: Ballantine, 2000.

Graham, Helen, and Gregory Vlamis. *Bach Flower Remedies for Animals.* Forres, Scotland: Findhorn Press, 1999.

Grainger, Janette. *Natural Insect Repellents for Pets, People, and Plants.* Austin, TX: Herb Bar, 1991.

Grosjean, Nelly. *Veterinary Aromatherapy.* Saffron Walden, England: C.W. Daniel Company, 2004.

Hunter, Francis. *Homoeopathic First-Aid Treatment for Pets.* London: Thorsons Publishers, 1984.

Kaslof, Leslie J. *The Traditional Flower Remedies of Dr. Edward Bach: A Self-Help Guide.* New Canaan, CT: Keats Publishing, 1988.

Klide, Alan M., and Shiu H. Kung. *Veterinary Acupuncture.* Philadelphia: University of Pennsylvania Press, 2002.

Kowalchick, Clare, and William H. Hylton, eds. *Rodale's Illustrated Encyclopedia of Herbs.* Emmaus, PA: Rodale, 1998.

Levy, Juliette de Baïracli. *The Complete Herbal Handbook for the Dog and Cat.* London: Faber and Faber, 1992.

Levy, Juliette de Baïracli. *Herbal Handbook for Farm and Stable.* London: Faber and Faber, 1991.

Lust, John. *The Herb Book: The Complete and Authoritative Guide to More than 500 Herbs.* New York: Bantam Books, 1979.

MacLeod, George, MRCVS, DVSM. *Dogs: Homeopathic Remedies.* London: Random House UK, 2005.

MacLeod, George, MRCVS, DVSM, VetFFHom. *A Veterinary Materia Medica and Clinical Repertory: With a Materia Medica of the Nosodes.* London: Random House UK, 2004.

McKay, Pat. *Natural Immunity: Why You Should Not Vaccinate.* Pasadena: Oscar Publications, 1997.

McTaggart, Lynne. *The Field: The Quest for the Secret Force of the Universe.* New York: HarperCollins, 2008.

Ogden, Donald I., DVM. *Natural Hygienic Care of Pets.* East Sussex, England: Society of Metaphysicians, 1986.

Palika, Liz. *Consumer's Guide to Dog Food: What's in Dog Food, Why It's There, and How to Choose the Best Food for Your Dog.* New York: Howell Book House, 1996.

Puotinen, C. J. *The Encyclopedia of Natural Pet Care.* Lincolnwood, IL: Keats Publishing, 2000.

Raymonde-Hawkins, M., and George Macleod. *The Raystede Handbook of Homoeopathic Remedies for Animals.* Saffron Walden, England: C.W. Daniel Company, 1985.

Scheffer, Mechthild. *Bach Flower Therapy: Theory and Practice.* Rochester, VT: Healing Arts Press, 1986.

Schoen, Allen M., and Susan Wynn. *Complementary and Alternative Veterinary Medicine: Principles and Practice.* St. Louis: Mosby, 1998.

Schoen, Allen, DVM. *Love, Miracles, and Animal Healing.* New York: Simon and Schuster, 1995.

Schoen, Allen M. *Veterinary Acupuncture: Ancient Art to Modern Medicine*. St. Louis: Mosby, 2001.

Schwartz, Cheryl. *Four Paws, Five Directions: A Guide to Chinese Medicine for Cats and Dogs*. Berkeley: Celestial Arts Publishing, 1996.

Scott, Martin J., and Gael Mariani. *Bach Flower Remedies for Dogs*. Forres, Scotland: Findhorn Press, 1999.

Snow, Amy, and Nancy Zidonis. *The Well-Connected Dog: A Guide to Canine Acupressure*. Larkspur, CO: Tallgrass Publishers, 1999.

Stein, Diane. *Natural Healing for Dogs and Cats*. Santa Cruz, CA: Crossing Press, 1993.

Stein, Petra. *Natural Health Care for Your Dog: Self-Help Using Homeopathy and Bach Flowers*. Hauppauge, NY: Barron's Educational Series, 1997.

Tellington-Jones, Linda, and Sybil Taylor. *The Tellington T Touch: A Revolutionary Natural Method to Train and Care for Your Favorite Animal*. New York: Penguin, 1993.

Tilford, Gregory L., and Mary L. Wulff. *Herbs for Pets: The Natural Way to Enhance Your Pet's Life*. Irvine, CA: BowTie Press, 2009.

Vithoulkas, George. *Homeopathy—Medicine of the New Man*. New York: Simon and Schuster, 1992.

Volhard, Wendy, and Kerry Brown, DVM. *Holistic Guide for a Healthy Dog*. New York: Howell Book House, 2000.

Winter, William G., DVM. *The Holistic Veterinary Handbook: Safe, Effective Treatment Plans for the Companion Animal Practitioner*. Lakeville, MN: Galde Press, 1997.

Yarnall, Celeste. *Natural Dog Care: A Complete Guide to Holistic Health Care for Dogs*. New York: Castle Book, 2000.

CHAPTER 9

Bach, Edward, MD, and F.J. Wheeler, MD. *Bach Flower Remedies*. New York: McGraw-Hill, 1998.

Council on Biologic and Therapeutic Agents, "Vaccination Principles (Oversight: COBTA; Approved by the AVMA Executive Board April 2001; revised April 2007)." American Veterinary Medical Association, http://www.avma.org/issues/vaccination/vaccination.asp (accessed January 3, 2009).

Cummings, Stephen, and Dana Ullman. *Everybody's Guide to Homeopathic Medicines*. New York: Jeremy P. Tarcher/Penguin, 2004.

Fishman, B., and J. Scarnell. "Persistence of Protection against Infectious Canine Hepatitis Virus." *Vet. Rec.* 99 (1976): 509.

Goldstein, Martin, DVM. *The Nature of Animal Healing*. New York: Ballantine, 2000.

Gorham, J.R. "Duration of Vaccination Immunity and the Influence on Subsequent Prophylaxis." *JAVMA* 149 (1966): 699-704.

Graham, Helen, and Gregory Vlamis. *Bach Flower Remedies for Animals*. Forres, Scotland: Findhorn Press, 1999.

HogenEsch, Harm, DVM, et al. "Effect of Vaccination on Serum Concentrations of Total and Antigen-specific Immunoglobulin E in Dogs."*AJVR* 63 (4) (2002): 611-616.

Janssens, Luc. *Acupuncture Points and Meridians in the Dog*. Fort Collins, CO: International Veterinary Acupuncture Society, 1984.

Levy, Juliette de Baïracli. *The Complete Herbal Handbook for the Dog and Cat*. London: Faber and Faber, 1992.

MacLeod, George, MRCVS, DVSM. *Dogs: Homeopathic Remedies*. London: Random House UK, 2005.

Messonnier, Shawn P. *Vaccination: What You Must Know before You Vaccinate Your Dog (The Best of Care for Your Best of Friends)*. Lincolnwood, IL: Keats Publishing, 1999.

Nambudripad, Devi S., MD, DC, LAc, PhD. *Say Goodbye to Illness: Nambudpriad's Allergy Elimination Techniques (NAET)*. Buena Park, CA: Delta Publishers, 2002.

Nambudpriad's Allergy Elimination Techniques, www.naet.com.

Palika, Liz. *Consumer's Guide to Dog Food: What's in Dog Food, Why It's There, and How to Choose the Best Food for Your Dog*. New York: Howell Book House, 1996.

Paul, Michael. "Report of the American Animal Hospital Association Canine Vaccine Task Force: 2003 Canine Vaccine Guidelines, Recommendations, and Supporting Literature. *JAAHA* 39 (March 2003): 119–131.

Plechner, Alfred J., DVM, and Martin Zucker. *Pet Allergies: Remedies for an Epidemic*. Inglewood, CA: Very Healthy Enterprises, 1985.

Puotinen, C. J. *The Encyclopedia of Natural Pet Care*. Lincolnwood, IL: Keats Publishing, 2000.

Scheffer, Mechthild. *Bach Flower Therapy: Theory and Practice*. Rochester, VT: Healing Arts Press, 1986.

Schoen, Allen M., D.M.V., and Susan Wynn, D.M.V. *Complementary and Alternative Veterinary Medicine: Principles and Practice*. St. Louis: Mosby, 1998.

Schultz, Ronald D. "Current and Future Canine and Feline Vaccination Programs," *VetMed* 93 (March 1998): 233-254.

Schultz, Ronald D. *Duration of Immunity to Canine Vaccines: What We Know and What We Don't Know, Proceedings. Canine Infectious Diseases: From Clinics to Molecular Pathogenesis*. Ithaca, NY: Elsevier, 1999.

Scott, Martin J., and Gael Mariani. *Bach Flower Remedies for Dogs*. Forres, Scotland: Findhorn Press, 1999.

Smith, C. A. "Current Concepts— Are We Vaccinating Too Much?" *JAVMA* 207(4) (1995): 421-425.

Stefanatos, Joanne, DVM. *Bioenergetic Medicine: Homeopathy and Acupuncture for Animals*. Bel Air, MD: American Holistic Veterinary Medical Association, 1990.

Ullman, Dana, M.P.H. *Discovering Homeopathy: Medicine for the Twenty-First Century*. Berkeley: North Atlantic Books, 1991.

CHAPTER 10
Goldstein, Martin, DVM. *The Nature of Animal Healing*. New York: Ballantine, 2000.

CHAPTER 12
Severino, Elizabeth. *The Animals' Viewpoint on Dying, Death, and Euthanasia*. Turnersville, NJ: The Healing Connection, 2002.

Recommended Products

Foods

DRY DOG FOODS

Addiction Foods
www.addictionfoods.com
Wild Kangaroo and Apples Formula

Artemis Pet Foods
www.artemiscompany.com
Power Formula

Azmira Holistic Animal Care
www.azmira.com
Classic Dog Formula

Back to Basics
Beowulf Natural Foods
www.beowulfs.com
Chicken Formula

**Bench and Field
Holistic Natural Canine**
www.benchandfield.com
Holistic Natural Canine Formula

Blue Buffalo
www.bluebuff.com
Chicken Formula

Burns Pet Health
www.burnspethealth.com
Brown Rice and Ocean Fish Formula

By Nature BrightLife
By Nature Pet Food
www.bynaturepetfoods.com
Bright Life Canine Formula

By Nature Organics
By Nature Pet Food
www.bynaturepetfoods.com
Chicken Formula

California Natural
Natura Pet Products
www.naturapet.com
Chicken Meal and Rice Formula

Canidae
www.canidae.com
Grain-Free All Life Stages Formula

Canine Caviar
www.caninecaviar.com
Lamb and Pearl Millet Formula

**Chicken Soup for the
Pet Lover's Soul**
Diamond Pet Products
www.chickensoupforthepetloverssoul.com
Adult Dog Formula

Cloud Star Kibble
www.cloudstar.com
Holistic Baked Kibble Formula

Drs. Foster and Smith
www.drsfostersmith.com
Lamb and Brown Rice Formula

Eagle Pack Holistic Select
Eagle Pack Pet Foods
www.eaglepack.com
*Anchovy, Sardine, and Salmon Meal
Formula*

**Evanger's Dog and
Cat Food Company**
www.evangersdogfood.com
Pheasant and Brown Rice Formula

EVO
Natura Pet Products
www.naturapet.com

Evolve
Triumph Pet Industries
www.evolvepet.com
Maintenance Formula

Firstmate Dog Food
www.firstmate.com
Ultra Premium Naturally Holistic Formula

Fromm Four Star Nutritionals
www.frommfamily.com
Chicken à la Veg Formula

Go! Natural
Petcurean Pet Nutrition
www.petcurean.com
*Chicken, Fruit, and Vegetable
Formula*

Hund-N-Flocken
Solid Gold Health Products
www.solidgoldhealth.com

Innova
Natura Pet Products
www.naturapet.com

Karma Organic
Natura Pet Products
www.naturapet.com

Lick Your Chops
Healthy Pet Foods, Inc.
www.healthypetfoodsinc.com
Adult Maintenance Formula

Life4K9 Pet Food Corporation
www.life4k9.com
Chicken and Barley Formula

Lifespan
PetGuard
www.*petguard.com*

Merrick Pet Care
www.merrickpetcare.com
Cowboy Cookout Formula

MMillennia
Solid Gold Health Products
www.solidgoldhealth.com

Natural Balance Organic
Dick Van Patten's
Natural Balance Pet Foods
www.naturalbalanceinc.com

Natural Balance Ultra Premium
Dick Van Patten's
Natural Balance Pet Foods
www.naturalbalanceinc.com

Newman's Own Organics
www.newmansownorganics.com

NutriSource
KLN Enterprises
www.nutrisourcedogfood.com
Adult Formula

**Organix Castor
and Pollux Pet Works**
www.castorpolluxpet.com
Organix Canine Formula

PetGuard
www.petguard.com
Organic Vegetarian Formula

Performatrin Ultra
www.performatrinultra.com
Chicken and Brown Rice Formula

PHD Viand
PHD Products
www.phdproducts.com
*Canine Growth and Maintenance
Viand Formula*

Pinnacle
Breeder's Choice Pet Foods
www.breeders-choice.com
Holistic Trout and Sweet Potato Formula

Prairie
Nature's Variety
www.naturesvariety.com
*New Zealand Venison Meal
and Millet Formula*

Premium Edge
www.premiumedgepetfood.com
Chicken, Rice, and Vegetable Formula

Prime Life Plus
Owen and Mandeville Pet Products
(203) 262-8003

Raw Instinct
Nature's Variety
www.naturesvariety.com

Royal Canin Veterinary Diet
Royal Canin
www.royalcanin.us
Potato and Rabbit Formula

Show Bound Naturals
Healthy Pet Foods, Inc.
www.healthypetfoodsinc.com
Chicken and Brown Rice Formula

Timberwolf Organics
www.timberwolforganics.com
Lamb and Barley with Apples Formula

Ultra Holistic Nutrition
Nutro Products, Inc.
www.ultraholistic.com
Ultra Adult Dry Kibble

VéRUS
www.veruspetfoods.com
Advanced Opticoat Diet

Wellness
Old Mother Hubbard
Super 5 Mix Complete Health
www.wellnesspetfood.com
*Whitefish and Sweet Potato
Formula*

**Wellness Simple Food
Solutions**
Old Mother Hubbard
www.wellnesspetfood.com
Rice and Venison Formula

Wenaewe
www.wenaewe.com.uy
*Puppy to Senior Organic
Formula*

Wysong
www.wysong.net
Anergen Formula

Zinpro
Lincoln Biotech
www.lincolnbiotech.com
Skin and Coat Formula

WET DOG FOODS
Addiction Foods
www.addictionfoods.com
Venison and Apples Entrée

**Advanced Pet Diets Select
Choice**
Breeder's Choice Pet Foods
www.breeders-choice.com
*Chicken and Rice Skin and Coat
Formula*

Artemis Pet Foods
www.artemiscomapny.com
Beef Formula

Avo Derm
Breeder's Choice Pet Foods
www.breeders-choice.com
Original Formula

Azmira Holistic Animal Care
www.azmira.com
Beef and Chicken Formula

Blue Homestyle Recipes
The Blue Buffalo Company
www.bluebuff.com
Chicken Dinner

By Nature Organics
www.bynaturepetfoods.com
Organic Turkey, Sweet Potato, and Peas

California Natural
Natura Pet Products
www.naturapet.com
Salmon and Sweet Potato

Canidae
www.canidae.com
*All Life Stages Formula
Chicken, Lamb, and Fish Meal*

**Chicken Soup for
the Pet Lover's Soul**
Diamond Pet Foods
www.chickensoupforthepetlovers
soul.com
Adult Dog Formula

Drs. Foster and Smith
www.drsfostersmith.com
Lamb and Brown Rice Adult Dog Food

Eagle Pack Holistic Select
Eagle Pack Pet Foods
www.eaglepack.com
Chicken Formula (with Oat Bran)

Entrée for Dogs
Three Dog Bakery
www.threedog.com
Chicken, Broccoli, Carrots, and Rice

**Evanger's Dog and Cat
Food Company**
www.evangersdogfood.com
Duck and Sweet Potato Dinner

EVO
Natura Pet Products
www.naturapet.com
EVO 95% Beef

Evolve
Triumph Pet
Industries Inc.
www.evolvepet.com
Turkey

**Fromm Four
Star Nutritionals**
www.frommfamily.com
Beef Entrée

Innova
Natura Pet Products
www.naturapet.com
Adult

Lamaderm
Natural Life Pet Products
www.nlpp.com

Lick Your Chops
Healthy Pet Foods, Inc.
www.healthypetfoodsinc.com
Adult Canned Dog Maintenance

Merrick Pet Care
www.merrickpetcare.com
Thanksgiving Day Dinner

Natural Balance Ultra-Premium
Dick Van Patten's
Natural Balance Pet Foods
www.naturalbalanceinc.com
Beef Formula

**Natural Balance Eatables for
Dogs**
Dick Van Patten's
Natural Balance Pet Foods
www.naturalbalanceinc.com
Irish Stew

Natural Life
Natural Life Pet Products
www.nlpp.com
Adult Complete

Newman's Own Organics
www.newmansownorganics.com
Chicken Formula

Nutro Natural Choice
Nutro Products Inc.
www.nutroproducts.com
*Chicken, Rice, and Oatmeal
Formula*

Organix
Castor and Pollux Pet Works
www.castorpolluxpet.com
Original Formula

Performatrin Ultra
www.performatrinultra.com
Chicken and Wild Rice Stew

PetGuard
www.petguard.com
*Organic Chicken and Vegetable
Entrée*

Pet Promise
www.petpromiseinc.com
Chicken and Brown Rice Formula

Pinnacle
Breeder's Choice Pet Foods
www.breeders-choice.com
Holistic Trout and Sweet Potato

Prairie
Nature's Variety
www.naturesvariety.com
Beef Stew

Precise Pet Products
www.precisepet.com
Adult Formula

Showbound Naturals
Healthy Pet Foods, Inc.
www.healthypetfoodsinc.com
Chicken Cuts in Broth

**Solid Gold Health Products
for Pets**
www.solidgoldhealth.com
Turkey and Ocean Fish

Spot's Stew
Halo, Purely for Pets
www.halopets.com

**Triumph Pet
Industries, Inc.**
www.triumphpet.com
Chicken, Rice, and Vegetable

VéRUS Pet Foods, Inc.
www.veruspetfoods.com
Chicken and Rice Formula

Wellness
Old Mother Hubbard
www.wellnesspetfood.com
Chicken and Sweet Potato Formula

COMMERCIAL RAW DIETS

A Place for Paws
www.aplaceforpaws.com

Aunt Jeni's Home Made
www.auntjeni.com

Bravo!
www.bravorawdiet.com

Canine Carnivore Raw Diet
www.canine-carnivore.com

Evanger's Game Meats
www.evangersdogfood.com

EVO
Natura
www.naturapet.com

Halshan Premium Raw Food
www.halshan.com

HomeMade4Life
www.pets4life.com
Manufactured in the United States
by Aunt Jeni's Home Made
www.auntjeni.com
Manufactured in Canada
by Pets 4 Life
www.pets4life.com

The Honest Kitchen
www.thehonestkitchen.com

Nature's Variety
www.naturesvariety.com

Oma's Pride
www.omaspride.com

Pet Orlando (Pat McKay)
www.petorlando.com

Purely Primitives
Teddy's Freezer
(888) 500-9589

Steve's Real Food for Dogs
www.stevesrealfood.com

Urban Wolf
www.urbanwolf.cc

COOKIE-TYPE TREATS

Bellyrubs Dog Treats
Meyer Country Farms
www.meyercountryfarms.com

Buddy Biscuits
Cloud Star Corporation
www.cloudstar.com

Charlee Bear Dog Treats
www.charleebear.com

Doggie Divines
Brunzi's Best Inc.
(845) 734-4490

Dudley's Do Right Training Treats
Bark Stix
www.barkstix.com

Grandma Lucy's Dog Treats
www.grandmalucys.com

Healthy Dog Bakery Treats
The Hand That Feeds You
www.healthydogbakery.com

Heidi's Homemade Dog Treats
www.heidisbakery.com

Henry and Sons' Vegetarian Dog Cookies
www.henryandsons.com

Howlin' Gourmet
Dancing Paws Bekery
www.dancingpaws.com

Latka's Treats
www.de-licioustreats.com

Lick'n Crunch Cookies
Three Dog Bakery
www.threedog.com

Liver Biscotti
Premier Pet Products
www.liverbiscotti.com

Mother Nature Natural Dog Biscuits
Natura Pet Products
www.naturapet.com

NatureNosh
www.nature-nosh.com

Newman's Own Premium Dog Treats
www.newmansownorganics.com

Old Mother Hubbard Dog Biscuits
www.oldmotherhubbard.com

Simon and Huey's Doggoned Tasty Treats
(888) 757-9663

Smooches For Pooches
The Honest Kitchen
www.thehonestkitchen.com

Sojos Good Dog Treats
Sojourner Farms
www.sojos.com

Toy Temptations
Dogchewz NYC
www.dogchewz.com

Wagatha's Dog Biscuits
www.wagathas.com

Waggers Original Dog Treats
www.waggers.com

Wellness Wellbars
Old Mother Hubbard, Inc.
www.wellnesspetfood.com

Wet Noses Herbal Dog Treats
www.wet-noses.com

MEAT-BASED OR JERKY-STYLE TREATS
Dogswell Dog Treats
www.dogswell.com

Dr. Becker's Bites
www.drbeckersbites.com

Dr-Chew Sweet Potato Treats
Landy Corporation
www.dr-chew.com

Etta Says! Liver Treats
www.ettasays.com

Liv-a-Littles
Halo, Purely for Pets
www.halopets.com

Nothing But . . . Treats
A Place for Paws
www.aplaceforpaws.com

Real Food Toppers
Complete Natural Nutrition
www.realfoodtoppers.com

Rosie's Rewards
Rosebud, Inc.
www.rosiesrewards.com

Waggers Champion Chips
www.waggers.com

Wellness Pure Rewards and Wellness Wellbites
Old Mother Hubbard, Inc.
www.wellnesspetfood.com

Whole Life Pet Treats
www.wholelifepet.com

ZiwiPeak Good Dog Treats
www.ziwipeak.com

Zuke's Natural Treats for Dogs
www.zukes.com

HERBS AND VITAMINS
Ambrican Enterprises, Limited
(541) 899-2080

Animals Apawthecary
(406) 961-8600

Avena Botanicals
www.avenabotanicals.com

Blessed Herbs
www.blessedherbs.com

California School of Herbal Studies
www.cshs.com

Deserving Pets
1-877-31-VITAL (318-4825)
www.deservingpets.com

East Earth Trade Winds
www.snowcrest.net/eetw

East Park Research, Inc.
www.eastparkresearch.net

Flora Inc.
www.florahealth.com

Frontier Cooperative Herbs
www.frontiercoop.com

Green Terrestrial
(802) 375-8087

Herb Pharm
www.herb-pharm.com

Island Herbs (Ryan Drum)
www.ryandrum.com

Mountain Rose Herbs
www.mountainroseherbs.com

Native Essence Herb Company
www.herbmed.com

Nutrimoor Company Inc.
212-6985-MOOR

Omega Nutrition
www.omeganutrition.com

Polysaccharide-polypeptide (PSP) and fucoidan
Charles Tom Schenck, DVM
(877) 835-5454

Prozyme
www.prozymeproducts.com

Richters Herb Specialists
www.richters.com.

Sage Mountain
www.sagemountain.com

Starwest Botanicals
www.starwest-botanicals.com

Swissette Herb Farm
(845) 496-7841

Tasha's Herbs
(800) 315-0142

The Vitamin Shoppe
www.vitaminshoppe.com

Timberwolf Salmon Oil
www.timberwolforganics.com

TransPacific Health Products
www.transpacificherbalproducts.com

Willner Chemists
www.willner.com

Young Living Essential Oils
www.youngliving.us

CALCIUM SOURCES
Animal Essentials Natural Calcium
www.animalessentials.com

NOW Bone Meal Powder
www.nowfoods.com

Solid Gold Steamed Bone Meal
www.solidgoldhealth.com

Solgar Bone Meal Powder
www.solgar.com

Wysong's Call of the Wild
www.wysong.net

HOMEOPATHIC AND FLOWER REMEDIES
Anaflora: Flower Essences for Animals
www.anaflora.com

Ayush Herbs, Inc.
www.ayush.com

Boericke and Tafel, Inc.
(800) 876-9505

Boiron Group
www.boiron.com

Deserving Pets
(877) 318-4825
www.deservingpets.com

Dolisos America, Inc.
(702) 871-7153

Ellon (Bach U.S.A.)
(800) 433-7523

Flower Essence Services
http://us.fesflowers.com

Homeopathy Overnight
www.homeopathyovernight.com

Minimum Price Homeopathic Books
www.minimum.com

Nelson and Company, Ltd.
www.nelsons.net

Standard Homeopathic Company
(800) 624-9659

GREEN BLENDS

All Systems Go! Total Health Aid for Pets
Aunt Jeni
www.auntjeni.com

Animal Essentials Organic Green Alternative Health Blend
www.animalessentials.com

Berte's Green Blend
B-Naturals
www.b-naturals.com

Solid Gold Seameal Powder
www.solidgoldhealth.com

ADDITIONAL RESOURCES

Deva Khalsa, VMD
(888) 446-9134
www.doctordeva.com

Dr. Johanna Budwig's cancer-curing diet
www.datadepo.com/cancercure/budwig.htm

Hemopet/Hemolife (Dr. Jean Dodds)
www.hemopet.org

Norfields Magnetics
(800) 344-8400

Poly-MVA—Advanced Medicine and Research Company
(800) 960-6760 or
www.polymvasurvivors.com

Polysaccharide-polypeptide (PSP) and fucoidan Charles Tom Schenck, DVM
(877) 835-5454

Index

A

acidic pH, 40–41, 43, 107, 173, 202
acupressure, 122
acupuncture, 118–22, 203
adenosine triphosphate (ATP), 38, 199
advertising, 22–23, 32
aflatoxins in peanuts, 162
afterlife of dogs, 214–15
alkaline pH, 40, 44, 88, 177–78, 202
allergies
  complications with, 147–54
  from conventional kibble, 139–40
  and GM foods, 28
  herbal rinse or spray for, 98
  holistic treatments, 142–47
  and immune system, 137, 141–42, 155–56
  to nutritional yeast, 73
  overview, 137–39, 140
  and pollution, 44
  skin allergies, 140–47
  and vaccinations, 138, 155–59
  See also itching
allergy elimination techniques, 134–35
aloe vera, 86–87, 145
alpha-glycan PSP, 166
alternative therapies, 114.
  See also holistic therapies
amaranth, 65
American Animal Hospital Association's Canine Vaccine Task Force, 155
American Holistic Veterinary Medical Association (AHVMA), 134
American Veterinary Medical Association, 120, 155
amino acids, 22, 28–29, 72, 107
anatomy
  cells, 38–41, 44–45, 82–83, 140, 166–67
  digestive tract, 35–38
  ear, 148

heart, 196
ligaments and tendons, 132
pancreas, 183
spine, 131
thyroid gland, 168
animal fat or digest, 33, 163
animal instincts and herbs, 81
animal protein in diet, 24, 43
antibacterial herbs, 85, 92, 96
antibiotics, 37, 82, 116, 152
antibiotic-resistant bacteria, 116, 148–49
antibiotics in meats, 43, 72
anticancer diets, 172–76
antioxidants
  beta carotene, 105, 109, 165, 171
  CoQ10, 109, 145, 171, 199
  overview, 39, 108–9
  vitamin A, 105, 109, 165
  vitamin C, 101–2, 106, 109, 144–45, 165
  vitamin E, 107, 109, 145, 165, 171, 199
  See also selenium
Apis mellifica, 127
apoptosis, 176, 179
apple recipes, 229, 259
applied kinesiology, 135
aquapuncture, 121
Aronoson, Linda, 206
arthritis and turmeric, 81
asparagus, 85, 200, 276
ATP (adenosine triphosphate), 38, 199
avocado, 62
Ayurvedic medicine, 80

B

B vitamins, 37, 105–6
Bach flower remedies, 130–31, 208, 214
bacteria
  antibiotic-resistant, 116, 148–49
  ear infections, 147–49, 150–51

in small intestine, 36–37
baking soda, 85, 145
bananas with yogurt, 62
barley, 65
barley stews, 240, 245
Barnes, Broda, 168
basmati rice, 65
beans and lentils, 61
beef, 21–22, 32–33, 62, 138
beef by-products, 30–32, 33
beef recipes, 185, 234, 235, 239, 240, 245, 256, 257, 266, 273, 276
beet pulp, 33
best friends, 15–16, 205–6
beta carotene, 105, 109, 165, 171
bile ducts, 38
bioelectric theory of acupuncture, 121
biotin, 67
birthday cakes, 270–71
biscuit, treat, and snack recipes, 260–69, 277
Blobel, Gunter, 167
blueberries, 174, 181
boarding kennels, 158–59
bone marrow, 76
bone meal, 107, 164, 169
bones for gnawing, 76–77
Bordetella vaccine, 158
botanical medicine
  berries, 174, 181
  cranberries, 43, 88
  for diabetes patients, 186–87
  for diarrhea, 192
  garlic, 60, 85–86, 165, 176
  Hawthorne berries, 80, 199
  in India, 80
  for kidney failure, 203
  neoplasene, 179
  for separation anxiety, 207
  See also herbs
breed-related problems
  fungal infections, 151
  vaccination risks, 156
brewer's yeast, 73, 269
bromelain, 109
brown rice, 65
Brusch, Charles, 175
Bryonia, 128, 129

buckwheat, 65
Budwig, Johanna, 173–74
by-products, 23, 30–32, 33, 162

C
cabbage leaf, 85, 146
Caisse, Rene, 175
calcium, 107, 254–55, 256
calendula, 91–92, 145
cancer
    and animal protein in diet, 24, 43
    anticancer diets, 172–76
    cancer salves, 172
    chemotherapy, 171, 179
    holistic remedies, 177–80
    overview, 161–62
    prevention of, 162–64
    prevention versus cure, 170–71
    supplements for fighting, 165–69
    symptoms of, 169–70
    treatment choices, 170–71, 180–81
Canine Café
    casseroles and loaves, 233–38
    eggs and omelets, 250–52
    fruits, 258–60
    holiday meals, 270–71
    muffins, 227–32
    overview, 221
    raw diets, 252–56
    special needs dogs, 272–80
    stews and soups, 238–45
    stocks, 256–58
    toppers, 50, 58, 222–27
    toss and serve meals, 246–50
    See also cooking for your dog
Canine Vaccine Task Force (AAHA), 155
caraway and digestion, 81, 85
carbohydrates and cancer tumors, 172–73
carob powder, 192
casseroles and loaves, 233–38
cells of your dog's body, 38–41, 44–45, 82–83, 140, 166–67
cellular communication, 167

Center for Veterinary Medicine (FDA), 30
chamomile, 90–91
cheese, 67, 68
cheese recipes, 224, 237, 248, 251, 270
chemical additives, 29–33
chewy toppers, 225–27
chicken, 71–72, 138, 264
chicken bones warning, 71, 77
chicken by-products, 23, 30–32, 33
chicken recipes, 185, 228, 236, 240, 241, 244, 248, 255, 258, 264, 275
children and dogs, 17
China and food recalls, 24–26
China Study, The (Campbell), 24, 70, 162, 163
Chinese medicine, 80, 81, 192
cholesterol, 68, 71
cinnamon and diabetes, 81
coat care, 76, 95, 97, 98–99, 154, 224
    topical for hot spots, 145–46
coconut oil, 75–76, 256
colloidal oatmeal, 145–46
commercial dog food
    advertising about, 22–24
    GM foods, 26–29
    in healthy diets, 50
    and Industrial Revolution, 21–22
    labels on, 29–33
    manufacturers' self-regulation, 31
    obesity from, 204–5
    prepared grain mixes, 66–67
    preservatives in, 31–32, 33, 139–40, 163, 167
    quality foods, 32–33, 54–55
    recalls, 24–26, 29
    safety and unsafety of, 29–33, 43, 163
communication, 16–17, 48
complementary medicine, 114
congestive heart failure, 196, 198–99, 213
connecting with your dog
    as best friends, 15–16, 205–6

communication, 16–17, 48
    dog's point of view, 14–15, 16, 18–19
    letting dogs be dogs, 17–18
    at mealtimes, 47–48, 55, 59
    overview, 13
    unconditional love, 14–15, 45, 211–12, 214–15
constipation, 66, 193–95
conventional medicine
    allergy testing, 141–42
    chemotherapy, 171, 177
    for ear infections, 147–48, 150, 151
    with holistic methods, 130, 181, 197, 198, 199
    itching treatment, 122–23
    overview, 114–17
    side effects, 113, 125, 170
    vaccinations, 138, 141, 154–59, 166–67
    See also pharmaceutical drugs
cooking for your dog
    finding a good kibble base, 32–33, 54–55
    fruits, 44, 62, 63, 258
    hassle factor, 49–54
    leftovers, 48–49, 48–50, 52–53, 62
    overview, 47–48
    raw versus cooked meat, 69–71
    vegetables, 61–62
    See also Canine Café; diet; nutrition
CoQ10, 109, 145, 171, 199
corn gluten contamination, 26
couscous, 65
cranberries, 43, 88
crunchy toppers, 224–25
cryomazine, 25
cucumbers, 85
Current Veterinary Therapy IX (reference book), 155
cyanuric acid, 26

D
dairy products
    alkaline pH from, 44
    cheeses, 67, 68
    egg recipes, 237, 242, 250–52, 274, 275

egg shells, 68, 251, 255
eggs, 67–68, 106–7
kefir, 37, 68
milk, 68
yogurt, 37, 62, 68, 173
dandelion, 80, 87–88,
200–201
Daniels, A. C., 22
*Death of the Tumor and
Cancer, The* (Budwig),
174
death of your dog
afterlife, 214–15
golden twilight, 212–14
overview, 211–12
saying good-bye,
216–19
diabetes, 81, 183–87, 273
diarrhea
dairy products for, 68
homeopathics, 190–91
overview, 188–90
pharmaceuticals for,
190
potassium depletion,
108
probiotics for, 37, 68,
189, 191, 195
recipes for, 188, 189,
274–76
diet
bones, 76–77
fish, 72–73
foods dogs shouldn't
eat, 24, 63, 164
fresh fruit, 62, 63
fresh vegetables, 60–62
grains, 64–67
meat in, 69–72
media myths about,
23–24
nutritional yeast, 73
organic produce, 62, 64
overview, 57–58
and pH balance, 40–41
portions and propor-
tions, 58–59
roughage in, 194, 195
See also cooking for
your dog; dairy
products; fruits; grains;
kibble; meats; nutrition;
oils; recipes; vegetables
diets
all-meat diets, 41, 52
for allergy relief, 143–44
anticancer diets,
163–66, 172–76, 181
Calming Diet, 280
Chubby Dog Chow, 279

for diabetes, 81, 184,
185, 273
Heart Diet, 276
high-protein diets, 43
for kidney failure,
202–3, 277–79
raw diet, 252–56
vegetarian diet, 24, 43,
232, 268
digestive system
anatomy of, 35–38
constipation, 66,
193–95
gall bladder, 38
herbs for, 81, 90, 94
intestines, 36–37
liver, 37–38, 40–41,
87–88, 90
and probiotics, 37, 68,
189, 191, 195
and variety in diet,
23–24, 41, 54
See also diarrhea
dill, 85
diseases
and cells, 44–45
coconut oil for, 75
diabetes, 81, 183–87,
273
distemper, 189
heart conditions,
196–200, 213
hypothyroidism, 168–69
kidney failure, 201–4
mad cow disease, 31,
71
parvovirus, 189
and pH balance, 40–41
from protein excess,
42–43
pulmonary congestion,
200–201
rabies, 157
recovery broth for, 272
vaccinations, 138, 141,
154–59, 166–67
See also cancer;
illnesses
dismutase (SOD), 108, 109
distemper, 189
distemper vaccination,
155–56, 159
diuretics, 87, 200–201
DNA and GM foods, 27
DNA damage and cancer,
165, 166
doctrine of signatures, 80
Dodds, Jean, 144, 168
Dodman, Nicholas, 206
dog biscuits, 21–22. *See*

also biscuit, treat, and
snack recipes
dog food, 48–49, 50, 52–53.
See also Canine Café;
commercial dog food;
diet
Dr. Budwig's Anticancer
Diet, 173, 174, 181

E
E. coli, 70, 71
ear infections, 147–49
echinacea (purple
coneflower), 82, 89, 93
egg recipes, 237, 242,
250–52, 274, 275
egg shells, 68, 251, 255
eggs and milk products,
67–68, 106–7
electroacupuncture, 121
Eliot, T. S., 17
ellagic acid, 174
emotional problems,
205–6, 208–9
emotions, human and
canine, 15
endocrine balance, 81
Environmental Protection
Agency (EPA), 25
enzymatic processes, 36,
39
enzymes
adding to food, 195
lysozyme, 36
overview, 36, 39
and pH level, 40–41
for protection from free
radicals, 108, 109
wobenzym N, 180
essential fatty acids. *See*
fatty acids
Essiac tea, 175
ethoxyquin, 31, 33, 163,
167
European doctrine of
signatures, 80
euthanasia, 213–14. *See
also* death of your dog
evolution of dogs, 41
evolving with your dog,
14–15
exercise, 169
extracellular fluid, 39–40

F
family meals, 47–48, 55, 59
farewell ceremonies,
216–19
fasting, 191

fat on raw meat, 71
fatty acids
    in coconut oil, 75–76
    in egg yolks, 67
    in flaxseeds, 74–75,
        145, 164
    omega-3, 67, 145,
        163–64, 199
    in raw meat, 70
feces and *Salmonella* or *E.
    coli* bacteria, 71
federal laws on dog food
    production, 29–30
feeding your dog, 58–59,
    227. *See also* Canine
    Café; cooking for your
    dog; diet; kibble
fennel, 81, 84, 85, 94
fish, 72–73
fish recipes
    mackerel, 247
    salmon, 236, 248, 250,
        262
    whitefish, 231, 247, 253,
        258
flagyl (metronidazole), 190
flax seeds and flax seed
    oil, 74–75, 145, 164,
        173–74
fleas, 60, 269
flounder, 72
fluid retention, 87, 88, 94,
    200–201
fluids for kidney failure,
    204
Food and Drug
    Administration, 26,
        29–30, 123
4-D ingredients, 30–31
Fox, Michael, 26–27
freezing raw meat, 71
frozen treats, 259
fruits
    in diet, 44, 62, 63, 258
    recipes, 229, 231,
        259–60, 273
Frumker, Sanford, 177–78
fucoidan, 175–76
fungal infections, 151–53

G
gall bladder, 38
game birds, 72
Gamett, Merrill, 179–80
Gandhi, Mahatma, 125
garlic, 60, 85–86, 165, 176
genetically modified (GM)
    foods, 26–29
Gentian violet, 149
Giardia, 189

Ginko biloba, 80, 109
ginseng root, 80
gizzards, 72
glycoforms, 167
GM (genetically modified)
    foods, 26–29
gold bead implants, 122
golden twilight of life,
    212–14
Goodhart, George, 135
grains
    adding to leftovers, 50,
        53
    alkaline pH from, 44
    cooking time chart, 65
    including in diet, 64,
        66–67
    overview, 64–67
    in raw-food diets, 254,
        256
    See also cooking for
        your dog
grapes, warning about, 63
grazing dogs, 42
Gulf War Syndrome, 156

H
Hahnemann, Samuel,
    123–24, 126–27
hassle factor, 49–54
Hawthorne berries
    (*Crataegus*), 80, 199
heart as dog food, 42, 72
heart conditions, 196–200,
    213
heart health, 67, 80, 94,
    108
heart murmurs, 196,
    198–99
Hemopet, 144, 168
herbs
    alkaline pH from, 44
    for diarrhea, 192
    as diuretics, 200–201
    and drug companies, 83
    drying, 89, 96
    for healthy skin, 98–99
    herbal gardens, 89–90
    herbal medicine, 80–83
    Hoxsey herbs, 177
    overview, 79, 83, 85
    in raw-food diets, 256
    for wounds, 91–92, 93,
        95
    See also botanical
        medicine
herbs, specific
    aloe vera, 86–87, 145
    calendula, 91–92, 145
    chamomile, 90–91

dandelion, 80, 87–88,
    200–201
echinacea, 82, 89, 93
fennel, 81, 84, 85, 94
lavender, 96–97
oregano, 85
parsley, 85, 94, 200, 234
rose hips, 113
rosemary, 81, 85, 95,
    109
sage, 85, 95
St. John's Wort, 89, 207
thyme, 96
    See also botanical
        medicine
high-protein diets, 43
Hillman, Noel, 26
hip dysplasia, 122
Hippocrates, 132
holiday meals, 270–71
holistic remedies for
    cancer, 177–80
holistic therapies
    acupuncture, 118–22
    allergy elimination
        techniques, 134–35
    Bach flower remedies,
        130–31, 208, 214
    and conventional
        medicine, 130, 181, 197,
            198, 199
    overview, 114–19, 135
    prolotherapy, 132–34
    spinal manipulation,
        118–19, 131–32
    topical preparations for
        hot spots, 145–46
    See also botanical
        medicine; homeopathy
homeopathy
    combination remedies,
        129
    founding of, 123–24
    individualized
        treatment, 127–28
    Law of Similars, 124–25
    method for using,
        129–30
    overview, 114, 122–23
    preparation of, 125–27
    See also homeopathic
        remedies
*Homeopathic
    Pharmacopoeia of the
    United States*, 123
homeopathic remedies
    for allergic reactions,
        146–47
    for cancer, 177–80
    for constipation, 194
    for diabetes, 187

for diarrhea, 190–91
for dogs on chemotherapy, 171, 179
for ear infections, 150
for fear of thunderstorms, 208–9
for grief, 214
for heart conditions, 199–200
for kidney failure, 203–4
for nervousness, 209
for pulmonary congestion, 200
for ringworm, 153
for separation anxiety, 207
for vomiting, 192, 193
homotoxicology, 127
hormones, 43, 72, 107
hot spots, topical preparations for, 145–46
Hoxsey herbs, 177
Humphreys, Frederick, 123
hypericum (St. John's Wort), 89, 207
Hypoallergenic Antiyeast Meal, 152
hypothyroidism, 168–69
Hypothyroidism (Barnes), 168

I
illnesses
    constipation, 66, 193–95
    ear infections, 147–49
    fluid retention, 87, 88, 94, 200–201
    as imbalance of Qi, 80
    recovery broth for, 272
    vomiting, 189, 192–93
    See also allergies; diarrhea; diseases; infections
immune system
    and allergies, 137, 141–42, 155–56
    and antibiotics, 82
    and cancer, 177
    echinacea for boosting, 82, 89, 93
    nutritional boost to, 162
    and raw meat, 70
    and vaccinations, 138
    and vitamin C, 106
Industrial Revolution, 22
infections
    ear infections, 147–49, 150–51

fungal infections, 151–53
in the heart, 196
homeopathics, 150
ringworm, 152–53
urinary tract infections, 88
yeast infections, 147–50, 152
injuries, prolotherapy for, 132–34
insulin, 184
integrative health care, 114
intelligence of dogs, 19
intestines, 36–37
IP6 supplement, 177
itching
    aloe vera for, 87, 145
    cabbage for, 85
    fungal infections, 151–53
    herbs for, 90, 92
    homeopathy for, 122–23
    from scabies, 153–54
    topical preparations for hot spots, 145–46
    See also allergies
ivermectin, 154

J
Journal of Current Biology, 19
Journal of the American Veterinary Medical Association, 155

K
kaopectate, 190
kefir, 37, 68
kibble
    additives in commercial brands, 31–32, 43
    building a meal with, 48, 50, 52–54, 62, 66
    as emergency ration, 52
    finding a good kibble, 32–33, 54–55
    and immune system, 139–40
    toppers for, 50, 58, 222–27
    vegetarian, 43, 55
kidneys (body parts)
    dairy products for, 68
    damage from melamine, 25–26
    diet for, 202–3, 277–79
    kidney failure, 201–4
    parsley for, 85, 94

and pH balance, 40–41
and thyroid, 205
kidneys as dog food, 72, 203
kinesiology, 135
Kudzu Root Recipe, 189, 274

L
L-tryptophan, 28–29, 72
labels on dog food, 29–33
lamb, 71, 72, 138–39, 144, 152
lamb recipes, 244, 257
large intestine, 36
laser acupuncture, 122
Last Hours of Ancient Sunlight, The (Hartman), 18
lauric acid, 76
lavender, 96–97
Law of Similars, 124–25
laxatives for humans, warning about, 195
leftovers, 48–50, 52–53, 62
lentils and beans, 61
ligaments, 132
lipoic acid, 179–80
liver (body part), 37–38, 40–41, 87–88, 90
liver as dog food, 72
liver recipes, 231, 235, 245, 249, 261, 267
loaves and casseroles, 233–38
lungs and pH balance, 40
Lux, Wilhelm, 123
Lymdyp rinse, 154
lysozyme, 36

M
mackerel, 72, 73, 247
mad cow disease, 31, 71
magnesium, 108
magnets, 177, 179
Malassezia, 151–52
March 2007 recall, 24–26, 29
Materia Medica, 128
McManners, H., 156
meal planning, 49–53. See also diet
meals in a muffin, 227–32
meat diets, 41, 52
meat preparation, 254
meats
    cooked versus raw, 69–71

lamb, 71, 72, 138–39, 144, 152
lamb recipes, 244, 257
organ meats, 72, 164
organic, 54, 72, 164
pork, 71, 243
rabbit, 71
raw meat and bones diet, 41, 52
turkey, 72, 229, 233, 247
See also beef; chicken; fish
medications. See pharmaceutical drugs
melamine in wheat gluten, 25
melatonin, 206
mental ability of dogs, 19
Menu Foods of Canada, 25, 26, 27
mercury in fish, 73
metronidazole (flagyl), 190
microflora or microbiota, 37
microwaves, warning about, 70
Milk Bone advertisement, 22
milk powder, 26, 68. See also dairy products
millet, 65
minerals
    calcium, 107, 254–55, 256
    for diabetes, 185–86
    overview, 107–8
    quality supplements, 103–4
    role in body, 39
    See also selenium; supplements
mitochondria, 38
mix and match meals, 253
modalities, 115. See also holistic therapies
monolaurin, 76
moxibustion, 122
muffin meals, 227–32
myths created by dog food manufacturers, 23–24

N
Nambudripad Allergy Elimination Technique (NAET), 134–35
National Cancer Institute, 163
National Institutes of Health, 162

Native American legend, 14
nature, your dog's experience of, 16, 18–19
neoplasene, 179
neurophysiological theory of acupuncture, 120–21
New York Times, 25
nonsteroidal anti-inflammatory drugs (NSAIDs), 115, 133
Nostradamus, 113
nutrition
    absence of, in commercially grown foods, 101
    and cells of the body, 38–41, 44–45, 82–83, 140, 166–67
    in dairy products, 68
    and digestive tract, 35–38
    flax seeds and flax seed oil, 74–75, 145, 164, 173–74
    in meats, 70–71
    overview, 35
    in seaweed, 62, 175–76, 254
    See also diet; pH; proteins; supplements
nutritional yeast, 73
nuts, 44, 164, 174, 265, 268

O
oat recipes, 228, 231, 266, 267
oatmeal, 65, 66
oatmeal poultices, 145–46
oatmeal recipes, 222, 224, 247, 256, 260, 265
oats (steel cut), 65, 66
obesity, 59, 204–5, 279
oil-controlling rinse and spray, 97, 98
oils
    calories from, 59
    coconut oil, 75–76, 256
    fatty acids in, 145
    flax seeds and flax seed oil, 74–75, 145, 164, 173–74
    including in diet, 74–76
    olive oil, 74, 195, 256
    organic, 71, 74
    for raw diets, 256
    walnut oil, 256
omega-3 fatty acids, 67, 145, 163–64, 199

omelets, 252
onions, warning about, 24, 61
oregano, 85
organ meats, 72, 164
organic foods, 28, 33, 82, 174–75
organic grains, 66
organic meats, 54, 72, 164
organic oils, 71, 74
organic plant-cell calcium, 103
organic produce, 50, 62, 64, 163, 244. See also fruits; vegetables
overweight dogs, 59, 204–5, 279
oyster shell, powdered, 107

P
pack mentality, 14, 17, 47–48, 55, 59
palladium, 179–80
Palmer, Volney B., 22
pancreas, 183
papayas, 62
parasites, 72, 153–54, 189
parsley, 85, 94, 200, 234
parvovirus, 189
parvovirus vaccination, 155–56, 159
Pauling, Linus, 102
peanuts and peanut by-products, 33, 162
Pedigree Pet Foods in Thailand, 29
people food, 24
pesticides
    in cells, 39–40, 72
    on dandelions, 88
    on grass, 42, 139, 168
    in liver of non-organic animals, 72
    melamine from, 25
    on produce, 62, 64
    See also toxins
pH (parts of hydrogen)
    acidic pH, 40–41, 43, 107, 173, 202
    alkaline pH, 40, 44, 88, 177–78, 202
    overview, 37
pharmaceutical drugs
    antibiotic-resistant bacteria, 116, 148–49
    antibiotics, 37, 82, 116, 152
    combining with holistic therapy, 114–15

conventional medicine and, 113–17, 122–23, 130, 141–42, 171
for diarrhea, 190
diuretics, 87
from herbs, 83
steroids, 115, 118–19, 141, 158
treating symptoms versus problems, 115, 117
phytochemicals, 89, 163
pollution, 38, 39–40, 44, 139, 167–68. *See also* pesticides; toxins
Poly-MVA, 179–80
polysaccharides, 166
pork, cooking, 71
pork stew, 243
portions and proportions, 58–59
potassium, 108
potato recipes, 235, 237, 247–49, 252, 276
poultry, 71–72. *See also* chicken; turkey
poultry by-products, 23, 30–32, 33
Preparation H cream, 146
preservatives in commercial dog foods, 31–32, 33, 139–40, 163, 167
prion proteins, 31, 71
probiotics, 37, 68, 189, 191, 195
prolotherapy, 132–34
proportions and portions, 58–59
proteins
amino acids from, 22, 28–29, 72, 107
and cancer prevention, 164
limiting amount of, 24, 42–43
mad cow disease, 31, 71
melamine contamination, 25
overview, 42–43
and pH balance, 40–41
role in body, 39
storage in the liver, 38
value of, in commercial dog foods, 30–31
pulmonary congestion, 200–201
pumpkin, canned, 194–95
purple coneflower

(echinacea), 82, 89, 93
pycnogenol, 109

Q
quercetin, 109, 145
quinoa, 65, 247, 248

R
rabbit meat, cooking, 71
rabies, 157
rabies vaccination, 157, 158, 167
raisins, warning about, 63
raw diet, 252–56
raw meat and bones diet, 41, 52
raw versus cooked meat, 69–71
recalls, 24–26, 29
recipes. *See* Canine Café
recommended daily allowance (RDA), 102–3
recovery broth, 272
red raspberries, 174, 181
rescue remedy, 214
Reston, James, 120
Revolution, 154
rice, cooking, 65, 66
Rice and Egg Drop Soup, 188
rice on label, 33
rice protein contamination, 26, 29
rice recipes, 241–42, 245, 250–51, 275
ringworm, 152–53
rites of passage for dog owners, 218
Rogers, Will, 215
root vegetable chicken stew, 240
rose hips, 113
rosemary, 81, 85, 95, 109

S
sage, 85, 95
salmon, 72, 73
salmon recipes, 236, 248, 250, 262
Salmonella, 67, 70, 71
salt and heart conditions, 196
sarcoptic mange (scabies), 153–54
"Scientists Link Gulf War Illness to Vaccines and Drugs" (McManners), 156
seafood stew, 245

seaweed, 62, 175–76, 254
selenium
bone meal versus, 165, 169
for cancer, 171, 180
for cancer prevention, 165
with chemotherapy, 171
overview, 108, 109
Selsun Blue shampoo, 154
semidry dog foods, 31–32, 33
separation anxiety, 205–7
Shulman, Ben, 217–19
skin allergies, 140–47
slaughterhouse waste products, 30–31
slippery elm, 192
small intestine, 36–37
snack, treat, and biscuit recipes, 260–69, 277
social work, 17
SOD (dismutase), 108, 109
sodium pentobarbital in dog food, 30
sodium selenite, 108, 180
soups and stews, 238–45
special needs dogs, 183, 205–9, 272–80. *See also* diseases; illnesses
spices, 44, 79, 81, 165, 256. *See also* herbs
spinal manipulation, 118–19, 131–32
Spratt, James, 21
St. John's Wort (hypericum), 89, 207
steroids (in non-organic meats), 43, 72
steroids (pharmaceutical), 115, 118–19, 141, 158
stews and soups, 238–45
stocks, 66, 256–58, 272
strawberries, 174, 181
sugars as energy source, 39
supplements
for allergy relief, 144–45
amino acids, 22, 28–29, 72, 107
for diabetes, 184, 185–86
for heart conditions, 199
IP6 supplement, 177
melatonin, 206
overview, 69, 81–82, 101, 109
Poly-MVA, 179–80
polysaccharides, 166

probiotics, 37, 68, 189, 191, 195
See also antioxidants; enzymes; fatty acids; minerals; nutrition; vitamins
sweet potatoes, 189, 237, 244, 274. *See also* yams

T
tarragon, 85
tea, black or green, 145
tendons, 132
Test and Grow Healthy (Frumker), 177–78
thunderstorms, fear of, 208–9
thyme, 96
thyroid function, 108, 144, 168–69, 205
tilapia, 72
tomato pomace, 33
topical preparations for hot spots, 145–46
toppers, 50, 58, 222–27
toss and serve meals, 246–50
toxins
  aflatoxins in peanuts, 162
  and antioxidants, 109
  in bone meal, 107, 164, 169
  in commercial dog foods, 43
  and digestive tract, 38, 39–40
  on fruits and vegetables, 62, 64
  minimizing, 167–68
  from pollution, 38, 39–40, 44, 139, 167–68
  See also pesticides
treat, snack, and biscuit recipes, 260–69, 277
trout, 72
Tuberculinum 100c, 177–78
tumeric, 81, 165
tumors, 172–73
tuna, canned, warning about, 73

turkey, 72
turkey recipes, 229, 233, 247

U
ultrasound test, 170
unconditional love, 14–15, 45, 211–12, 214–15
urinary tract infections, 88
U.S. Food and Nutrition Board, 103–4
USA Today, 26

V
vaccinations, 138, 141, 154–59, 166–67
vaccine titer tests, 157–59
vegetables
  adding to leftovers, 50
  alkaline pH from, 44
  grass versus, 42
  including in diet, 60–62, 163, 189
vegetables in recipes
  asparagus, 276
  broccoli, 223, 234–35, 237, 252, 273
  carrots, 223, 226, 231, 233–34, 256, 270, 280
  cauliflower, 224, 247, 273
  mixed, 226, 239–45, 257–58, 277–79
  potatoes, 234–35, 237, 247–49, 252
  pumpkin, 227, 230
  spinach, 251
  squash, 223, 227, 230, 256
  string beans, 235
  sweet potatoes or yams, 237, 246, 248, 256, 261, 274–75
vegetarian diet, 24, 43
vegetarian recipes, 223–24, 232, 238, 252, 268
venison, 33, 71, 138, 144, 249
vitamins
  B vitamins, 105–6
  in commercial dog

foods, 23
  for diabetes, 185–86
  overview, 52, 53, 102–4, 104–5
  role in body, 39
  vitamin A, 105, 109, 165
  vitamin C, 101–2, 106, 109, 144–45, 165
  vitamin D, 106–7
  vitamin E, 107, 109, 145, 165, 171, 199
  See also antioxidants; supplements
vomiting, 189, 192–93

W
walnut oil, 256
wart removal with garlic, 86
watermelon, 62
Western herbal medicine, 81
wheat (cracked), 65
wheat, GM, 27
wheat berries, 65
wheat bran, 66
wheat gluten contamination, 25–26
wheat on label, 32–33
whitefish recipes, 231, 247, 253, 258
wild dogs, 41, 42
witch hazel, 85, 145
wobenzym N, 180
World Health Organization, 81, 123
wounds, herbs for healing, 91–92, 93, 95

Y
yams, 189, 246, 248, 261, 275. *See also* sweet potatoes
yawning, 48
yeast infections, 147–50, 152
yogurt, 37, 62, 68

Z
zinc, 109

About the Author

Dr. Deva K. Khalsa, a licensed doctor of veterinary medicine, earned her VMD degree from the University of Pennsylvania. She is a member of the American Veterinary Medical Association, the American Holistic Veterinary Medical Association, and the International Veterinary Acupuncture Society. She has studied homeopathy for more than twenty-five years, as well as other alternative therapies, and she lectures nationally and internationally on her fresh and successful approach to veterinary medicine. She is the coauthor of *Healing Your Horse: Alternative Therapies* (Howell Book House, 1993). Her work stems from her belief that animals are at their best and happiest only when they are in a healthy and natural state. Dr. Khalsa focuses on empowering people to discover and nurture this natural state in their pets and, in doing so, to connect with and celebrate the true spirit of animals.